EQUALITY AND DIVERSITY

Value incommensurability and the politics of recognition

Steven R. Smith

First published in Great Britain in 2011 by

The Policy Press
University of Bristol
Fourth Floor
Beacon House
Queen's Road
Bristol BS8 1QU
UK

t: +44 (0)117 331 4054
f: +44 (0)117 331 4093
tpp-info@bristol.ac.uk
www.policypress.co.uk

North American office:
The Policy Press
c/o International Specialized Books Services
920 NE 58th Avenue, Suite 300
Portland, OR 97213-3786, USA
t: +1 503 287 3093
f: +1 503 280 8832
info@isbs.com

© The Policy Press

British Library Cataloguing in Publication Data
A catalogue record for this book is available from the British Library.

Library of Congress Cataloging-in-Publication Data
A catalog record for this book has been requested.

ISBN 978 1 84742 607 9 hardcover

Cover design by The Policy Press.
Front cover: Many thanks to Ernesto Lozada-Uzuriaga Steele for giving permission to use his painting 'Siempre' for the design of the front cover. He is also author of the book
Five stones & a burnt stick: Toward the ancient wisdom of intimacy, which is cited in the dedication.
Printed and bound in Great Britain by TJ International, Padstow.
The Policy Press uses environmentally responsible print partners.

For Lyn

'... the wisdom of intimacy teaches that we must not need the other person to be like, to speak like, to think like, to feel like, and to dream like ourselves. The path of intimacy embraces and nurtures the difference between ourself and the other. It respects and nourishes this uniqueness and difference. The path of intimacy creates a sacred space in which the other is encouraged and enabled to find their own path, be their own self, think their own thoughts, speak with their own voice, acknowledge their own feelings, and dream their own dream. Intimacy celebrates the difference between the self and the other. The richness of your difference will always surprise, delight, challenge, and teach you. These differences will never be exhausted in the brevity of life. Every day will be one of great discovery and wonder.'

Ernesto Lozada-Uzuriaga Steele (2009) *Five stones and a burnt stick: Towards the ancient wisdom of intimacy*, New York, NY: Strategic Book Publishing, p 28.

Contents

Preface

One of the primary objectives of this book is to redefine elements of contemporary Anglo-American liberal egalitarianism that promote the universal values of liberty and equality, however conceptualised, and to articulate how these elements are central to the radicalised political agendas of new social movements. The concern is that these agendas have become too firmly associated with the 'identity politics' of postmodern and poststructuralist thought, and what has been dubbed continental philosophy, which frequently rejects the universal claims of liberal egalitarianism. Despite some benefits explored here, both philosophical and political, the other troubling by-product of this association is the disregard of proper discussions about values, as the attack on universal principles often leads to value and cultural relativism. For social movements especially, this attack is self-defeating, as these forms of relativism also reject radical critical perspectives that claim some kind of privileged position for seeing the world, which many forms of relativism deny is possible. In addition, the error of self-defeat is compounded by philosophical and political duplicity, as continental positions, while often seemingly anti-universal and anti-liberal egalitarian, are frequently committed to universally opposing social and economic systems that exclude and disadvantage relatively powerless individuals and group members – a commitment that liberal egalitarians also wholeheartedly endorse.

This diagnosis of at least some aspects of continental thinking does not mean, of course, that Anglo-American liberal egalitarianism is immune to criticism. Analytical philosophy underpins the general approach of liberal egalitarianism, and is often based on overreaching claims about the efficacy of reason and theoretical explanation regarding questions of value, and what can be said about the human condition. There are, however, well-established strands within liberalism itself that have curtailed these claims – recognising that, although reason and notions of reasonableness may healthily constrain the exercise of individual agency and freedom, there are limits to what reason and theory can offer in explaining and justifying value commitment, and the complex and often paradoxical character of human experience and social relations. Certainly, acknowledging the force of these constraints is due in part to the legacy of continental philosophy, especially perhaps from existentialism and elements of postmodernism and poststructuralist thought. However, it is also due to the profundity of liberalism itself and the issues it grapples with concerning value pluralism and the right to pursue lives that are different to others. These issues and the liberal responses to them, in turn, have influenced some of the main preoccupations of continental philosophy and the positions taken by supposedly more radical political positions that often pose as anti-liberal and anti-egalitarian.

More specifically, four propositions are defended throughout the book: first, that promoting value pluralism accommodates the right to pursue values that are often incommensurable and incomparable both between persons, and within and across one person's life; second, that the exercise of individual agency when making particular choices and commitments, while properly constrained by reason and notions of reasonableness, has no ultimate or foundational rational justification or explanation: third, that legitimately promoting equality and unity between persons and group members produces a conflict, both philosophically and politically, with the similarly legitimate promotion of diversity and separateness between these same persons and group-members; and fourth, that establishing reciprocal relations between differently situated 'others' is a basis for instituting just social relations, given that persons can learn, both dialogically and non-dialogically, from the way others positively engage with their lives, whatever circumstances may be experienced, and even if these lives radically differ.

The central argument is that these propositions are defendable from certain interpretations of liberalism and liberal egalitarianism, and are often explicitly or implicitly endorsed by social movements – such as the disability rights movement, the women's movement and those defending multiculturalism. However, as a result, it must also be acknowledged that the values associated with promoting equality and diversity are often deeply conflicting, leading to policies and practices that pull in opposite directions. For example, in relation to disability, policies and practices encouraging the positive assertion of highly particularised and diverse individual and group-member identities associated with impairment often profoundly conflict with those egalitarian policies and practices that seek to rectify disadvantage derived from these impairments – that is, disadvantage understood as being caused by medical or social conditions, or a mixture of both.

Following this analysis, the more general claim is that egalitarian policies and practices, intending to alleviate disadvantage and what is objectively defined as obstacles to human flourishing, are often irreconcilable with those policies and practices that recognise that disadvantaged individuals and group members can subjectively respond to their experiences in ways that are surprisingly life-enhancing. The further argument made is that efforts to 'solve' this irreconcilability should be resisted, accepting instead that it reflects not only the inevitable messiness of implementing policies and practices derived from political compromise and conflicting interests, but also intractable philosophical conundrums, delimiting what can be explained or spoken about regarding matters of value, identity and the finite and transient character of human experience. These conundrums also produce various normative paradoxes concerning how these matters should be viewed and responded to. For example, experiencing social disadvantage and high levels of flourishing can both be shaped and created via oppressive social relations; so being viewed and treated as an outsider or 'the other' can be at once oppressive and liberating. Possessing an outsider status is oppressive because the structural features of exclusion means that an excluded person is likely to experience systemic disadvantage regarding the potential future lives that might be led by that person. The main normative argument here is that this state of affairs ought to be remedied by universal egalitarian redistributive policies and practices, on the grounds that unequal opportunities to live a range of different lives is socially unjust. Nevertheless, possessing an outsider status leading to disadvantage as regarding limited opportunities may be liberating in other ways, the main normative argument being that positive identity formation is not often based on contemplating potentiality as related to lives that could have been led, but rather is, quite rightly, forged from a positive engagement with transient and highly particularised lived experiences as these occur presently. These experiences include those that are objectively and universally defined as disadvantaged or oppressed, but, according to many within social movements, can paradoxically often lead to enhanced subjective levels of well-being and human flourishing.

This enhancement may occur for a number of reasons, some of which are problematic for the position defended here. For example, many liberal egalitarians have explored what has been termed 'adaptive preferences' – the claim being that expectations of the worse-off are often reduced precisely because of their disadvantaged social position. Consequently, the subjective enhancement of well-being and human flourishing is not necessarily the answer to questions of injustice and exploitation, as it may be that certain social relations cause more easily fulfilled expectations as these expectations are unjustifiably lowered for the worse-off. However, the argument here is that while the problem of adaptive preferences should be taken very seriously in many circumstances, it is certainly not the end of the story regarding the way marginalised individuals and group members actively engage with their experiences. For example, and using the language of existentialism and poststructuralism to make the point, excluded 'otherness' can operate as a spur to increased identity authenticity, as excluded individuals and minority group members often see themselves as being more free than the included to live a life outside of oppressive dominant norms and practices. When recognising this kind of subjective and highly particularised perspective of the excluded, the limits of liberal egalitarianism are most acutely felt. Liberal egalitarians, in order to justify redistributive policies and practices, often appeal to an empathic engagement with the disadvantaged through, for example, the emotions of pity or sympathy, that makes comparisons between the lives of the 'better-off' and 'worse-off', thus ignoring or at least underplaying these more nuanced and ambivalent subjective responses to oppressive or disadvantaged conditions. The principle recommendation, then, is that the 'better-off' should resist making these axiomatic comparative assumptions about the lives of 'worse-off' individuals and groups, and how the latter respond to their social and other circumstances. Instead, a 'disposition of surprise' should be encouraged, remaining open to the idea that an individual or group member may respond to adverse circumstances in surprisingly positive ways. The point is that this surprise is not necessarily caused by adapted preferences, but can be derived from the paradoxical manner in which a person positively engages with what might objectively be defined as bad experiences – acknowledging that her identity is positively transformed in the present, but without unjustifiably lowering expectations about what could be achieved by her in the future.

Finally, recognising this type of paradox in identity formation helps to establish a moral principle of learning from 'the other' in various dialogic and non-dialogic forms, wherever someone is placed in the social strata now, and whatever potential lives may, or may not, be led. This principle also underpins promoting reciprocity as a central value for socially just policies and practices – establishing equal opportunities to live a variety of potential lives for the future, emphasising the importance of redistributive policies and practices, but where mutually beneficial relations between persons who lead incommensurable lives are now celebrated, emphasising those policies and practices that positively recognise particular identities as these occur presently. Promoting this variety of forms of life across communities also leads to a positive engagement with the radically different other, where a full-blooded liberal society can emerge that recognises and positively affirms identities as these are actually formed and created – at the same time developing policies and practices that are robustly egalitarian in their aspirations, dynamically transforming social and economic structures in the future so as to be non-oppressive and liberating.

Acknowledgements

I would like to offer heartfelt thanks to my colleagues at the University of Wales Newport, most particularly to members of the Social Ethics Research Group (SERG), of which I am extremely proud to be a part. Those members to whom I am especially indebted, former and current, are Gideon Calder, Phillip Cole, David Morgans and Enzo Rossi, who have all taken trouble to make constructive criticisms on the various themes explored throughout the book, whether in writing or in discussion. The other thanks due relate to the development of particular chapters.

Sections of Chapters One and Two appeared in a paper I presented at the 'Toleration and respect: concepts, justifications and applications' workshop at the Seventh Annual Conference of Political Theory Workshops at Manchester Metropolitan University in 2010. This workshop was also part of a Framework Seven European Union-funded project RESPECT, of which SERG is a member. More specifically, I would like to thank the main organiser, Emanuela Ceva, for her responses to earlier drafts of the Manchester paper, as well as to the participants at the workshop for their very insightful and thought-provoking comments, especially Peter Balint, John Horton, Tariq Madood and Enzo Rossi. An earlier version of Chapter Two also was given as a paper to the University of Brighton's Philosophical Society in 2007. I would like to thank the organiser, Bob Brecher, as well as the participants at this event for their various contributions.

Chapter Three is a revised and extended version of S. R. Smith (2008) 'Agency and surprise, learning at the limits of empathic-imagination and liberal egalitarianism' *Critical Review in International Social and Political Philosophy*, vol 11, no 1, pp 25-40 (the journal website can be found at www.informaworld.com). I would like to thank the editor, Richard Bellamy, for his very useful suggestions for revisions to the article, and any other individuals associated with the referring process, as well as the Taylor and Francis publishing group for giving me permission to reproduce parts of this article here. Earlier versions of this article were also presented to the University of Lampeter's Philosophy Colloquium in 2007 and to the Politics of Misrecognition conference at the University of Bristol in 2010. Again, I would like to thank the participants at these events for their positive engagement and constructive criticisms.

Chapter Four is a revised and extended version of S. R. Smith (2005b) 'Keeping our distance in compassion-based social relations' *The Journal of Moral Philosophy*, vol 2, no 1, pp 69-87. I would like to thank the editor, Thom Brooks, for his useful suggestions for revisions, and any other individuals associated with the referring process, as well as Brill Publications for giving me permission to reproduce parts of this article here. Earlier and later revised versions of this article and chapter were also presented to the University of Cambridge's Von Hugel Institute annual conference in 2005; to the Priority and Practice conference at University College London (UCL) in 2005; to the University of Cardiff's Philosophy Department in 2005; to the Association for Legal and Social Philosophy annual conference at University College Dublin (UCD) in 2006; and to the South-West Bio-Ethics Workshop organised by the SERG at the University of Wales, Newport in 2010. Again, I would like to thank participants at all these events for their insightful and thought-provoking comments, most particularly Jo Wolff and Catriona MacKinnon at the UCL event, Harry Brighouse at the UCD event, and Gideon Calder, Enzo Rossi and Phillip Cole at the Newport event.

Chapter Five is a revised and extended version of S. R. Smith (2009) 'Social justice and disability, competing interpretations of the medical and social models', pp 15-29, in the collection *Arguing about disability: Philosophical perspectives*. I would like to thank the editors, Kristjana Kristiansen, Simo Vehmas and Tom Shakespeare, for their very useful suggestions for revision, and the publisher Routledge for giving me permission to reproduce parts of the chapter here. An earlier version of this chapter was also presented to the launch conference for the Centre for Applied Philosophy, Politics and Ethics at the University of Brighton. Again, I would like to thank Bob Brecher, as well as the other participants at this event, for their various contributions.

Finally, Chapter Six is a revised and extended version of S. R. Smith (2005) 'Equality, identity and the disability rights movement: from policy to practice and from Kant to Nietzsche in more than one uneasy move' *Critical Social Policy*, vol 25, no 4, pp 554-76. I would like to thank the editors and those associated with the refereeing process for their very useful comments, and to Sage Publications for giving me permission to reproduce parts of the article here. An earlier version of this article was also presented to the Social Policy Association annual conference, at the University of Nottingham in 2004. Again, I would like to thank participants at this event for their insightful and thought-provoking comments. Of course, I take full responsibility for all the material presented and arguments defended throughout the book.

ONE

Equality, diversity and radical politics

Introduction

There are two central premises of this book: first, that the values worth promoting across communities, including those associated with equality and diversity, are often conflicting and incommensurable – so are values that pull in opposite directions and cannot be measured against one scale, or, most strongly, cannot be compared; and second, that individuals in these communities are agents who have lives that reflect commitments to many incommensurable 'valued objects' both between individuals and group members and across one individual's life. My main argument is that this type of value conflict and incommensurability is philosophically defensible and, with some elaboration, helps make plausible the normative claims associated with the political slogan that 'differences should be celebrated'. This slogan, endorsed by, among others, those within contemporary social movements, to be sure, is a political gambit to protect what might be termed the 'identity interests' of the marginalised and disadvantaged, but, I argue, is one that can be understood philosophically insofar as it reflects the incommensurability of promoting the values of both equality and diversity. Following this understanding, I defend my other main normative claim, that through various social and political policies and practices, we should encourage and engage in reciprocal or mutually beneficial relations with equal others, while recognising that we also often lead incommensurably different lives.

Moreover, once value incommensurability in these forms is acknowledged, other matters, concerning the relationship between individuals and group members living in liberal communities, become clearer. First, I argue that the character of individual attachments to incommensurable valued objects, both across one individual's life and between individuals and group members, provide reasons to promote certain types of equality and diversity within these communities. So the liberal egalitarian principle of having equal respect for others is made more substantial if it is acknowledged that the different 'other' who leads a life that is incommensurable with yours, nevertheless, like you, has committed to deep-felt attachments.

Second, a universal principle supporting diversity is allowed, where different individual and group-member 'life forms' are viewed as often being incommensurable, implying that many are neither better or worse than, nor equal to or otherwise on a par with, others. Respect for 'the other' is derived, then, at least in part, from suspending or at least limiting judgments about the comparative worth of lives led. Therefore, promoting incommensurable life forms is distinguished as a particular brand of value pluralism; that is, supporting the liberal claim that values worth promoting are often not only many, conflicting and immune to lexical ordering, but also incomparably and so comprehensively different, occupying qualitatively different 'value streams' and unable to be traded off against each other without unjustifiably compromising the merit of each value. In social and political spheres, a wide range of different identities and 'conceptions of the good' can be promoted across this incommensurable rubric, with the view that those identities that seek to impose conceptions of the good on others are ruled out as oppressive.

Third, and following specific claims about the character of reciprocal relations, the equal respect ensuing is not subsequently gained from the abstract Kantian universal attribution of equal status to persons as choosers, and/or who have beliefs or identities that matter to them, but instead is founded on promoting the very particularised but positive relational dynamic that can occur between incommensurably differently situated others living in a liberal community. However, I do not give an overriding normative and political priority to deliberative rational dialogue being facilitated in the public realm, contrary to many other authors who have some sympathy with these conclusions (Parekh, 2000, 2008; Honneth, 1992, 2007; Taylor, 1992; Habermas, 1994; Tully, 2004). Although facilitating dialogue with others is a very important aspect to how this dynamic is generated, the highly relational aspect to the reciprocal exchange recommended derives at least as much from very specific and particular emotional and physical encounters with others, as from facilitating rational and reasonable public discourses between those who hold radically different conceptions of the good.

Fourth, from the latter, I argue that the subsequent diversity promoted is not merely a by-product of a cognitive disposition, seen as a platform for deliberative tolerance and inclusion, nor is it an aesthetic or quasi-aesthetic ideal to be achieved by liberal communities, assuming a celebration of diversity can be asserted bluntly, as it were, without further justification.[1] Rather, diversity is promoted to facilitate a richness in reciprocal exchange that, I argue, can be achieved by a more general openness to otherness that would be less possible in more homogenous communities, or in communities that may have diverse cultures and identities but have a more or less inert status in relation to each other. So, reflecting many themes in contemporary social theory and philosophy, particularised identities, beliefs and characteristics, albeit strongly held, are not seen as entirely fixed or essential (Hughes and Lewis, 1998; Saraga, 1998; Foucault, 2001; Faubion, 2003). Instead, they are viewed, to lesser or greater degrees, as continually changing and changeable, as these reciprocal encounters with radically different others within this type of liberal community both affirm and challenge who we are, what we do and what beliefs we hold,

Fifth, however, on a different tack, I argue that acknowledging the presence of diverse and incommensurable lives so described also puts healthy limits on empathic imagination regarding the condition of 'the other', but considerably complicates conventional interpretations of liberal egalitarian political philosophy and contemporary social theory and philosophy. These limits are derived, in the first instance, from the way individuals are viewed from many liberal perspectives at least, as separate from each other – relating both to differences in individual experiences, and to how individuals as agents respond differently to these experiences. Therefore, it might be said that the incommensurable aspects of individual lives are based not only on the often different commitments made to valued objects, but also on the very particularised and unpredictable way persons respond to their experiences, which are highly diverse, surprising and frequently incomparable – so producing the comprehensive incommensurability defined earlier.

I argue further that these various considerations reflect both Kantian and Nietzschean/existentialist philosophical themes, and problematise many contemporary liberal egalitarian conceptions of justice, as distributions to the disadvantaged or marginalised often presuppose a common understanding or empathic connection, eliciting, for example, the emotions of sympathy and pity for those people defined as worse off. This presupposition is especially problematic for disabled people, a group that is typically and often unambiguously assumed as being comparatively worse off and worthy targets for compassion or pity, but who regard this attitude as patronising and disempowering. My main philosophical response is that acknowledging these descriptive limits to empathic imagination puts proper normative constraints on the role of empathic sympathy and pity when promoting socially just societies. These constraints, both descriptive and normative, imply a reconceptualisation of luck in liberal egalitarian theory, recognising that individuals often engage with their 'bad luck' in ways that can paradoxically positively transform lives, and that therefore cannot be fully compared with a life that might have been lived otherwise. I argue that via this reconceptualisation we can better articulate the political demands of the disability rights movement (DRM), which has fiercely resisted defining disabled people as tragic and passive victims of circumstances beyond their control, and so becoming 'objects of pity' for having comparatively worse lives than non-disabled people.

More specifically, using disability as a platform for discussion throughout much of the book, one of my central claims is that the conflicts associated with promoting the values of equality and diversity are especially highlighted through what I term an unsynthesised dual endorsement of both Kantian and Nietzschean/existentialist philosophies by the DRM. The former allows for a liberal promotion of equal rights to choose an independent and separate life to others, an important cornerstone for many of the political demands of new social movements, while the latter leads to a more radical philosophical and political critique of any universalised moral frameworks, including those that relate to promoting rights and Anglo-American liberal egalitarianism. This critique is found in much contemporary European social theory and philosophy, and is also highly influential on other social movements, such as the women's movement, the gay and lesbian movement, and the promotion of multiculturalism and anti-colonialism.

Finally, this dual endorsement leads to other conflicts, both philosophically and politically, again, I would contend, reflecting the incommensurability of values promoted across liberal communities. For example, the tension between these two different philosophical traditions reveals further the incommensurability of equality and diversity when both values are promoted, establishing important limits to reason and theory in resolving the conflict between them. Consequently, instead of using reason and theory to solve the problems of value conflict in liberal societies, I argue that the presence of value incommensurability reflects certain paradoxes concerning the human condition, in the context of asserting particularised identities as these relate to what is important to persons, at the same time maintaining universal values in human relations. My central claim is that fully acknowledging these conflicts and paradoxes, allows for a practical engagement with 'the radically different other', out of which a healthy plural society can more fully emerge and develop.

As a prelude to these discussions, I will now outline the wider political and philosophical backgrounds to the equality and diversity debate. This will contextualise further my explorations of what has been called the 'universalist' and 'particularist' emphases within this debate, as these relate to the arguments just rehearsed, and the demands of radical political positions – especially the demands of new social movements.

Establishing the parameters of the equality and diversity debate

The value of equality is central to most, if not all, Anglo–American contemporary political philosophy, but is notoriously difficult to define substantially with any degree of consensus (Nagel, 1995, pp 63-74; Sen, 1992; Arneson, 1993; Cohen, 2000, pp 101-15; Heywood, 2004, pp 284-315). Consequently, rival theories of equality span vast political and philosophical landscapes. Libertarians of both right and left, liberal egalitarians, utilitarians, various analytical Marxists and neo-Marxists all claim an 'equality space' for their positions but conceive this space in very different ways. Despite these differences, egalitarian theorists have made a lot of the common characteristics between human beings, arguing that these imply the principle of equal treatment in certain morally relevant respects. This principle then leads to universal rules being applied equally to all, according to these specific conceptions of equality.

There is a great appeal, both politically and philosophically, to making these universal claims. The political reasons for endorsing this type of universalism has been variously motivated, but probably gained most momentum after the Second World War, when human rights abuses became so apparent. This resulted in the 1948 United Nations Universal Declaration of Human Rights, which has subsequently been used as a normative benchmark for other similar frameworks, such as European Human Rights legislation. Philosophical arguments for these rights have been defended since at least the 17th century found in, among many others, John Locke, Immanuel Kant, John Stuart Mill and John Rawls (Birch, 1993, pp 113-34; Knowles, 2001, pp 155-74). Reasons for defending these universal rights and their associated values are of course various, but that a defence ought to be made is endorsed by those working in this universal rights-based tradition, often defined as liberal. The point is that the value of equality is also readily endorsed, given that these rights are equally attributable to all.

However, egalitarian positions have been complicated, not only by disputes among liberals and egalitarians, but also by the rise of what has been dubbed the 'politics of recognition'. Born from equality movements, but based on a radicalised assertion of specific or particularised identities, this new politics emphasising differences between people has profoundly disrupted traditional egalitarian agendas (for example, see Young, 1990; Honneth, 1992; 2007; Taylor, 1992; Fraser, 1997; Parekh, 2000; Fraser and Honneth, 2003). However equality is conceptualised, universal liberal claims that all persons are equal and should be ascribed certain rights, while not necessarily entirely rejected, are now often viewed with suspicion, judged as ignoring, or at least underestimating, the normative significance of being different (that is, differences that relate to group membership and/or personal characteristics that are said to comprise specific identities and matter deeply to particular persons).[2] For example, elements of feminist theory, being traditionally concerned with establishing equality between men and women, have recently been highly critical of these liberal and egalitarian assertions. Often informed by postmodern and poststructuralist theory from continental Europe, the argument roughly states that the value of equality, while represented as a liberating and universal goal for all, merely serves to justify dominant masculanised cultural norms exercised through these liberal justifications, denying gender difference and so excluding and suppressing interests particular to women (for example, see Butler, 1990; Young, 1990; Whelehan, 1995; Squires, 1999; Bryson, 2003). More generally, universal equality claims, often derived from Anglo-American political philosophy, are seen to obscure the concrete negotiation of differences between these various identities, as its universalism overemphasises the similarities between people, and so, quoting Iris Marion Young, 'by claiming to provide a standpoint which all subjects can adopt denies the difference between subjects' (Young, 1990, p 10).

Again, there has been great appeal, both politically and philosophically, for making these particularist claims. The political motivation for endorsing particularism is from a variety of social movements arising in the 19th and especially 20th centuries, leading to radicalised assertions of marginalised group-member identities opposed to dominance and oppression by other social and cultural groupings (Young, 1990; Fraser, 1997; Ellison, 1999; Fraser and Honneth, 2003; Honneth, 2007). Colonised national identities have been opposed to colonial rule; women's identities have been opposed to patriarchal rule; black identities have been opposed to white rule; homosexual and 'queer' identities have been opposed to heterosexual rule; and more recently, disability identities have been opposed to non-disabled rule. Philosophical arguments for this stress at least on particularism have been defended by a growing number of commentators addressing both Anglo-American and continental audiences and concerns (for example, see Butler, 1990; Young, 1990; Honneth, 1992, 2007; Taylor, 1992). But these positions have also often been profoundly influenced by continental philosophy, past and present, and are found in, among others, the works of Friedrich Nietzsche, Emmanuel Levinas and Michel Foucault (Nietzsche, 1975a, 1975b; Levinas, 1985, 2006; Foucault, 2001; also see Honderich, 1995; West, 1996). Reasons for defending these forms of particularism are again various, but those working within this tradition tend to problematise universal or 'objective' principles, or, as sometimes referred to, 'totalising' principles, so as to recommend the assertion of specific values as related to those characteristics that comprise these particular and highly 'subjective' identities and characteristics.

Given this apparent disjunction between universalism and particularism, a central question of contemporary political thought is how the conflict between equality and diversity principles should be viewed and understood. One response is to entrench in either camp. Consequently, some analytical Anglo-American egalitarian philosophers promote the universal values of equality and impartiality as an alternative to what they see as the often philosophically incoherent, and politically dangerous, promotion of cultural particularism and value relativism (see, for example, Nussbaum, 1992, 2000; Barry, 1995, 2001). Conversely, those influenced by continental philosophy often robustly defend cultural particularism, resisting what they see as the oppressive imposition of universal identities, regardless of whether these identities relate to individual 'subjects' or 'groups' and are being expressed and reinforced via these liberal principles of equality (see, for example, Butler, 1990; Young, 1990; Saraga, 1998).

Nevertheless, from a relatively small base in the early 1990s, an increasing number of commentators have tried to establish a middle or at least partially synthesised ground, by accommodating particularism and the assertion of specific identities, but also preserving what is seen as the universal value of equality, however conceptualised (for example, Taylor, 1992, 1997; Fraser, 1997; Fraser, in Fraser and Honneth, 2003; Ellison, 1999; Parekh, 2000).[3] My response, here and throughout the book, while generally sympathetic to the latter strategy in offering an alternative to entrenchment, does not promote a synthesised *middle* ground between them, as if political theory can find solutions to both the philosophical and political conflict between the values associated with promoting equality and diversity.[4] Instead, I adapt arguments from the continental tradition, found mainly, but not exclusively, in the existentialism of Soren Kierkegaard, Friedrich Nietzsche and Jean-Paul Sartre, and from within an orthodox strand of liberal thinking that promotes value incommensurability and found in, for example, the work of Isaiah Berlin, Joseph Raz and William Galston. My main claim, reflecting, I believe, central themes within both these traditions, is that the values associated with equality and diversity should be promoted in liberal plural societies, but are often neither commensurable nor comparable, and nor is the conflict between them synthesisable. However, before elaborating these arguments, I will first provide a brief exegesis of the advantages and disadvantages of universalism and particularism as identified by political philosophers and policy analysts who are committed to political positions that might be loosely described as radical. It is in this latter context that a wider understanding of the political and policy positions promoted can, I contend, be better appreciated, in particular as they relate to the philosophical concerns and issues just outlined.

Radical positions, as I am defining the term here, seek to reconfigure and even transform social, political and economic relations reflecting some kind of universal egalitarian value base. These include liberal egalitarian positions that typically justify redistributing resources from the 'better-off' to the 'worst-off', given the presence of, for example, material inequalities across free market economies, as well as more full-blooded socialist positions that seek to dismantle capitalist systems, replacing them with more collective forms of provision. In addition, radical political positions, again as I am defining the term, directly challenge dominant norms and practices through positively asserting a wide range of different and particularised identities, in part so the value of these identities are positively recognised in the public realm. Here, liberal egalitarian positions would often see this process of recognition broadly reflecting the value of freedom, as individuals, being members of groups, are ascribed certain rights to choose particular and different identities and values that matter to them. They would also include other less liberal positions most typically promoted within contemporary social movements, representing the various identities and interests of minority group members, giving voice to their experiences and concerns, and often opposing other more dominant group interests.[5] However, reflecting the political and philosophical debates outlined previously these two emphases within radical politics, according to Nancy Fraser at least, raise a number of difficult issues, given 'an absence of any credible overarching emancipatory project despite the proliferation of fronts of struggle; a general decoupling of the cultural politics of recognition from the social politics of redistribution; and a decentering of claims for equality in the face of aggressive marketization and sharply rising material inequality' (Fraser, 1997, p 3). Acknowledging these issues, I now intend to briefly sketch how emphasising either universalism or particularism has both advantages and disadvantages for radical political positions, suggesting, I believe, a *pro tanto* dilemma or conflict for political philosophers and policy analysts committed to radical politics. I explore the possibility of subsuming one side of this conflict to the other as a way of 'solving' the dilemma. However, as a prelude to the remainder of the book, I conclude that these solutions, both politically and philosophically, are inadequate.

Radical politics and universalism versus particularism

To roughly paraphrase Raz, there are three principal conditions for universal claims; they can be stated without use of singular reference points such as place or time, or to any particular individual or group; they can be articulated in any place and at any time and in principle be comprehended by any person or group; and, in principle they can be displayed or expressed by any person or group (Raz, 2001, pp 54-6). Given these conditions, for those committed to radical political positions, the first obvious advantage of universalism is that it is unifying and inclusive. Recognising cultural and other differences may be accommodated within this universal rubric, but these differences are secondary to what human beings have in common regarding what we can abstractly state, understand and articulate about our lives (that is, abstracted from our particular identities, social conditions and personal characteristics). However, the corresponding disadvantage of these universal claims is that they may say little or nothing about the particularised character of moral domains and human experiences, because these are necessarily depersonalised by this very process of universalised abstraction. For example, if normatively legitimate relationships are largely defined by the extent to which universal rules are followed, specific relational commitments that inevitably differ between individual persons and cultural and social groupings are likely to be ignored. The response from particularism comes in various guises, from postmodern positions to different versions of communitarianism, for example, but with the advantage being that emphasising specific relational commitments reflected in, say, cultural identities, prevents this over-abstraction found in universal rule following (Sandel, 1982; Young, 1990; Taylor, 1992; Ellison, 1999; Salih, 2003). This emphasis, in turn, provides a radical platform for asserting these differences against dominant norms and practices. Conversely, the disadvantage in making these particularised claims is that it can often lead to cultural conservatism and insularity, as it becomes difficult to critique prevailing orders if morality is increasingly grounded in existing social relations and practices (Taylor-Gooby, 1994; Fitzpatrick, 1996; O'Brien and Penna, 1996; Barry, 2001; Nussbaum, 1992, 2000, 2006). At its most extreme, some forms of particularism collapse into epistemological and value relativism, with its radical critique of universal theorising being self-defeating as a result. Briefly put, this is because any radical critique asserts a privileged position or vantage point for seeing the world, occurring outside of the paradigmatic framework being critiqued. Nevertheless, claiming a privileged position is precisely what universal theorising is being critiqued for by these particularists (Habermas, 1990; West, 1996, pp 200-1; also see Hales, 1997, pp 34-5).

The second advantage to making universal claims for radical political positions is that moral priority can be given to the condition of the worse-off (Rawls, 1973; Nagel, 1995, pp 65-9; Arneson, 2000; Cohen, 2000). Here, universal claims about the descriptive condition of all persons are distinguished from but *lead to* further normative claims of impartiality, substituting personal and particular interests for impersonal ones, which then allow for the prioritisation of the worst-off's universal interests, needs and so on, even if this means sacrificing, at least to some degree, one's own particularised interests as a member of a better-off group (for example, see Nagel, 1995, pp 63-74). The corresponding disadvantage is that subsequent policy and practice risks undermining the positive identity and self-respect of the worse-off, by defining worse-off people as passive victims of their circumstances, and even as 'objects of pity', given the initial universal judgments concerning the diminished condition of the individual lives of those in this group compared with the better-off (Anderson, 1999; and see my arguments in Smith 2002a, 2005a, 2005b, 2009 and here in Chapters Three, Four, Five and Six). These judgments also often reinforce the exclusion and oppression of these groups, according to many spokespersons within social movements (Saraga, 1998; Ellison, 1999; Heredia, 2007). In contrast, particularist claims often allow for a radicalised assertion of specific identities and characteristics, recognising the positive and thriving character of individuals as members of certain groups who face adverse social, political and economic circumstances. However, the corresponding disadvantage of particularism for radical political positions is that this understanding of identity assertion risks romanticising the condition of the worse-off, where universal debilitating handicaps and obstacles to the development and enhancement of, for example, human well-being, can be ignored in an effort to democratise or give voice to these positive personal and/or group-member experiences (Nussbaum, 1992, 2000, 2006; Arneson, 2000; Phillips, 2004).

The third advantage to making universal claims is their intended determinate and non-arbitrary content. Operating as general guides to specific action, universal rules determine principles of decision making based on rational or reasonable calculations understood as impartial (for example, see Nagel, 1995, pp 1-20; Barry, 1995). These are reflected in the universal formal rule of equality that 'like cases be treated the same and unlike cases differently' – with the meaning of what are relevant similarities and differences being informed by specific understandings of impartiality. For example, if two persons have equal ability for performing certain types of work, arbitrary differences based on, say, gender, race and ethnic origin are regarded as irrelevant to whether someone should be employed or not. The formal rule is interpreted in these like cases via job performance or capability, effectively ignoring other irrelevant differences between persons (Clarke, 1994, p 1; Smith, 1998, pp 138-41; Calder and Smith, 2011). However, identifying relevant similarities and differences in like and unlike cases are often indeterminate. Even in limited examples, where what determines a like case may seem self-evident, these are difficult to justify without relying on certain givens about persons and group characteristics which are often question-begging. For example, diminished job performance and capability can often be related to gender, race and ethnic origin when generalised characteristics of group members are mediated via a social context that systematically discriminates against these members (Smith, 1998, pp 136-45; Phillips, 2004; see also Calder and Smith, 2011). If a woman's job performance is detrimentally affected by lack of childcare facilities, or by an overburdened social expectation regarding the role of women in caring for children, it could be argued that being a woman is relevant to job performance and capabilities, given these social conditions. The controversial substantive normative question then arises as to how gender differences are caused and in turn how these are addressed, which is clearly not answerable by referring to the formal equality rule.

In response to these problems, some forms of radical politics, influenced by contemporary social theory, use particularist arguments to critique all categories of, for example, gender, race and ethnic 'group', when describing and representing personal experiences, viewing them as products of homogenising myths, misrepresenting the different lives of particular individuals (for example, see Butler, 1990; Saraga, 1998; Heredia, 2007). However, the counter-response from liberal egalitarians is that, without any recourse to universal categories for defending general normative principles of impartiality, it seems difficult to avoid treating individuals and group members arbitrarily and unfairly. For example, while it may be important for liberal egalitarians to recognise that a person has particular obligations and attachments peculiar to her and relating to, for example, family and friendship loyalties, such situations should not be regarded as immune to impartial judgment, lest nepotism and other forms of unjustifiable partial privilege intrude. These obligations and attachments are instead delimited by more general and universal principles, such as 'all persons should prioritise family and friendship loyalties' that in turn allow impartial judgments to prevail even in specific circumstances (Barry, 1995, 2001; Haworth, 2005). For example, it might be morally defensible for a daughter to first save her father from drowning, and not another person's father, thereby upholding particular obligations, but only provided the same daughter recognises the universal justification of all daughters saving their fathers first, that is, in other circumstances where *her* father could not also be saved. However, the disadvantage of this strategy for radical political positions is that accommodating particular obligations through this form of universal deliberation, which considers each specific circumstance, again can appear question-begging. Many people's circumstances are themselves shaped by unjust social and political arrangements, and are therefore subject to criticism, as these unjust arrangements could in turn diminish a person's ability to aid someone close to them.

Consequently, to summarise, universalism and particularism, and the associated values of equality and diversity, seem to be in profound conflict when defending radical political positions. This conflict is represented in Box 1.1, where the respective advantages and disadvantages *between* each stance are regarded as incompatible when matched horizontally, whereas the advantages and disadvantages *within* each stance seem to cancel each other out when matched vertically. Therefore, there seems to be a *pro tanto* or intransigent dilemma for radical political positions seeking to promote the values of equality and diversity: in short, the more an advantage is emphasised from one stance, the greater disadvantage within this stance is exposed by the other.

Box 1.1: Universalism versus particularism

Equality and the universalist stance	Diversity and the particularist stance
Advantages for radical politics	*Disadvantages for radical politics*
i. Unifying and inclusive	i. Culturally conservative/value-relative
ii. Priority to the worse-off	ii. Ignores disadvantage and handicap
iii. Determinate and non-arbitrary	iii. Indeterminate and morally arbitrary
Disadvantages for radical politics	*Advantages for radical politics*
i. Overly abstract and impersonal	i. Cultural relevance and specificity
ii. Label disadvantaged as victims	ii. Positive voice to oppressed minorities
iii. Uses question-begging substantive categories	iii. Avoids stereotyping/fixed categories

I will now briefly outline three contrasting philosophical responses to the dilemmas and conflicts outlined in Box 1.1. First, the conflicts and dilemmas are viewed as *prima facie*, where conflicting values implied in each stance can be ranked according to a philosophical system or theory, with each set of advantages outweighing or assuming priority over the corresponding disadvantages. Second, in the absence of a foundational philosophical system or theory of value arbitrating between these advantages and disadvantages, value scepticism holds, where substantial judgments about values and their relationship to each other are considered impossible to make. Third, the conflicts and dilemmas are viewed as *pro tanto* and incommensurable but this is not cause for philosophical or political alarm or wholesale value scepticism, as the presence of incommensurability is philosophically coherent, given the proper limits ascribed to theory and reason in ranking values, and that as a political consequence lives can be enriched in a plural society through positively engaging with radically differently situated others. Throughout this book, I defend the third response, but first I provide an outlined critical examination of those various philosophical attempts at resolving the conflicts, through promoting mutual respect, equal concern, and what is referred to as the positive recognition of 'the other'.

Resolving the conflict between the values of equality and diversity

Notions of self-respect, respect for others, equal concern and the positive recognition of 'the other' often overlap in their conceptual relationship and practical application. For example, it might be argued that a necessary condition for maintaining and promoting self-respect is a confidence that you, as a person, are treated alongside other persons with equal concern, and that you will positively recognise and respect others similarly (see, for example, Darwall, 1977; Bird, 2004). Much Kantian and neo-Kantian liberal moral and political philosophy assumes that respect for 'the other' as a different and separately choosing person or agent must be promoted alongside self-respect, implying that respect should be mutual between persons and so, to cite John Rawls, is 'reciprocally self-supporting' (Rawls, 1973, p 179).[6] In this context, a situation where individuals choose a plurality of conflicting goods is delimited, first by recognising the equal right of all persons to choose, which then provides a basis for respecting and so positively recognising these differences between persons. Briefly put, this respect and recognition is therefore due if, and only if, the equal right of all to choose their own understanding of a 'good life' is upheld as a first principle (also see Rawls, 1993, 2001). In Kantian parlance, the priority of the homogenous 'right' (reflected in the universal value of attributing equal rights between persons) over the heterogeneous 'good' (reflecting the value of difference in promoting particularised identities and personal characteristics) adjudicates between what is seen now only as a *prima facie* conflict between equality and diversity. For example, if rational persons pursue their own self-interest and various conceptions of the good in a world of scarce resources, on grounds of Kantian reasonableness these persons would also be open to maintaining political and social systems guaranteeing rights to secure these interests equally, such as those rights found in various forms of liberal social contract (again, see Rawls, 1973, 1993, 2001; also see for example, Gauthier, 1990; Scanlon, 1998). Given this understanding, rationality and reasonableness perform modest instrumental functions in managing the conflict between equality and diversity, that is, without retreating to an extreme particularist subjectivism, which recognises only individual wants, desires and perspectives, but resisting the unadulterated objectivism of universal ends defined by, say, nature, God or even reason itself – ends that, in their philosophical or theological application, often do not sufficiently accommodate particular wants, desires and perspectives, as previously highlighted (Nagel, 1989, pp 26-7; 1993, pp 10-20; Gauthier, 1990, pp 343-4).

However, there are notorious problems with adopting these types of strategy, reflecting schisms over how the relationship between values and reason are viewed, with these often being ignored, or at least downplayed, by Kantian and/or contractarian moves. First, the relationship between personal identities and attitudes to difference is complex, with various ambiguities arising over how substantive notions of mutual respect are properly understood. How do notions of respect relate to, for example, other important political concepts such as tolerance, where individuals in liberal societies are asked to tolerate behaviour, beliefs and other characteristics they may deeply disapprove of or otherwise object to (Mendus, 1999; Parekh, 2000; Raz, 2001; Bird, 2004; McKinnon, 2006)? In response, many Kantians ground the value of self-respect, and its correlate, respect for others, not in recognising or giving merit to differences reflecting a person's particularised identity or personal characteristics, but rather in the person's more generalised rational and deliberative capacity to choose different 'conceptions of the good'. But this understanding of mutual respect, which bypasses personal characteristics or qualities, raises other problems concerning the over-abstraction and over-generalisation explored previously. Individual identity and/or personal characteristics become disembodied from the person as 'subject', if these substantial features of persons are subsumed under universal abstract categories, in this case the universal category of deliberative person as chooser (Sandel, 1982; Galston, 2002, pp 15-27). The point for radical political positions is that this move is problematic when specific characteristics are deemed as oppressive in relation to other characteristics viewed as oppressed. Consequently, charges of over-abstraction have substantial normative bite when it is acknowledged that concrete political experiences often have a profound and detrimental bearing on the way persons, belonging to oppressed groups, are treated by others.

Second, when disembodied subjects stripped of particular interests are universally and hypothetically postulated for the sake of defending impartial conceptions of justice (Rawls, 1973; 1993; 2001), partial commitments are often smuggled in, so to speak, and sully the argument on its own terms (Munoz-Darde, 1998; Parekh, 2000, pp 80-113). For example, Rawlsian understandings of justice depend on highly particularised commitments to forms of family life that, for many feminist writers, are often unstated in his arguments, masking the sociological realities of patriarchal societies that depend on families being promoted in certain oppressive ways (Munoz-Darde, 1998). Another related empirical problem concerns what some have highlighted as a universal human inability to be wholly impartial, given our partial commitments (Nagel, 1989; 1995; Griffin, 1997). If 'ought' implies 'can', as it must do in Kantian and other moral theory, a universalised moral injunction that we should be wholly impartial is in danger of losing plausibility when we acknowledge fully the kind of persons we are universally. Certainly, Kantians do acknowledge this problem in, for example, Rawls' earlier and especially later work, where individual self-interest is prioritised in his theory of justice (Rawls, 1971, 2001). However, it might be countered that this masks the deeper tensions between promoting impartiality through equal respect and universally promoting diverse and particularised interests – that is, when recognising the legitimate and rational deep-felt commitments relatively well-off people have to particular 'valued objects', alongside the conflicting universal but legitimate demands of reasonableness when living in a world of scarce resources, acknowledging many people are very badly off (again, see Nagel, 1989, 1995).

Third, and on a different tack, upholding self-respect and respect for others as choosers does not recognise the many conceptions of the good that do not value choice, or at least regard choice as secondary to other values (Galston, 2002, pp 20-3). Many particularised identities and personal characteristics are not chosen but still are highly valued because they are underpinned by, say, family and community upbringing or cultural heritage (Sandel, 1982; Gray, 1996; Galston, 2002, pp 15-27). It might be counter-argued by Kantians that valuing choice, or more precisely, the universal choosing person as deliberative self-legislator, means it is possible to allow the pursuit of unchosen values or values other than choice, and still be consistent with Kantian ethics, provided it is possible to freely disengage from these commitments, whatever their cause. However, this seems to underplay the import from Kantians themselves concerning *why* persons are valued – namely that persons are authors of their own conceptions of the good, and so value choice as the foundation for other values, which then provides the basis for respecting persons *as* choosers who have autonomously chosen their conceptions of good – that is, considered separately to any freedoms a person might also have to disengage from commitments that are socialised.

One liberal universalist response to these problems is to state that a person's differences should be respected and recognised, not because she has chosen a difference that matters to her, but because it matters to her whether or not she has chosen it (for example, see Jones, 2006). A further advantage of this strategy for many liberals and Kantians is that equality is maintained as a first principle, affording equal *status* to different identities and cultural characteristics, again without making controversial normative claims about the particular *merit* of these identities and characteristics (also see Laegaard, 2005). It might also be argued, on less Kantian grounds perhaps, that general epistemological uncertainty regarding what is or is not a good life for all girders this form of liberalism (Nagel, 1989, 1995; Barry, 1995; Parekh, 2000, pp 338-43). Therefore, the liberal state recognises a variety of commitments, characteristics and identities by providing impartial institutions that allow the expression of particularised or partial commitments, none of which have privileged epistemological status (also see Taylor, 2003, pp 246-71). Conflict between impartial and partial values may still be present after these procedures are established, and so to this extent there is no complete or total solution to the conflict between these values. Nevertheless, most of the conflict has been dissolved through impartial institutional practices derived from these prior assumptions regarding individual identities and these commitments to various conceptions of the good and value scepticism.

However, I contend that these solutions, although they meet some of the Kantian problems highlighted previously, run into difficulties for radical political positions, derived in part from sociological claims that I think are uncontroversial and that are explored throughout the book. Related to the broadly Rousseauian concern (explored by Gauthier, 1990, pp 78-109) that over-dependence on the opinion and respect of others for status can itself be oppressive, the status of particular identities is often mediated through prevailing social, political and economic relations. Consequently, radical political positions often assert that negative judgments concerning marginalised identities ought to be challenged, especially by those who bear these identities. Moreover, it is within this wider political context that other philosophical and normative questions are raised about the character of identity, self-consciousness, agency and group recognition. These issues are explored further in subsequent chapters; suffice it to say here that the Hegelian-type claim that identities are often formed from asserting what individuals as members of a group are not, and so are formed negatively, is pertinent to my arguments (also see Cullen, 1979; Camus, 1982, pp 106-8). The main contention here is that these social relations have a profound effect on what individuals think of themselves, and what they also think of others who are defined as different. For example, various normative distinctions are often made between particularised identities as a result of these social processes, where according to radical political positions at least, and as stated previously, some identities are consequently oppressed while others are viewed as oppressive (see also Fraser, 1997, pp 189-235; Fraser and Honneth, 2003). The difficult question, avoided by the Kantianesque move just described, is precisely how these latter judgments are made, as judging the lesser merit of, for example, a fascist or racist or homophobic belief or identity held by a particular person or group is legitimate from radical perspectives wanting to maintain equal respect, *even if* these particular beliefs and identities matter a lot to those who hold them.

According to radical political positions, parallel problems for liberal contractarians emerge, given that some oppressive relations are entered into by contractual agreement, a difficulty that, albeit often disregarded by right libertarians such as Nozick (1974, pp 297-334), cannot be so readily ignored by leftist universalist liberal egalitarians such as Rawls (1973) and Scanlon (1998). This difficulty leads to other troubling questions concerning the relationship between consent and rationality within these institutional procedures, but again is often unstated, or at least is in danger of being understated by these liberal egalitarians (also see Lovett, 2004). For example, can just procedural systems be legitimated via voluntary agreement and democratic process that may render these legitimations theoretically indeterminate as politically obnoxious outcomes can be justified by voluntary consent? Certainly, procedures that do not pre-empt any particular outcome may be formulated such that the quality of interaction between persons effectively rules out politically obnoxious outcomes, but this then forces a wedge between proceduralism and voluntarism that may be normatively plausible, but can also be problematic for certain contractarians and proceduralists. This is because substantial judgments concerning what is not permissible is suggested in any subsequent theory of justice, and so renders certain forms of voluntary agreement superfluous. It also implies an outcome of sorts, relating to the quality of social relations that ensue via certain types of procedure (also see Ceva, 2009). Either way, substantial normative conceptions of justice are again allowed, but are neither an outcome of agreement nor procedure and so need to be explicitly defended. Certainly, radical political positions often promote substantial conceptions of justice, on the grounds that leaving justice to voluntary agreement and/or procedures within liberal democratic societies is insufficient for maintaining just institutional practices, given the presence of powerful vested interests. But this suggestion again is in danger of leaving difficult normative questions unanswered concerning what specific *forms* of justice are permissible or not, and, moreover, what bearing this permissibility has on diverse identity formation and the pursuit of different 'conceptions of the good' and 'forms of life'?

According to Nancy Fraser, for example, some forms of difference tend to be consistent with radical demands for cultural recognition, such as those based on homosexual and gay identities: 'their mode of collectivity is that of a despised sexuality, rooted in the cultural-valuational structure of society. From this perspective, the injustice they suffer is quintessentially a matter of recognition'

(Fraser, 1997, p 18). Other forms of difference, meanwhile, tend to reflect oppressive political and economic relations, such as class inequalities, and are therefore often seen by radical political positions as eradicable through redistributive policies and practices. So, from Fraser's analysis of Marxian understandings of class, '[T]he last thing it needs is recognition of its difference. On the contrary, the only way to remedy the injustice is to put the proletariat out of business' (Fraser, 1997, p 18). Even putting aside that some forms of 'despised sexuality' are indeed oppressive, such as those relating to, say, child sexual abuse, it is not immediately obvious on what normative grounds the distinctions between these other forms of identity and difference are made. For Fraser, making judgments concerning what identities ought to be eradicated produces a dilemma regarding some social categories, such as gender. Here, the logic of redistribution is to eradicate gender distinctions, given that women are often exploited politically and economically, but this is an outcome that may be regretted on the radical feminist assumption that patriarchal societies devalue women's identities and so the latter should be asserted and recognised in the face of dominant masculanised norms (Fraser, 1997, pp 19-20). However, even for gender differences, for Fraser the likely best finesse of what she calls the redistribution-recognition dilemma is 'socialism in the economy plus deconstruction in the culture' (p 31). Nevertheless, she also acknowledges that 'for this scenario to be psychologically and politically feasible [it] requires that all people be weaned from their attachment to current cultural constructions of their interests and identities' (Fraser, 1997, p 31). Despite Fraser having some reservations about this strategy, given the attachment many oppressed people have to their existing identities (see Fraser, 1997, p 39),[7] it would still allow her primary recommendation for 'social equality' where 'cultural differences can be freely elaborated and democratically mediated ...' (Fraser, 1997, p 186).[8] Establishing social equality as a 'first principle' is also consistent with her later work. According to Toppinen, as a result '... she treats recognition as a question of justice, and so is able to overcome the presumption of incompatibility between the recognition paradigm and the redistribution paradigm and makes it feasible to position both terms in a single framework' (Toppinen, 2005, p 427; see also Fraser, in Fraser and Honneth, 2003, especially pp 7-109). So again, as with class differences, there is, in the final analysis, no *pro tanto* dilemma for Fraser, even for those groups who demand both redistribution and recognition.

However, reflecting the themes presented so far, these arguments from Fraser are, I believe, proceeding too hastily, as they risk ignoring or at least downplaying (acknowledging Fraser's reservations) how particularised forms of difference – including those based on class identities – are often highly valued by the holder, even if these differences are produced by oppressive political and economic relations. Following the Marxian interpretation by Fraser, for example, what really matters in terms of justice is eradicating the disadvantage connected with holding this specific identity rather than the identity itself. This is again, I contend, question-begging. Briefly put, my counter-claim is that the basic structure of these arguments, despite Fraser's caveats, commits a similar error to the Kantian universalist explored previously, that is, they take for granted precisely what has been critiqued by particularists by assuming 'that there is a single conception of the person [or class] and there is a common currency of justice' (Laegaard, 2005, p 348). To reiterate, the thoroughgoing deconstructionist argument, which is at least entertained by Fraser, is that all persons should be weaned from their individual attachments, allowing for the promotion of justice as 'social equality'. Consequently, reflecting the Marxist analysis, any positive valuation by the holder of her class identity is in danger of exhibiting false consciousness, preserving transitory differences and distracting attention from the long-term political and economic goal of eradicating class and other similar differences. Paralleling this argument, on more liberal egalitarian Kantian grounds, the greater the divergence in the 'conceptions of the good' present in any one society, leading to a wider range of positively affirmed identities, the fewer the reasons to redistribute resources from the 'better-off' to the 'worst-off' (Van Parijs, 1995, pp 58-85). For example, high levels of well-being can be experienced by the worst-off, who may positively adapt their preferences and aspirations, and subsequent conceptions of the good, according to their circumstances, thus reflecting the positive assertion of their particularised identities (Nussbaum, 2000, pp 160-1). In both cases, particularism and difference is rejected in favour of more universal judgments and recommendations, based either on promoting classlessness as a socialist ideal, or in the Kantian abstraction of the generalised person, the deliberative chooser.

These latter questions and conundrums, and others beside, raise various philosophical and political issues explored throughout the book, concerning the character of 'disadvantage' and what this disadvantage specifically means for persons who experience it. Suffice it to say here, there is a more general counter-claim I will now outline, based on what I believe is a plausible assumption about the way we tend to give value and moral priority to our existing identities and lives led, however these lives are related to social and economic structures. More specifically, I contend that if we do not have full knowledge of future identities or lives to inform what we should be concerned for currently, and have only limited connections with past identities, given that political struggles have changed over time the specific types of group identity and persons we have now become, a positive affiliation to present identities is likely to take priority over other identities that have existed in the past or will exist in the future. It is important to be clear that I am not claiming that a positive affiliation to current identities and characteristics *necessarily* takes priority over past or future identities, as some persons and group members may deeply regret aspects of, or even all of, their present identities and lives led, only that a moral presumption in favour of the present will often occur, given these epistemological limitations. My main argument is that failing to acknowledge this 'bias toward the present', concerning identity formation and a life that is now being lived, has, I believe, contributed to Marxists', and to a lesser extent, Fraser's, inability to recognise sufficiently the normative importance of oppressed groups, whether related to class or not, positively asserting particular differences and identities as they presently exist.[9]

Consequently, while opportunities for future lives may be unjustifiably restricted for those group members defined as disadvantaged and historically oppressed, all of us only have one life to lead, and so are profoundly embedded in the present as we gain value primarily from the lives we actually lead – that is, separate from the political and economic circumstances we experience.

This bias towards the present leads to other questions and conundrums that I argue also produce various normative paradoxes concerning how these matters should be viewed and addressed. For example, experiencing social disadvantage and high levels of flourishing can both be shaped and created via oppressive social relations – so being viewed and treated as an outsider or 'the other' can be at once oppressive *and* liberating. Possessing outsider status is oppressive because the structural features of exclusion mean that an excluded person is likely to experience systemic disadvantage regarding the potential lives that might be led by that person. My main normative argument is that this state of affairs ought to be remedied by robust egalitarian redistributive policies and practices, on the grounds that unequal opportunity to live a range of different lives is socially unjust. Nevertheless, possessing outsider status leading to disadvantage in respect of limited opportunities can be liberating in other ways. My main normative argument here is that positive identity formation is not often based on contemplating potentiality as related to lives that could have been led, but rather is, quite rightly, forged from a positive engagement with actual and highly particularised lived experiences. These experiences include those that are objectively defined as disadvantaged or oppressed, but, according to many within social movements, paradoxically often lead to enhanced subjective levels of well-being compared with what kind of life might otherwise have been led.

Following on, then, from these various arguments and from my critique of the supposed solutions to the conflict between universalism and particularism, and the associated values of equality and diversity, the response here, and throughout the book, is to refuse such solutions both on philosophical and political grounds. In short, I argue that the values underpinning these conflicts or dilemmas are often incommensurable and incomparable, but that this state of affairs is to be recommended both philosophically and politically.

Value incommensurability and celebrating difference

Following the previous discussion, my central claim is that the value conflicts underpinning the equality and diversity debate produces a *pro tanto* dilemma – that is, a dilemma that exists after all the philosophical arguments are in, so to speak. This type of dilemma contrasts with a *prima facie* dilemma solvable by reference to particular philosophical systems, leading to the kinds of solution explored and critiqued so far (see also Smith, 1998, pp 214-45; 2007a, pp 11-18). The point here is that if the conflict between equality and diversity reflects a *pro tanto* dilemma, it contains both moral gains and losses for radical political positions. These gains and losses are made apparent in the corresponding advantages and disadvantages of universalism and particularism outlined in Box 1.1, which then affect the answers given by political philosophers to identity-related politics concerning political values such as respect, tolerance, recognition and redistribution. But how might a radical political position respond to these gains and losses, as related to the main themes I explore in this book?

According to those commentators I sympathise with, we should not necessarily jettison one conflicting value in favour of the other, but rather reject the idea that moral adjudicating principles can always be used to resolve such dilemmas. There may be no theoretical solution to these dilemmas – they could be irresolvable 'all the way down' and this assumption ought to be incorporated within political practice and in the wider complex moral world human beings subsequently occupy (also see Urmson, 1974; Dancy, 1993, pp 109-15; Fishkin, 2002). The assumption in this case is that often the values associated with the equality and diversity debate conflict at this ground level and so cannot be solved by philosophical argument. More specifically, the assumption underpins this book in my arguments for the incommensurability of values.

For Joseph Raz, 'A and B are incommensurate if it is neither true that one is better than the other nor true that they are of equal value' (Raz, 1988, p 332).[10] If two values are not equal but one is not better than the other, any conflict arising from accepting both these values cannot be solved by comparing and ranking each. Given this definition of incommensurability, where comparative weightings are rejected, trade-offs are also blocked where the increase of one value is permitted as the other reduces (see also Sen, 1985; Barry, 1990; Chang, 1997). It might be conceded by incommensurabilists that trade-offs are politically an inevitable aspect of policy and practice implementation, as will be explored further in Chapters Two and Six, and even that some forms of identity are positively recast as a result, but this concession does not entail rejecting the philosophical claim that values underpinning the promotion of equality and diversity are often at fundamental odds, because they cannot be ranked and/or weighted against each other. Briefly put, they are comprehensively different, occupying qualitatively different 'value streams', and so cannot be traded off against each other without unjustifiably compromising the merit of each value. But what are the implications for other kinds of theorising and rational deliberation, assuming the presence of incommensurable values?

Aligning myself with liberal philosophers such as Berlin (1969), Raz (1988, 2001) and Galston (2002), I dispute the claim that reason and moral theory can solve the problem of incommensurable values. It is a claim that takes for granted the capacity rational deliberation has to deliver a single philosophical principle or grading method for ranking values that then can be readily applied to policy and practice. In short, according to incommensurabilists, this falsifies the specific character of moral decision making as being 'calculable' and therefore 'definitive'. For Isaiah Berlin, 'to assume that all values can be graded on one scale, so that it is a mere matter of inspection to determine the highest, seems to me to falsify our knowledge ... to represent moral decision as an operation which a slide-rule could, in principle, perform' (Berlin, 1969, p 171). Similarly, William Galston asserts that if 'there is no *summum bonum* that is the chief good of all individuals. It means there are no comprehensive lexical orderings amongst types of goods. It also means that there is no "first virtue of social institutions"'(Galston, 2002, p 5). However, putting these constraints on rational deliberation to solve value conflict is often not countenanced by theorists who argue that values associated with, say, distinctive cultures can be compared and ranked without restriction. Andrew Shorten, for example, in his recent discussion on toleration, anticipates that 'incorporating the concepts of "fairness" and "cultural commitments" can … move the terms of debate away from accounts of the incommensurability of rival moral and cultural traditions, and instead to a more coherent account of the standards of public justification required by a potential overriding reason for tolerant restraint' (Shorten, 2005, p 289). Certainly, agent-based accounts of incommensurability and accounts of cultural traditions that might be thought of as incommensurable should not be confused (as will be explored later). However, to the extent that incommensurability implies a range of values that are considered worth pursuing by agents, and are values that can also be reflected across different cultures and traditions, highlights some of the inadequacies of theories that try to *unrestrictedly* compare alternative value systems. Developing Berlin's insight, Raz argues that these theories are profoundly question-begging:

> Theories which provide general recipes for comparing values …
> begin by establishing people's actual judgments on the relative value of
> options, and extrapolate principles which can be applied generally and
> without restriction to any pair of alternatives. Unrestricted generality
> is built into the theory forming process as a theoretical desideratum.
> The question of incommensurability is begged without argument.
> (Raz, 1988, p 335)

Of course, it might be conceded that some conflicts over values between agents and cultures are solvable through rational deliberation, and/or that the pressure of everyday decision making requires that 'solutions' are found in certain cases. However, this should not preclude incommensurable values remaining, where further philosophical digging is neither required nor possible to complete rational deliberations and make 'perfect' the outcomes of these conflicts (also see Rajezi, 2002, pp 373-83). Again, to cite Raz:

> There is a strong temptation to think of incommensurability as an
> imperfection, an incompleteness … the mistake in this thought is that
> it assumes that there is a true value behind the ranking of options….
> Values may change, but such a change is not the discovery of some
> deeper truth. It is simply a change of value. Therefore, where there is
> incommensurability it is the ultimate truth. There is nothing further
> behind it, nor is it a sign of imperfection. (Raz, 1988, p 327)[11]

Another strong temptation is to think of incommensurability as a form of value relativism, where the incompleteness indicates that the significance of a particular value or set of values is seen as valuable *merely* relative to the holder, whether as an individual agent or as part of a cultural grouping, and so has no significance across time and between cultures. However, this again is question-begging as it falsely implies that ranking and comparing values is the only alternative to value relativism. Incommensurabilists argue that while values are often many and incomparable, they are values worth pursuing across time and between cultures, thereby positing the possibility of an incommensurable range of values that are in principle beneficial to all, but find their various expressions across a gamut of cultures and values that are also incommensurably different (also see Berlin, 1991, pp 70-90, and Chapters Two and Seven in this book).

Finally, one other philosophical 'solution' to the 'imperfection' of incommensurability is to follow a monistic commitment to utilitarianism. This promotes one highest principle, allowing for a systematic adjudication between other lower or secondary values (for a thorough discussion of the monistic character of utilitarianism and its relationship to alternative pluralistic value positions, see Gowans, 1987, pp 4-31). Relating to those values associated with promoting equality and diversity, for utilitarians maximising human welfare can be the yardstick for deciding which policy should be pursued. Conflicting values, such as reducing inequalities and positively asserting particular identities, are dealt with as a means to the end of serving the utilitarian principle, where the appropriate balance between the two turns on whether it maximises welfare and/ or well-being for the greatest number. However, I have argued elsewhere that while utilitarianism might appear superficially attractive, providing a philosophical and political solution of sorts to dilemmas in decision making, it is an inadequate normative response to these debates for a number of reasons (Smith, 1997; 1998, pp 214-45; 2002b; 2007a, pp 1-18). Briefly put, my argument is that although overall justifications for policies can be incorporated under generalised higher principles such as 'maximising human welfare is desirable' or 'social assistance is necessary to attain individual and social welfare', these principles are notably unhelpful when articulating and addressing questions concerning justifications of specific policies and practices. For example, addressing the question of who should be responsible for delivering welfare outcomes involves examining 'states of affairs' (as related to overall consequences) and 'moral agency' (as related to individual responsibility), where positions need to accommodate both domains to make proper sense of the moral claims being made (see also Sen, 1985, pp 213-16; Parfit, 1987, p 430). However, the principle 'maximising human welfare is desirable' risks defining a particular state of affairs without necessarily accommodating issues relating to moral agency, concerning who should deliver particular welfare outcomes. I contend here, and throughout the book, that it is during these finer points of distinction in policy and practice debate that philosophical discussions concerning value conflict are usefully applied, and arguments defending the view that values are often incommensurable are especially helpful. I will now begin to apply this contention to those issues explored so far, and, as a prelude to the remainder of the book, most especially to how difference is 'celebrated' via my understanding of value incommensurability, and how specific notions of reciprocal exchange are understood and promoted in any ensuing liberal society.

Celebrating difference and justice as reciprocity

> To the extent that hope for the future depends on philosophical enlightenment it depends on no small measure on understanding the limits of universality, and the source and nature of diversity. It depends on reconciling belief in universality with a correct understanding of the real diversity of values. (Raz, 2001, p 3)

Of course, the reconciling here does not involve reconciling the diversity of values as these are frequently incommensurable; rather, it involves proposing the value of diversity for all while also recognising the often, but not always, incomparable character of people's lives, whether understood as lives pursued by individual agents *and/or* as participators in particular cultural communities. Following this latter claim, there are three separate but related propositions I wish to distinguish regarding value incommensurability: the philosophical or meta-ethical claim that conflicts between universalism and particularism, and the values associated with promoting equality and diversity, are often incommensurable; the empirical claim that lives led by individuals and groups, reflecting their particularised identities and/or the agent-based values they are committed to, are often incommensurable; and the normative claim that understanding these values, whether derived from cultural traditions or agency, as incommensurable should allow us to view the presence of radically different lives as potentially enriching and positive for all – that is, more enriching and positive than if these conflicting and incommensurable values did not exist.

Therefore, to recommend the slogan that we 'celebrate difference' implies at least three types of argument relating to the position so far defended. First, value incommensurability permits a thoroughgoing particularism, so limiting the claims of universal theorising, but is also paradoxically based on diversity being promoted as a value potentially beneficial for all. In short, promoting highly particularised and incommensurable differences is presumed a morally preferable state of affairs to promoting uniformed, or even strictly prioritised, goods among human beings.[12] Second, a very liberal appeal might then be made to the value of equality operating as a universal moral principle – that is, if this appeal invites different individuals and group members not only to assert their own particularised differences, but also to promote the equal capacity of other individuals and group members in asserting their particular difference – whether these relate to recognition or redistributive claims. Third, institutional arrangements are established where social relationships between radically differently situated others are seen as potentially reciprocal or mutually beneficial. Acknowledging this reciprocity in turn underpins social cohesion and cooperation, heightened by the presence of value incommensurability, and given what can be reciprocally learnt from these differences (see Chapters Two, Three and Four for examples of where this reciprocity occurs).

By way of summarising my position so far, I now explore in more detail the third claim to contextualise further the subsequent themes of the book. John Rawls famously argued that reciprocity is central to liberal egalitarian notions of justice and fairness (for example, see Rawls, 1973, pp 494-9; 2001, pp 122-4). For Rawls, reciprocal benefits occur between persons in any just society through acts of cooperation and mutual exchange. The commitment to reciprocity is derived from what he calls a 'tendency to answer in kind', without which the claim from Rawls is that 'fruitful social cooperation is [made] fragile if not impossible' (Rawls, 1973, pp 494-5). Inevitably, there are many criticisms of the Rawlsian position that cannot be explored in detail here (see, for example, Barry, 1995, pp 28-51; Cohen, 1995, pp 187-98 and pp 224-56; Arneson, 1997, pp 339-40). However, I have argued elsewhere that political philosophers, defending what on the face of it might seem like more radical political causes, have moved too swiftly in criticism of the Rawlsian defence of justice as reciprocity (Smith, 2001a, 2001b, 2002a, 2002b). Briefly put, my response has been that there is much more to reciprocity than first meets the eye, when examining how productivity, understood as the production of valuable objects, is managed and structured through social cooperation and mutual exchange. Whether through individual or collective forms, giving and receiving between persons while characterising reciprocal relations does not, I argue, solely depend on the production of valuable objects that can then be used by others. Certainly, a central aspect of establishing reciprocal relations concerns the value of things produced for mutual exchange, but this value cannot be assessed independently from what I have called the 'ontological stance' of givers and receivers. In other words, it is how people *are* with others, not just what they produce *for* others, that defines and shapes reciprocal relations. For example, if a person defines herself, or is defined by others, as having little or nothing to contribute in mutual exchanges, possibilities of both acknowledging and developing reciprocal relations are reduced. First, contributions might already be made by this person but will go unrecognised; and second, potential contributions will often be prevented on the possibly false assumption that the person's lack of productive capacity renders mutual exchange impossible.[13] On the contrary, if a person is open to receiving a wide variety of benefits from what another person has to offer, reciprocal exchange is more likely than if that person is less able or willing to receive, even if the giver has the same to offer in both cases. How, then, does this understanding of reciprocity relate to the arguments presented here concerning value incommensurability?

If incommensurability is promoted as underpinning the slogan that 'differences should be celebrated', the specific forms of recognition and redistribution required in reciprocal exchanges need not make comparative judgments about the relative worth of individual identities or lives led. The suspension of comparable judgment is justified via the definition of incommensurability offered earlier, where the worth of identity x is viewed as neither equal to, nor better than, nor worse than, nor on a par with, the worth of identity y. This allows individuals and group-members, as Sartre puts it, to escape 'the point of view of the other' (Sartre, 1995, pp 527-8), so providing space for the openness to receiving benefits from 'the other' just described. However, in what sense, then, do identities merit recognition, given this suspension of judgment? The recognition is not gained from the abstract universal attribution of equal status to persons who have identities that matter to them (as defended by certain forms of Kantian liberal universalism critiqued previously), but is instead, I argue, founded on the very particularised but positive relational dynamic that can occur between radically differently situated others living in a liberal community. Indeed, acknowledging this type of relational dynamic I believe makes better sense of the particularist demands of commentators such as Iris Marion Young (for example, see Young, 1990, pp 12-13). In her reflections on city life, she argues that '... ideally city life embodies four virtues that represent heterogeneity rather than unity; social differentiation rather than exclusion, variety, eroticism and publicity' (Young, 1990, p 13). My argument here is that these ideals are entirely consistent with those orthodox strands of liberalism promoting value incommensurability and reciprocity; that is, fully accommodating Young's stress on the value of difference and particularity, but not abandoning commitments to what Raz calls 'limited universalism'. For example, acknowledging incommensurability implies that identity x is seen by the holder as valuable for an undefeated reason, but not for a reason that defeats all others (Raz, 1988, pp 338-40). In this context, it is possible to attribute merit to particular identities without judging other identities as worse or better , which then, I argue, allows mutual benefits between different individual and group identities to more likely result. Briefly put, this attribution maintains a robust and highly particularised assertion of identity promoted by Young, but also allows a universal claim for respecting 'the other' as both giver and receiver, and in the process providing liberal flesh to Young's defence of 'an egalitarian politics of difference' (Young, 1990, p 157).

However, committing to incommensurability might work well for those who are open to benefit from those who are radically different, but what about those who, say, have zealously held religious and other beliefs? Surely, they would claim that their lives are better than other lives led, and that this assertion cannot be compromised, otherwise it risks undermining the belief itself as a deeply held conviction. I will now argue that this claim, although often made, does not necessarily follow from deeply held convictions in general, but rather from a particular type of conviction that puts considerable faith in having overwhelming reasons for believing x *as opposed* to y. It is important here to make a distinction between attitudes to other beliefs or religions based on the content of a belief, and the strength of the belief as related to certain forms of personal conviction. Consequently, a very committed religious person can also have strong beliefs based on what she regards as undefeated reasons, but, echoing Raz, not necessarily perceive these as reasons that defeat all others. Indeed, the strength of her belief may reflect a faith that grounds belief, only partly in reasons, and may not even ground faith in reasons at all.[14] Of course, the implications of this type of position are unsatisfactory for the religious fanatic intent on imposing her conception of the good on others, for what she sees as good reasons that defeat all others. However, it is still a position that allows the holding of deeply held religious convictions that may, in principle at least, acknowledge the positive presence of other incommensurable 'forms of life', even if these do not share the same convictions.[15]

So, how does this relate to my conception of reciprocity and the positive relational dynamic that might come about as a result of living in such a liberal society? First, establishing reciprocal relations in large part relies on fostering an attitude of mutual self-worth, derived from a positive assessment of what the first person can offer to the other, and what the other can contribute for the benefit of the first person. In this type of political and social environment, any incommensurable differences between individuals can be positively promoted, anticipating the possibilities of increased reciprocity, even when existing social relations might unjustly reinforce particular forms of social disadvantage. Second, the normative significance of a liberal community committed to 'celebrating differences' across incommensurable forms of life suggests the possibility of people being unified through various social practices by their mutual preparedness and openness to learn from or be enriched by these differences. These practices would include cultivating deliberative and conversational abilities between different persons with radically different beliefs and viewpoints, but also would encourage more emotional and physical encounters with others. The latter would include, for example, non-cognitive or non-deliberative experiential engagements with others – through art, personal relationships, cultural celebrations, the exploration and sharing of particular habits, customs and the like. Third, I contend that acknowledging the presence of incommensurable values within these engagements helps us to understand who we are now with some measure of confidence that being attached to a particular form of life will not be judged as worse than others – underpinned by a principle of reciprocity that we positively learn not only from our own deep-felt attachments, but also from the experiences and perspectives of others with attachments that are also equally deep-felt but radically different to our own. In other words, the incommensurability I promote is delimited, allowing the assertion of radically different forms of life that are in certain important respects incomparable as related to the worth of lives led described previously, but still providing space for mutual understanding between persons and groups based on the assumption that the presence of these differences is conducive to maintaining shared group values beyond those that are incommensurable. This mutual understanding, while allowing me to judge that your life is worth learning from, does not need to provide theoretical or philosophical comparisons regarding the proper relationship between particular values and/or cultural traditions, seeing these as largely, or at least often, immune to value rankings and other comparable weightings.

Finally, it might be tempting at this point to declare that promoting incommensurable values and diversity is merely instrumental to some other greater good, such as promoting well-being through relational enrichment and reciprocal exchange – similar to, say, John Stuart Mill's promotion of diversity and individuality as a means to the end of enhancing happiness (Mill, 1991, pp 62-82; also see Galston, 2002, p 27). However, while recognising that this raises some important questions about the relationship between well-being and other values, I believe it misdescribes what is meant by value incommensurability as a non-monistic alternative to utilitarianism. In Chapters Four, Five and Six, I reject homogenous and uniform goods of the kind promoted by utilitarianism, while recognising that persons and group members might be enriched and unified in their joint promotion of incommensurable diversity, including those diverse forms of life that do not promote well-being as a 'master value'. Following Parekh, my main claim, then, is that the unity to be promoted is certainly not the same as homogeneity, and that the equality to be promoted is certainly not the same as uniformity. Instead, I advocate what I call 'particularised universalism', which promotes both equality and diversity as incommensurable and conflicting goals. In other words, I accommodate 'the political demands of deep and defiant diversity' (Parekh, 2000, p 9) by promoting value diversity and incommensurability as a universal human value. As a result, my argument, 'unlike multiculturalism … does not have ethno-cultural identity as its goal, or the "recognition" of present self- or group-perception as its means' (McClennan, 2008, p 103). Therefore, while I disrupt certain assumptions of recognition politics and multiculturalism, I also acknowledge the importance of asserting specific and radically different identities as they currently occur. For example, I would not ascribe to universally promoting 'hybrid identities' (see also Madood, 2007), where persons are encouraged to abandon specific, deeply held convictions and beliefs in favour of more eclectic identities (Gilroy, 1993, 2004; Bhabha, 1994).[16] Although this preference may be taken up by some individuals in the type of liberal community I recommend, if applied universally, they would, I believe, be likely to lead to the promotion of sameness and homogeneity. In short, this is because hybrid identities can level out the deepness of difference through a process of eclectic assimilation and integration.[17] Instead, my contention is that the presence of incommensurable values and the celebration of these differences, while helping us to continually reshape our personal identities and beliefs in reference to more widely held communal goals, also allow individuals to be attached deeply to specific forms of life across their whole lives.

In Chapter Two, I explore the specific character of these individual attachments, again as related to value incommensurability. My central claim is that understanding individual attachments opens up conceptual and normative space for promoting value incommensurability, given that individuals will attach themselves to a range of specific 'valued objects' that are often incommensurable. However, this highlights further various philosophical and political questions and issues raised in this chapter, concerning not only the form of these objects and how they are imbued with value, but also the nature and causes of individual attachments, again as these relate to the values of equality and diversity.

Notes

[1] I would like to thank John Horton for helping me clarify this point in our discussion of value pluralism during the 'Toleration and respect: concepts, justifications and applications' workshop at the Seventh Annual Conference of Political Theory Workshops at Manchester Metropolitan University in 2010.

[2] I am aware that a number of issues are being glossed over here concerning the distinction between the meaning of identity as related to personal characteristics, such as belief, behaviour, social habits and customs. Suffice it to say, my concern in this chapter is not so much over the meaning of identity – although to be sure this is an important question explored throughout the book – but that the impact of 'recognition politics' means that specific questions relating to the particular characteristics of persons and group members have in various ways problematised traditional egalitarian agendas. It is enough for my outlining at this point to highlight how what matters to us as particular persons and members of certain groups in *some* way relates to our identity – that is, how the things we are attached and committed to reflect our beliefs, behaviour and customs.

[3] Inevitably, these classifications oversimplify positions, and some of these commentators might object to being placed in any one of these camps. However, my intention here is merely to outline the parameters of the debate, rather than to strictly categorise positions as such.

[4] Following on from note 3 above, admittedly even those who promote this middle ground will often delimit their 'solutions' to subsequent dilemmas and conflicts in policy and practice. For example, according to Fraser: 'The redistribution-recognition dilemma is real. There is no neat theoretical move by which it can be wholly dissolved or resolved' (Fraser, 1997, p 31). However, she still sees this as a problem to be solved, albeit partially: 'The best we can do is to try and soften the dilemma by finding approaches that minimize conflicts between redistribution and recognition in cases where both must be pursued simultaneously' (Fraser, 1997, p 31).

[5] It might also be claimed that these assumptions concerning radical political positions are question-begging for my arguments regarding value incommensurability, as they by definition promote value pluralism or the promotion of diverse values. To counter, it is important to make clear that these assumptions are not promoting any particular *type* of pluralism, such as value incommensurability, which in turn I seek to defend. It also might be claimed that this definition of radical politics covers such a range of political philosophies, including liberal egalitarian positions, which would be better described as

reformist rather than radical. This charge is, I believe, partly justified, although my defence for using the term 'radical' is that the challenge these positions offer to inequalities and dominant or monolithic norms does demand considerable change, especially in the long term, and so is not *merely* reformist in policy and practice. These positions also exclude large elements of conservative thinking found in, for example, the conservatism of Roger Scruton (2001) and unequivocally rejects full-blooded, free-market justifications for increasing inequalities found in, for example, Nozick (1974) or Hayek (1993).

[6] In *A theory of justice*, Rawls, for example, states: 'Furthermore, the public recognition of the two principles gives greater support to men's (sic) self-respect and this in turn increases the effectiveness of social cooperation.... It is clearly rational for men to secure their self-respect. A sense of their own worth is necessary if they are to pursue their conception of the good with zest and to delight in its fulfilment. Self-respect is not so much part of any rational plan of life as the sense that one's plan is worth carrying out. Now our self-respect normally depends on the respect of others.... Hence for this reason the parties would accept the natural duty of mutual respect which asks them to treat one another civilly and to be willing to explain the grounds of their actions.... Moreover, one may assume that those who respect themselves are more likely to respect each other and conversely. Self-contempt leads to contempt for others and threatens their good as much as envy does. Self-respect is reciprocally self-supporting' (Rawls, 1973, pp 178-9).

[7] This reservation is clearly articulated, albeit perhaps rather buried, in note 46 of her chapter 'From redistribution to recognition?' (Fraser, 1997): 'This has always been the problem with socialism. Although cognitively compelling, it is experientially remote. The addition of deconstruction seems to exacerbate the problem. It could turn out to be too negative and reactive, i.e., too *deconstructive*, to inspire struggles on behalf of subordinated collectivities attached to their existing identities' (Fraser, 1997, p 39; emphasis in original, and see my argument later). However, in this publication, and in her later work, she maintains that '... the *ultimate* cause of class injustice is the economic structure of capitalist society" (Fraser, 2003, p 23; emphasis added). Consequently, the socialist/Marxist claim that class differences should be eradicated remains largely intact with again no *pro tanto* dilemma emerging around the continued recognition of class identity, given the political and economic exploitation experienced by the working classes.

[8] See also Lister (2007) for a development of Fraser's arguments concerning social inequality and social justice.

[9] See also Parfit (1987, pp 149-86) for an interesting discussion about the different attitudes that might be had towards time, given what is important to us in the present, as distinct from the past and future.

[10] Ruth Chang (1997) explores in considerable depth the character of incommensurable claims, some of which rely on a weaker understanding that two items cannot be precisely measured by a single scale, while others are based on a stronger claim that two items cannot

be compared. She argues that 'Joseph Raz, for example, has used "incommensurability" as synonymous with "incomparability"' (Chang, 1997, p 1). My understanding of incommensurability, unless otherwise stated, uses the latter understanding as reflected in the definition just outlined by Raz.

[11] In a later publication, Raz states the point more succinctly: 'Explanations by reference to reasons do not explain everything. Our chemistry rather than our rationality explains why some like it hot' (Raz, 1997, p 127).

[12] See Chapters Three, Four and Six for examples of where disabled people's lives cannot be unrestrictedly compared with non-disabled people's lives, supporting my argument that the incommensurable differences that this lack of comparability produces is a morally preferable state of affairs to one that promotes non-disability as an 'idealised' uniformed or monistic norm.

[13] I have argued elsewhere that the former judgment is often made with respect to lone parents (Smith, 1999, 2002a), whereas the latter judgment is often made with respect to disabled people (Smith, 2001a, 2002a).

[14] For example, Christian existentialists reflect this latter understanding of the relationship between faith, religion and reason, which is found in Soren Kierkegaard's work and others following in his wake (Kierkegaard, 1994, pp 29-32; also see West, 1996, pp 117-26). The basic position of a Kierkegaardian Christian is that any reasons, however well formulated, can never, and should never, offer explanatory justifications for faith in Christ and God.

[15] Even within the same faith, the values promoted are often seen as incommensurable. Charles Taylor explores how Mary of Bethany, according to Jesus, is wrongly criticised by his disciples for spending money on expensive perfume to demonstrate her love for him, when it could have been better spent on the poor (Taylor, 1997, pp 176-8). Given that in other passages Jesus recommends giving resources to the poor, it can be concluded that this reflects the incommensurable character of values, at least as these are presented in the Gospels. That is, based on maintaining conflicting and often incomparable qualities of personal integrity and relations with others, the quality and integrity of Mary and her relationship with Jesus is incomparable and in both cases conflicts with their relations with poor people; see also Parekh's analysis of Thomas Aquinas (Parekh, 2000, p 24) and Chapter Two of this book.

[16] I am very grateful to Tariq Madood, in a conversation I had with him at the Manchester Political Theory Workshops conference in 2010, for highlighting this problem of hybrid or eclectic identities.

[17] I am very grateful to Peter Balint at the same conference for identifying this possible outcome for a society committed to value pluralism – an outcome I would obviously be keen to avoid for the reasons just stated.

TWO

Value incommensurability

Introduction

Following in part Joseph Raz (1988, 1997, 2001), my central claim in this chapter is that understanding individual attachments opens up conceptual and normative space for promoting value incommensurability, given that individuals are attached to a range of incommensurable 'valued objects' as defined in Chapter One. However, these attachments raise various questions and issues concerning the character of valued objects, how and why these objects are imbued with value, and subsequently the nature and causes of individual attachments – which I explore via four main propositions and subsequent arguments.

First, behind many of our moral intuitions about conflicting values, there are, I contend, incommensurable values promoting the potential quality or quantity of human life – for example, between spending resources on saving art and, more generally, aesthetic values, so promoting the quality of human life, or on saving innocent lives who are in dire need, so promoting the quantity of human life. However, although we are often required in practice to make moral choices between these values, my main claim is that making this choice does not necessarily imply that these values are commensurable or fully comparable, only that choosing is often unavoidable. That is, often unavoidable, given the presence of scarce resources, and that some moral weight should be attributed to partial plans and ambitions, even if these are instigated by the relatively well-off, and that saving innocent lives is also considered important. Indeed, I argue that most of our moral intuitions, when considered, demonstrate the incommensurability of these quantitative and qualitative values, even when choices are made between them.

Second, representing two poles of debate about value, there are, broadly speaking, structural and non-structural ways of understanding how choices are made between values, moral or otherwise, which I call, in their idealised forms, Platonic and Nietzschean/existentialist respectively. My main contention is that it is generally easier to establish incommensurability when tending towards the latter Nietzschean/existentialist understanding. I argue that with those gravitating towards Platonic understandings, full-blown comparisons are usually more readily and thoroughly made via structured moral theory when illuminating the rational justification of particular choices, with the essential meaning and purpose of value subsequently offered through what are viewed as intrinsically valued objects that have the 'objective character' of value revealed through observing the object itself. Alternatively, with those gravitating towards Nietzschean/existentialist non-structural understandings, particular valued attachments are more likely to be viewed as a product of life happening randomly and accidentally, with limited or no essential value being revealed through observing intrinsically valued objects. Instead, persons are seen to 'subjectively commit' to valued objects, which then largely creates, or at least provides an origin, for their valued characteristics, and, in the absence of an underlying rational structure fully comparing them, such objects are often appropriately regarded as incommensurable. Liberal egalitarian theories of value often oscillate between these two poles of understanding, but consistent with my arguments presented here and in Chapter One, those liberal egalitarians who promote incommensurability often tend towards the Nietzschean/existentialist rather than the Platonic viewpoint, at least in certain relevant respects.[1]

Third, assuming incommensurable subjective commitments can be made by persons to at least a certain range of valued objects, I examine the nature of regret, recognising that regretful responses to lives led and choices made initially seem to suggest that thoroughgoing comparisons are occurring between particular lives and choices. However, my argument is that while some types of regret do suggest commensurability – where a choice or life is judged as better or worse than, equal to, or on a par with, another – many forms of regret can accommodate the presence of incommensurable values, again when considering issues relating to the potential quality or quantity of life experiences. I conclude that it is reasonable to regret that we only have one life to lead, given that we might feel a genuine loss for the quantitative finiteness of life, even if we can do nothing about the limits of the human condition, and that no qualitative comparisons can be made with those other potential lives that could have been led by one person, but were not. Moreover, this lack of comparability is not only because many valued 'objects' in our lives are often so qualitatively different, relating, say, to career choice, friendships made, lovers chosen, and so on, but also because someone becomes a qualitatively different *person* as a result of the life actually led, to what she might have become if she had lived a different life. In short, the overall quality of the one life that is actually led in many respects is incommensurable, and so cannot be fully compared with the quality of potential lives that a person may imagine she could have led.

Fourth, I argue that because actual subjective attachments, incommensurable or otherwise, matter to all persons living in the singular, this prompts universal reasons for valuing attachments, as meaning and purpose is created and recreated over time by all persons through what might be termed 'acts of attachment making'. However, this universality is paradoxical because these attachments, being finite, often reflect highly partial and particularised commitments that seem often to only have value relative to the holder (suggesting a value-relativist position), but at the same time a less transient impartial commitment is made to others who have similar commitments (suggesting a universalist position). My position is that any theory of value should incorporate both these partial/impartial and subjectivist/objectivist accounts of value to make proper sense of what is being claimed, but recognising that these accounts are often pulling in opposite directions (see also

Nagel, 1989, 1995, for a similar position, explored in more detail later). Finally, I argue that we often appreciate and understand our partial and subjective deep-felt commitments and attachments better when we critically engage with a process of personal change or development and reciprocal engagement with others who lead radically different lives, providing a political and normative platform for defending a delimited universal and impartial account of liberal community, and reflecting themes explored throughout the book.

Value incommensurability and 'covering values'

Value incommensurability sometimes refers to there being no single measure to adjudicate between two or more conflicting values (Chang, 1997, pp 1-10; Anwander, 2001; see also Chapter One of this book). However, this weaker understanding of incommensurability is probably more accurately described as value pluralism, with value incommensurability, used in a stronger sense, being one version. The stronger sense implies not only that there is more than one value that cannot be measured with one scale or weighting, as Berlin, for example, variously stresses,[2] but that they are also incomparable (Chang, 1997, pp 1-2, and pp 1-66; Raz, 1988, pp 321-68). Ruth Chang (1997) explores in considerable detail the character of incommensurable claims, some of which rely on the weaker understanding that two items cannot be precisely measured by a single scale, while others are based on the stronger claim that two items cannot be compared. She then argues that 'Joseph Raz, for example, has used "incommensurability" as synonymous with "incomparability"' (Chang, 1997, p 1).

Again, as highlighted in Chapter One, for Raz, 'A and B are incommensurate if it is neither true that one is better than the other nor true that they are of equal value' (Raz, 1988, p 332). Consequently, two conflicting incommensurable values understood in this strong sense cannot be ranked in a lexical order, or traded off against each other, as with other pluralist understandings of value. This is because one does not have a higher priority over the other, as implied in lexical orderings of values (Rawls, 1973, pp 41-2), although neither are they equal, or otherwise comparably weighted, as implied in trade-offs (Barry, 1995, pp 5-10; Chang, 1997). Rather, the claim is that incommensurable values are qualitatively different such that no comparison is possible (Raz, 1988, pp 330-40; Lukes, 1997, pp 194-5; see also Smith, 1998, pp 214-45; 2007a, pp 11-18). For example, the 'valued objects' of money and friendship are often viewed as incommensurable in this stronger sense (Raz, 1988, pp 337-40; Anderson, 1997). So, Jane might choose to further her financial interests, knowing that friendships will be sacrificed, when choosing to move location for better-paid work, understanding that her relationships with existing friends will probably suffer. However, for incommensurabilists it is an inappropriate description of the choice Jane makes to say money is being chosen over friendship (Raz, 1988, pp 337-40; Anderson, 1997). Rather, aspects of Jane's life as related to these values are in what might be termed qualitatively different 'value streams'. In other words, they are valued independently of each other and so are not being traded off or placed in a lexical order. Hence, financial gain is not more important to her than friendship, but nor are they equal in value, or on a par, or otherwise comparably weighted; they are instead incomparable.

However, we need to be clear about why comparisons are not being made in these instances. Refusing to compare two valued objects does not mean they cannot be compared, as comparisons, although often difficult, are not necessarily impossible to make. For example, again according to Ruth Chang (1997, pp 1-65), when two objects are judged as incommensurable their 'covering values' are often mistakenly ignored. So, chalk is better than cheese when compared with the covering value of writing, while cheese is better than chalk when compared with the covering value of nutrition (see also Chang, 1997, pp 2-7; 2002, 2005). Once covering values are specified, then for Chang, many, if not all, incommensurable values, at least understood in the stronger sense, disappear. Instead, we should consider the merit of two valued objects as reflected in each covering value. For example, with money and friendship, it might be said that the value of having more money reflects the covering value of increased economic self-reliance and opportunity, whereas the value of having good friendships reflects the covering value of developing healthy relationships with others. Consequently, if Jane values economic self-reliance and opportunity as a means to the end of supporting healthy relationships with family members and others close to her, it seems that, despite first appearances, relationships do matter more to her than money – even if she moves to secure a better-paid job knowing that this will lead to other friendships being undermined. In short, friendships sacrificed as a result of moving are traded off against other gains made in her personal relationships. A related argument can be made for other common instrumental goods, such as peace and security, based on a distinction between 'values' that are particular to persons and 'goods' that are common to all. For David Gauthier, 'values are subjective, but peace is a common instrumental good, since it is a necessary means to each man's chief good, his own preservation' (Gauthier, 1990, p 17). Here, it seems that common goods and subjective values are being compared and rank ranked accordingly, so that securing these objective common goods will generally trump the promotion of subjective values if and when they conflict, as the former is necessary for the latter to pursue.

However, while I believe that these arguments for commensurability are persuasive in some circumstances, they are not all pervasive, as they ignore other factors that might be taken into account in establishing whether values or goods are incommensurable or not . Some of these factors, I contend, reflect the way quantitative and qualitative life values are often incommensurable, even if covering values are fully specified and the stronger sense of incommensurability is used. For example, the quantitative value of having a certain number of opportunities might increase for a person if she moves to secure a better-paid job (reflecting the first covering value specified), but this still might not be comparable with the qualitative value of supporting existing healthy relations with others when maintaining good-quality friendships (reflecting the second covering value specified).[3] That these values are not comparable is, I believe, reflected in the way friends who live relatively close to each other often respond to one of their group moving to secure better financial and career opportunities. First, there is cause for celebration among these friends, knowing that the person who has chosen to leave will experience increased opportunities for herself and possibly others. Second, these friends are also sad because they know that the quality of their friendship is being sacrificed, or at least are likely to diminish as a result. However, these friends usually do not resent the choice, as if the person moving is choosing increased opportunities *over* these friendships. Indeed, if there were such resentment, good friends would often remind themselves that the person leaving is precisely not choosing opportunities over their friendship, only choosing to increase her opportunities, even if these friendships are being sacrificed or diminished. In other words, they will in effect be reminding themselves of the incomparability between these two valued objects, despite the choice being made between them. More broadly, then, the 'choice' between money and friendship is not made commensurable simply by specifying covering values, as Chang claims, for this still begs the question about the character of the choice made and how values relate to each other. In this case, I argue that the character of the choice made, quite appropriately, refuses to compare money and friendship because comparing the value of money (promoting the quantitative covering value of increased opportunity) and the value of friendship (promoting the qualitative covering value of healthy relationships) misdescribes the way these values relate. That friends understand this refutation when one of their group moves to secure better-paid work also suggests that this incomparability is consistent with our moral intuitions.

Moreover, as a result of this lack of comparability, my claim is that ethical arguments should not only consider how values and goods relate to each other, but also what type of person an individual *becomes* with valued attachments, possessing certain goals and ambitions. My main contention is that a person often, to varying degrees, changes her own character and even identity, as well as the character of the valued objects she is partially attached to, through her changing experiences and commitments. Therefore, from a range of potential lives that might be lived in the plural, she may develop into a qualitatively different person, lived in the singular, than she would otherwise be. This type of personal development and change I believe gives an added nuance and complexity to the way values and/ or goods are said to relate, again allowing greater conceptual and normative space for promoting value incommensurability. However, before exploring these issues further, I will examine in more detail how many other moral choices reflect values that promote either the quantity or quality of human life, again reflecting choices that are often incommensurable.

Values and quantity versus quality

Can values be incommensurable when referring even to their covering values? My answer so far is 'yes', in particular when covering values reflect a *moral* choice between the potential quantity or quality of life experiences.[4] I will explore two other values that I believe also illustrate how quantitative and qualitative considerations are often incommensurable, even if moral choices are made between them – namely, the value of saving the life of a starving child and the value of saving a priceless work of art. Let us assume that resources for the latter can be transferred to accomplish the former and vice versa. Following Chang's argument, saving the priceless work of art is better than saving the life of a child in respect of the covering value that we ought to preserve aesthetic objects, while saving a starving a child is better than saving a priceless work of art in respect of the covering value that we ought to preserve innocent lives. However, this is not all that can or should be said on the matter, for as with the money versus friendship example, the merits of each as a moral value still seems to be pulling in very different directions, suggesting in turn, I believe, their possible incommensurability. My main argument is that when choices are made, as they often are in these circumstances, it is not necessarily because one option is morally better than the other, nor because both are equal, or on a par, or can be comparably weighted – their lack of comparability reflects, again, the incommensurability of values associated with promoting the quantity or quality of human life. In this example, saving a starving child reflects quantitative values, in the sense that the numbers of lives led is valued. The principal concern is that one person will not be living if action is not taken, and that this life as a quantitative entity therefore should be saved, while saving works of art reflects qualitative values, in the sense that enhancing the quality of lives led is usually valued when aesthetic objects are preserved. Here, no reference need be made to the numbers of people who can enjoy an aesthetic object, only that this enjoyment enhances the quality of life experienced, *whatever* the number enjoying it. My main point is that qualitative considerations concerning the saved object of art can and should be viewed separately from quantitative considerations concerning the amount of people living to experience art's enrichment. Moreover, I claim that this conclusion again seems consistent with our moral intuitions, as for most people it would seem wrong to demand that all art remain unpreserved until all starving children are fed, and yet also wrong to demand that physical objects of any kind should be preserved over preserving human life. These intuitions viewed separately can be subject to ethical scrutiny, and often are, but I contend that it is not immediately obvious why one intuition should be maintained *over* the other, only that both intuitions seem to hold weight even though they are pulling in opposite directions. But in what way are these intuitions reflecting values that are incommensurable?

Commensurabilists might argue that even choosing to save art for the sake of the previously stated qualitative value is still prioritising the quantity of human life in general, in that preserving humankind is a necessary condition before it is qualitatively enjoyed and appreciated. However, this, I believe, ignores what is morally deliberated in this case. It is misleading to claim that art is being saved for the sake of humankind, so prioritising quantity over quality in general terms, as in this choice art is being preserved for the sake of some people – those who are relatively better-off – thereby sacrificing the interests of those who are starving. Reflecting Derek Parfit's 'Mere Addition Paradox' (1987, pp 419-54), choosing the quality of art's enrichment, when put *this* way, intuitively seems morally unacceptable, given its elitist implications of preferring the interests of the better-off over the worst-off. It could also be argued that this preference unjustifiably sidelines the natural exercise of compassion for the worst-off, given their dire circumstances (Piper, 1991; Nussbaum, 1996; Whitebrook, 2002; these and related issues are also explored in Chapter Four of this book). Nevertheless, I would claim that always choosing to save the lives of starving children and sacrificing the preservation of art is also intuitively morally unacceptable, as when put *this* way, art, and indeed aesthetic value of any kind, would have to be sacrificed until all innocent lives are saved. On first glance, choosing the starving child might seem to many to carry more moral weight than saving the work of art, but, even if this were the case (which I readily concede it might well be), it again misses the point about what is being valued in this case. The unacceptability comes from choosing to save the starving child in such a way that it is viewed as trumping *all and every* claim for preserving aesthetic objects. However, this I believe also misdescribes the problem and fails to reflect the other side of Parfit's paradox (1987, pp 419-54), namely, if quantitative choices are applied consistently, more lives would always be considered better than fewer lives, even if the quality of everyone's life were radically reduced – this also being morally unacceptable and so producing the paradox. To repeat, though, the question is, if either of these choices is unacceptable, does it seem plausible to claim that the values underlying a commitment to both the quantity and quality of life experiences are not only pulling in opposite directions, but are also incommensurable?

My response is that, holding to *both* intuitions while recognising that they conflict is at least consistent with the suggestion that one option is not morally better than the other, but they are also neither equal, nor on a par, nor otherwise comparably weighted. The point here is that if they are incomparable, this might explain the force of the paradox as our intuitions seem to be not only conflicting but also in different 'value streams' (these and related issues will be explored further in Chapter Seven). However, one response would be to concede that one option is not morally better than the other, but that it is morally acceptable that some art is preserved and some innocent lives be saved – in other words, a trade-off should occur between quantitative and qualitative values, assuming they are equal, or can be otherwise compared and weighted against each other, but are often conflicting. Here, the unacceptability of not preserving any qualitative values until all innocent lives are saved reflects in part the moral principle that while innocent lives should be preserved, we should also allow persons, within reasonable limits, to implement their partial plans and commitments, including the plans and commitments of relatively well-off persons (see also Nagel, 1989, 1995, and Chapter One of this book). Certainly, in policy and practice, trade-offs of this kind often occur, subsequently leading to compromises between these competing interests when distributing scarce resources. But again, I believe, it is proceeding too quickly to assume that this indicates that these values are equal, or on a par, or that they can be compared in some other way.

First, we may regret aspects of any choice made in this example because in practice it requires sacrifice, but the choice itself does not indicate that *moral* trade-offs have been made between these values. Therefore, the presumption is not necessarily that we ought to trade off each, given that these values are equal or on a par with each other, or in some other way can be compared and weighted in relation to each other, only that in real life we often must choose between values that conflict. We therefore need not, and ought not, to claim that when saving some starving children and some works of art that a morally acceptable balance between these values has been established. Second, when choices are made, this reflects not only the value of what is being chosen, but also the particular attachments made by persons to human and non-human objects. The point here is that both forms of attachment may enhance the life of persons, but as these attachments include non-human objects, preserving these objects will also have value that may be independent from the value that might be found in persons more generally. The latter, to be sure, is a controversial claim, but given these various types of attachment, I will now explore why objects are valued, again reflecting these quantitative and qualitative considerations. I examine further the implications this valuing has for the structure of moral theory, the specific role played by incommensurable values when making choices, and the competing conceptions of personhood and identity that subsequently result.

Objects and structure: the Platonic versus Nietzschean viewpoints

One understanding of how and why things are valued is to start with the valued object itself. For example, an object might be valued because it is said to have intrinsic value that is counted as a reason for the object's preservation. Consider the assertion that a view of the countryside is worth preserving because such landscapes have an intrinsic value related, say, to an essential quality of natural beauty. Here the claim is that naturalness and beauty are contained within the valued object that is then appreciated by a human viewer. In its idealised form, call this the Platonic understanding of value in objects, as it assumes that the object has an intrinsic valued quality of *Naturalness* and *Beauty*, which can be called 'essentially good' or a 'good in itself', existing separately to the viewer but appreciated by her. In contrast, a very different understanding of how and why things are valued is to at least start with the way human beings *create* value by their attachments to objects. For example, consider the assertion that a beautiful view is worth preserving because a person values it as beautiful from the viewer's perspective. Here the claim is that an object has value because the viewer perceives it as valuable. In its idealised form, call this the Nietzschean understanding of value in objects where subjective perspectives shape and determine how and whether objects are valued, creating value via the perception itself, thereby rejecting the Platonic assumption that a valued object is good 'in itself'.[5]

Making this albeit simplified distinction concerning how objects are valued, recognising that many other positions are variously placed between those two poles, is hardly new in the philosophy of aesthetics (Blackburn, 1994, p 8), but I believe it provides insight into how incommensurable values are properly understood. In short, I contend that it is usually easier, or at least more direct, to argue for incommensurability the closer one is to the Nietzschean rather than the Platonic understanding of value. This is because the Platonic view, in establishing what is valuable 'in itself', often uses philosophical structure to illuminate what is 'good' and so is more likely to provide, through the work of reason and theory, a systemic ordering of values, leading to their commensurability and thoroughgoing comparison. It might be possible to envisage a philosophical structure revealing the incommensurability of values, but the analogy of structure as a coherent and ordered system providing a full explanation of the relationship between values, means that incommensurability is often not countenanced. Structures, by implication, consist of parts that can be related to and then compared – where one part, for example, is considered a means to the end of supporting another, and so on. Certainly, a degree of philosophical incompleteness and vagueness may be allowed, as these positions will variously reflect this structuralist assumption, but according to those tending to this position, this does not necessarily imply value incommensurability (see also Broome, 1997, and my discussion in Chapter One and later in this chapter). Rather, any incompleteness or vagueness is philosophically relatively unimportant, anticipating a more refined structured theory of value, provided through increasingly nuanced philosophical enquiry, that will illuminate better the nature of 'goodness' and the subsequent relationship between values.

More specifically, where are these tendencies towards Platonic or structuralist understandings of value promoted? Again, at the risk of over-simplification, I have in mind a disparate tradition of moral and political thought that includes Plato, Kant and other more contemporary theories of value such as utilitarianism and certain elements of post-Rawlsian Anglo-American political philosophy. While from Kant onwards, theories of value would not necessarily assume a Platonic understanding of intrinsic value, at least in its unadulterated Platonic form, all those within this tradition assume that some kind of value structure exists behind an appearance of uneven, plural and disconnected values, and that this structure is accessible via scientific and/or rational enquiry. Moreover, this accessibility is derived from the work of theory and empirical investigation that articulates, via a network of intelligible concepts, not only what is of value, but also the relationship between values. For example, classical utilitarians assert that enhancing happiness is the prime value or good, derived from rationally reflecting on what are seen as fixed empirical attributes of human nature, where individuals generally seek happiness and avoid pain. Values are ranked and ordered according to their instrumental usefulness in fulfilling this prime value, so providing a clearly defined and objective value structure related to the production of happiness or well-being.[6] Consequently, what might first appear as uneven, plural and disconnected instrumental values can, in the final analysis, be compared and deemed better than, worse than, equal to, or on a par with each other, reflecting the degree to which each value promotes the one prime value. More sophisticated utilitarians, from John Stuart Mill onwards, promote various conflicting instrumental values to enhance happiness, and so in this weaker sense defend value pluralism (Sen and Williams, 1982; Chang, 1997, pp 16-18). Indeed, they may even argue that some values, for example certain qualitative dimensions of pleasure, are incomparable, insofar as they produce very different kinds of happiness or well-being (Chang, 1997, pp 16-18). Nevertheless, sophisticated or otherwise, utilitarians seek to maximise happiness – even if what comprises happiness is viewed as complex and multi-dimensional – which in turn defines the parameters of an objectified value structure, consistent with what utilitarians see as the universally shared nature of human beings.

In addition, for all value structuralists, then, including utilitarians, the underlying structure of values is generally constant across time and between cultures. In other words, the relationship between values has horizontal structure as truth claims about value, the production of happiness, for example, are fixed *between* temporal and cultural domains (although what specifically produces happiness may considerably vary across time and between cultures). The structure also has an identifiable procedure for deciding a particular value hierarchy, even if more than one instrumental value is promoted, given that values exist in one true relation to each other, being ordered and so producing, again in the case of utilitarians, the greatest happiness. Consequently, the relationship between values also has vertical structure that is fixed *within* specific temporal and cultural domains. Despite profound disagreements with utilitarians concerning the way values are viewed and justified, the same general overall structural analysis can be made of Kant's moral system (for example, see Kant, 1993, 1997). The categorical imperative operates as a fixed universal rule to which all specific moral decision making refers, accessible via rational introspection and given universal conditions attributable to 'being a person' (see also Louden, 2000, and Chapter One of this book). A similar analysis can be made of Kantian and utilitarian hybrids such as David Gauthier, who argues that the structure of practical reasoning proposed by Kant can be used to justify and explain a person seeking happiness (Gauthier, 1990, pp 110-28); of Rawls's Kantianism (1971; 1993; 2001), which offers a lexical ordering of values through his principles of justice, providing a structure for understanding the relationship between the social values of liberty and equality, with the former being the first value to be fulfilled, after which the latter comes into play; of Barry (1995b), who trades off conflicting values where one is promoted at the expense of another but where both carry weight, with an appropriate balance being found between them; and of Chang (1997, pp 21-33), who argues that values, although they may not be equal, or better than or worse than one other, can be considered on a par, that is, still allowing the adjudication of values via, among other things, what she calls a covering theory of value, outlined and critiqued previously (also see Chang, 2002, 2005).

The point here is that when values are structured in moral theory, they are usually seen as mainly or wholly commensurable, where rational enquiry and scientific reasoning supposedly illuminate a procedure for measurement, value ranking or appropriate balancing. Certainly, those in this tradition often concede some limits to the illuminating scope of reason and science. For example, if moral scepticism or vagueness is acknowledged, as is often the case in contemporary moral theory, all conflicts between values may not be resolvable (Barry, 1995; Broome, 1997; Cohen, 2000, pp 12-13, 2003; Sugden, 2009). Nevertheless, for all these theorists, when choices are made they are still rationally justifiable through a value structure, which, however fuzzy at the edges, provides human beings with universal yardsticks to make calculated and calculable moral choices, judged as either better than, worse than, equal, or on a par with others.

My central claim here, though, alongside other incommensurabilists, is that non-structural possibilities of understanding values are unjustifiably marginalised or rendered incoherent as a result. This includes the notion that many, albeit not all, objects find value, not in philosophically decipherable value structures, but from the highly particularised subjective attachments made by human beings, reflecting, to varying degrees, the Nietzschean/existentialist perspective outlined earlier. I will now explore the implications of this latter understanding of value by examining the character and causes of many of our particular attachments, recognising that life happens randomly and accidentally, without intrinsic value or meaning, but nevertheless provides a specified experiential arena for valuing particular attachments that matter deeply to specific persons.

Accidents, attachments and the creation of value or meaning

My main contention is that the random and accidental character of what often happens in our lives has profound implications for how valued objects and subjective attachments are understood, and reflect the Nietzschean/existentialist perspective outlined previously. First, though, it should be noted that there is a distinction between those valued objects chosen by someone, and so initiated by consciously committing to the object as part of that person's 'life plan', and those valued objects that are committed to through socialised norms – parental upbringing, prevailing cultural influences and so on. The reason for making this distinction is explored further in the conclusion to this chapter, and in Chapter One. Suffice it to say here that although in practice commitments to valued objects derive from both deliberate choice *and* socialisation, the distinction allows for a range of commitments that do not depend on liberalised accounts of individual choice and agency that might, mistakenly in my view, associate all causes of commitment with conscious and reflective individual decision making. Second, it is also important to emphasise that the motivation for seeking value commensurability within the wider political arena could also be socialised. According to Cohen and Ben-Ari, modern western societies, in their political socialisation, often unquestioningly assume that theory and scientific understanding can readily compare values in the ways just explored, so tending to exclude political positions that accommodate incommensurable values, dilemmas and conflicts (Cohen and Ben-Ari, 1993). Therefore, given the causes of attachments are various, and a sociological or political bias toward value commensurability, an important question to address is precisely how this process of reasoning and calculation is understood, in particular when subjective and highly partial attachments are made.

For those who gravitate toward the Nietzschean non-structuralist perspective, humans create meaning and coherency in their lives, at least in part, through the subjective attachments made that matter to them. Stressing the difference with the value structuralists, it is these subjective attachments that are said to largely give *shape* to a person's life – where humans experience value and 'meaning' not so much from accessing a universally rational or objectively meaningful value structure that then informs their lives and choices accordingly, but rather from subjective commitments that are created and deemed by specific persons as worthy of attachment. Setting aside issues concerning the socialisation of attachments just outlined, a further existentialist-type distinction can also be made to explain how choices are made between objective contingent facts that are valueless and meaningless, and subjective commitments based on 'free acts of attachments' that are meaningful and value-laden. Thus, according to Sartre, for example, 'the fundamental act of freedom is discovered; and it is this which gives meaning to the particular action which I brought to consider' (Sartre, 1995, p 461; see also Warnock, 1970; Blackham, 1989; West, 1996, pp 154-88; Flynn, 2006; Reynolds, 2006). My main point here is that this existential premise that stresses the subjectivity of value creation is also variously found in those strands of liberal Anglo-American political philosophy that promote value incommensurability. According to Raz, 'meaning is invested in the world by our attachments to it' (Raz, 2001, p 16). My further claim, drawing again on this existentialist theme, is that if these attachments are made via a background of objective factual contingencies or 'accidents', this will also affect how we more generally view ourselves and the world we occupy, and in turn what can now be seen as the *creation* of incommensurable values. However, before I explicate and defend this latter claim in more detail, I will now explore the nature of the contingency or accident, referring to another liberal commentator, Thomas Nagel, and his analysis of what he calls objective and subjective 'standpoints', which again resonates, in certain important respects, with these Nietzschean and existentialist themes.

Nagel considers the contingent nature of our births. That I happen to be born from a single sperm fertilising a particular egg is purely accidental from a factually objective or outside perspective, and so for Nagel has no special or meaningful significance considered from this objective standpoint. Indeed, it is an event that is objectively meaningless, even absurd, having no factual importance or value in itself (Nagel, 1989, p 209). However, from an inside subjective perspective, the standpoint is utterly different, where 'my life seems monstrously important, and my death catastrophic' (Nagel, 1989, p 209) and as such has enormous significant meaning and value *for me*. Acknowledging the latter has various implications for the way human life is understood, the main point being, for Nagel, to recognise that these objective and subjective standpoints both have moral weight but fundamentally conflict, this conflict being integral to how we should understand morality, social relations and notions of selfhood (also see Nagel, 1995, for example pp 21-32). For example, one response to this conflict would be to abandon the particular and subjective and immerse oneself in the universal and transcendental, but for Nagel this is deeply unsatisfactory: 'I would rather lead an absurd life engaged in the particular than a seamless transcendental life immersed in the universal' (Nagel, 1989, pp 218-19). But also for Nagel, immersing oneself in the particular and subjective is self-indulgent and morally repugnant, as it over-inflates the significance of 'me' as related to the lives of 'others'. Instead, Nagel recommends what he calls humility in our moral thinking, and a disposition that 'falls between nihilistic detachment and blind self-importance' (Nagel, 1989, p 222). How, though, does this understanding of the conflict between objective and subjective standpoints reflect or not the Nietzschean and existentialist perspectives of value just outlined?

First, according to Nagel, meaning or value cannot be derived from observing objective facts of the world that happen to include the natural contingency of my birth. From this objective standpoint, my birth is, as stated, a meaningless and valueless factual event. Instead, meaning and value is derived from my being 'placed' in the universe from which position I subjectively relate to and value the world, making sense of myself and my life in a world that I imagine includes me, but understanding that others have a more objective regard. Consequently, I recognise that the world exists only as I subjectively know and value it, but also understanding 'myself' as an objective self that is part of the world. So, as with the universalism and particularism explored in Chapter One, these objective and subjective viewpoints as related to value and meaning, are not either/or corollaries but two sides of the same coin of human experience. I therefore experience an objective world that includes me, but recognise that it is a world that exists only in relation *to me*. For Nagel, then, 'to fully imagine the world without me, I have to get rid of the objective self as well, and this begins to feel like getting rid of the world itself rather than something in it' (Nagel, 1986, p 212).[7] Reflecting the view found in the Nietzschean/existentialist position, it is impossible to derive meaning and value from objective perspectives, whether these perspectives are related to rationality, structured theories of morality or scientific investigation. Instead, the subjective attachments I make in my life create meaning and value, including the world as I know and experience it, but this is also to acknowledge that the objective natural accident of my life has 'in fact' no intrinsic meaning or 'good in itself'.

Second, as well as these objective natural contingencies of birth and life, there are other social contingencies that help define the arena in which particular attachments are made. For example, I am attached to a valued object – my career as university professor, researcher and teacher. From an idealised Nietzschean perspective, I create this value through subjectively identifying with what I value in my work, relating to the joy I find in philosophical enquiry and education. But this attachment, even if it is said to be uniquely and subjectively 'mine', is only made possible by the objective presence of certain accidentally occurring social environments or events, which endorses the value of education and its associated activities and provides opportunities for me to participate in them. Following this observation, however, a further Nietzschean and existentialist point is that these specific attachments to valued objects that are freely made give a particular subjective shape and value that is specific to my life but that often changes as social circumstances alter (see also Warnock, 1970, pp 1-22; Blackham, 1989; West, 1996, pp 154-88; Flynn, 2006; Reynolds, 2006). Therefore, it might be argued that personal identity is also in a state of flux, where subjectively engaging with particular social contingencies creates value or meaning from a direct engagement within the world, which in turn profoundly shapes and re-shapes what is a socially contextualised person or person*s*. This conclusion also raises important questions about what the 'I' itself means, as there is no necessarily fixed or essential 'I' behind these contingencies, deriving meaning from its own objectified character, based on, say, abstract rational laws and/or facts about 'the self'. Rather, selfhood becomes radically contextualised such that the 'individual subject' effectively disappears, or at least becomes highly fragmented. Certain strands of continental philosophy as a result have radically decentred the 'subject' or 'I' and focused instead on the way meaning is socially created through culturally specific uses of language (West, 1996, pp 154-88). Other decenterings of the subject include the work of communitarian thinkers such as Michael Sandel, who argues that personal identity is generally discovered through social introspection, rather than being chosen by abstract individual agents (Sandel, 1982; see also Chapter One for further exploration of these and related issues). In any event, the notion of a single or essential 'I' or 'self', while not necessarily entirely abandoned, has become increasingly problematised in contemporary philosophical analysis, and is a recurring theme throughout this book.

Third, there are what might be termed personal contingencies, which also help define the arena in which attachments occur. For example, commitments to long-term relationships, where intimate attachments are made to a valued object such as a lover or friend, often occur after chance encounters. Again, when gravitating towards the Nietzschean non-structuralist and existentialist perspective, these attachments are uniquely and subjectively mine, but are facilitated by accidental and meaningless first-time objective factual events – such events defining the range and type of specific personal attachments that can and are made (also see Raz, 2001, for an exploration of how random personal attachments affect our view of the world and others). Consequently, when committing to a lifelong partner, it is not that one right person had to be found, as if the 'rightness' can be objectively known and deciphered from facts about the world, but rather that after an accidental and intrinsically meaningless initial event of meeting another person, a relationship is born where both persons create meaning and purpose in their subjective commitments to each other. More generally, it therefore becomes impossible to sustain an impersonal indifference to things and persons that matter in my life, not because of any objective meaning within things and persons, but because of my subjective commitments to them (also see Nagel, 1995, pp 10-20; Raz, 2001). The central political and moral problem is that if I were able to sustain an impersonal indifference to these personal meanings, it would leave others no reason to take my life seriously – that is, given the objective meaninglessness and valuelessness of these contingent events.

Finally, there are what might be termed physical contingencies relating to, for example, individual capabilities that also help define the arena in which attachments occur. A man with a small frame and below-average height is not usually attached to the valued object of aspiring to be a heavyweight boxer. Indeed, if he were attached to this valued object, it would be considered highly irrational, given these objective physical constraints. More plausibly, he may be attached to the valued object of aspiring to be a jockey, say, which, given his physical stature, would be possible to fulfill, and as such would be part of a reasonable range of lives that he might lead. The main point here is that what is defined as a reasonable range is at least partly shaped by these objective physical contingencies, namely the accident of having one particular body size and not another. But, again following the Nietzschean/existentialist perspective, we might recognise that this accident has no intrinsic meaning or value as an objective fact. Rather, the subjective commitment creates meaning and value, allowing the man to pursue one kind of life rather than another. As I will argue in Chapters Four, Five and Six, this understanding also has important implications for the experience of disability and impairment, going some way to explain why disabled people often do not regret having their impairments, but instead have positively incorporated this objective physical contingency or fact into their lives, from which subjective meaning and purpose is subsequently created (see also Smith, 2001a, 2002a, 2009).

But how do these various contingencies relate to my earlier discussions concerning value incommensurability? To repeat, from the Nietzschean and existentialist perspective and from the viewpoint of those who gravitate toward this position, the reason why an object is often valued, in this context at least, is not so much derived from accidental and objective circumstances, but instead is created from the subjective commitment of persons to particular valued objects. The natural contingency that I happen to be born and not another, or the social contingency that education and philosophical enquiry is valued in one society and not another, or the personal contingency that I meet a particular lover or friend and not another, or the physical contingency that I can pursue one sport or pastime and not another, has no intrinsic meaning or value. Instead, the meaning and value of committing to certain valued objects is principally derived from subjective and particularised attachments – that is, it is created *after the fact* of these objective contingencies. Certainly, objective facts have a bearing on these subjective attachments, as explored earlier, and as such the latter are therefore not entirely free-standing where value is *entirely* self-created. Nevertheless, subjective individual attachments give flesh to accessible and comprehensible meaning, not vice versa, and so literally making sense of the latter's objectivity. Once meaning is viewed from this dual perspective, it seems question-begging to simply assume that valued objects are commensurable through a theorised value structure, given that numerous subjective attachments to these objects are made and re-made after the objective occurrence of meaningless and highly diverse accidental events and circumstances. Objectified theory might use reason to justify why certain values are chosen, so explaining the rational intelligibility of choices made. But this does not imply that theory, via moral and/or value structures, can explain why one choice is made *over* others. Again, to cite Raz, 'here our reasons explain why we did what we did, but they do not explain why we did this rather than the equally eligible alternative. Intelligibility does not extend that far. It does not go all the way' (Raz, 2001, p 75; see also Malone, 1993). Developing this idea in an earlier publication, Raz states that an agent's will operates separately to reason, albeit attached to an option that is consistent with reason. Consequently, an individual agent usually does not consider all the options first, before a clear and rational answer is found about what to do. Instead, an agent simply chooses an appealing reasonable attachment and then pursues it:

> ... the will plays a role in human agency separate from that of reason, a role that neither kowtows to reason by endorsing its conclusions nor irrationally rebels against it by refusing to endorse it ... human experience ... teaches us that quite commonly people do not survey all the options open to them before choosing what to do. Rather, they find an option that they believe not to be excluded by reason and that appeals to them and pursue it. (Raz, 1997, pp 127-8)

Following this understanding, subjective attachments to valued objects are therefore freely created but are derived from non-rational motives that cannot necessarily be compared. So, interpreting Raz, Anwander concludes that 'Raz ... welcomes incomparability as making room for the exercise of the will and the free-play of non-rational motivations' (Anwander, 2001, p 194). Reinforcing this view, Elizabeth Anderson also argues for value incommensurability: 'our need to make space for the free play of non-rational motivation could thus be seen as a rational ground for not seeking to make comparative value judgments at every turn' (Anderson, 1997, p 100; see also Taylor, 1997, pp 178-80; Galston, 2002, pp 56-64). This latter position is confirmed in Raz's additional claim that '... a proper understanding of human agency ... presupposes that there are widespread incommensurabilities of options' (Raz, 1997, p 110).[8]

This presupposition, however, raises many other questions, explored further in Chapters Three and Four, concerning competing understandings of agency and will.[9] Briefly put here, and again at the risk of over-simplification, human will and agency can be viewed as distinct and different from reason, or as directly mirroring the reasoning process itself, with many positions in between (see also Millgram, 1997, pp 151-64; Regan, 1997, pp 129-43). That incommensurabilists tend toward the former view and commensurabilists the latter should be apparent from what has been explored so far. Value incommensurabilists promote the freedom to pursue various and incommensurable goals, seen as reflecting the character of human beings as unpredictable and self-transforming, who, although they may use reason to explain their choices, should not assume reason provides an 'ideal' system or structure to justify the choices made over others. In Isaiah Berlin's original argument defending value pluralism and incommensurability, he states:

> ... pluralism ... seems to me truer and more humane.... It is truer because it does, at least, recognise the fact that human goals are many, not all of them commensurable ... it is more humane because it does not (as the system-builders do) deprive men in the name of some remote, or incoherent, ideal, of much that they have found to be indispensable to their life as unpredictably self-transforming human beings. (Berlin, 2002, pp 216-17).

These arguments from Berlin Raz, and Anderson are also echoed by commentators who would not necessarily describe themselves as full-blooded incommensurabilists. For example, G.A. Cohen (2000, pp 11-13) highlights how being brought up in a certain way (this, he points out, being an accident of birth) is no reason to believe in principle p, and yet we also do not give up beliefs as a result of knowing this, even though we also know our reasons for believing p do not conclusively defeat reasons to not believe in p (compare Raz, 1988, pp 339-40; 1997). The general point here is that various subjective attachments to valued objects, be they relationships with significant others, career paths, the cultivation of particular aesthetic tastes and so on, form part of what a person becomes, where the plurality and often incommensurable character of these acts of attachment largely create meaning and value for that individual as a person or agent as she subjectively commits herself to these objects throughout her life. Given this plurality and diversity within and across a person's life, assessing human achievement via a value structure seems therefore inappropriate, or at least misses important aspects of the complex and inconclusive dynamics of personal development and identity creation. Indeed, this latter understanding, I believe, goes some way to explaining Amartya Sen's comments concerning egalitarian principles and the nature of freedom: 'if human diversity is so powerful that it makes it impossible to equalize what is potentially achievable, then there is a basic ambiguity in assessing achievement, and in judging equality of achievement or of the freedom to achieve' (Sen, 1992, p 91). I would contend, alongside the incommensurabilists, that this 'basic ambiguity' occurs because subjective meanings, understood in the non-structuralist Nietzschean and existentialist sense outlined, often cannot be fully compared via an objective theory of value, even if the latter has a legitimate role to play in any understanding of value. These meanings cannot be compared with another life or path that could also have been chosen and/or achieved had other accidental events occurred, as these events would have produced a qualitatively different shape to the whole life led. In other words, the number of lives that *might* have been led as a quantitative summation cannot be compared with the quality of a person's life *actually* led. Comparable judgments in respect of the 'achievements of life', as Sen puts it, are often therefore ruled out, leaving the Razian presupposition of incommensurability, in the strong incomparable sense, intact (see also Chapters One, Three, Four and Five for further developments of these and related issues).

Regret and incommensurability

However, what of feeling regret for a life or path that might have been led or chosen, but was not? Certainly, this feeling is common, which perhaps suggests that lives and choices are comparable, assuming regret makes apparent that a potential life led or path chosen is judged as better than the actual life led or choice made. This argument for commensurability, though, is again proceeding too hastily. To assume all regret is produced by legitimate comparisons between lives led or paths chosen discounts the possibility of a person regretting the loss of an unrealised life or choice simply because it is unrealised, but not necessarily because it compares favourably with another life or path chosen that has been realised. Regret does not always signify that one potential life or choice is better than another, only that some other life or choice could have been made but was not. In other words, the quantitative possibilities arising from the potential lives led or choices made are often extinguished, or at least diminished, by living a real life and making real choices, because living an actual life will tend to exclude or at least restrict the possibility of living another kind of potential life. What is regretted, therefore, is the finitude of life, not necessarily that one life is better than, worse than, equal to, or on a par with another. Of course, it might be argued that this type of regret is wasted because it is derived from what are the insurmountable limits of the human condition. However, it is a regret that is not, I contend, irrational, as it is quite understandable that we might regret the finitude of life, even if we are powerless to overcome it.

But before these issues are explored further, what types of reasonable regret do legitimately compare lives led or choices made? I will outline two such types of regret without suggesting they are exhaustive. First, there are moral regrets – regretting the ethical or non-ethical content of behaviour, or what might be termed virtuous or non-virtuous 'states of being' – the latter recognising that, for some commentators, living an ethical life is about being virtuous, as distinct from merely behaving well (Hursthouse, 1999; Oakley and Cocking, 2001;

Calder, 2007). For example, a Kantian who has broken a promise he could have avoided breaking would regret the action and the ill will that led to it, because it offends the first formulation of the categorical imperative, that we should only will those actions that can in principle be willed by all, which, according to Kantians, excludes the breaking of promises. Similarly, an act utilitarian would regret an avoidable action that reduced happiness, given the prime value or good that happiness should be maximised (Honderich, 1995, pp 890-2). In both cases ought implies can, suggesting that legitimate comparisons can be made between actions taken and those that could have been taken. Second, there are pragmatic regrets – regretting inefficient actions when implementing specific objectives. For example, a person who does not take an opportunity to achieve an objective she is committed to, because of momentary but avoidable negligence or complacency, could later regret the outcome because the non-action undermines achieving this objective. Someone in a similar situation who used her resources inefficiently could also reasonably regret the failed outcome if another more efficient option had been available. Again, given that in both cases ought implies can, a legitimate comparison is made between these actions or non-actions that are worse than those actions that could have been taken.

However, while recognising that these forms of regret may plausibly reflect commensurable values, I will now explore in more detail those other forms of regret that do not necessarily involve comparing lives or choices made. For example, Raz argues that there is no comparison between choosing to be a moderately successful graphic designer or a livestock farmer (Raz, 1988, pp 343-5). Neither choice is better or worse than or equal to the other, 'they are simply incommensurate' (Raz, 1988, p 343). According to Raz, this is because 'we lack any grounds for judging a career as a graphic designer to be intrinsically better or worse for those engaged in it than as a livestock farmer … assuming that they are likely to be equally successful and content in them' (Raz, 1988, p 343). There are many questions contained within the last qualification concerning the specific character of success and contentment related to notions of, say, well-being or happiness (see my exploration earlier and Chapters Three, Four and Five; see also Raz, 1988, pp 288-320). The point here, though, is that Raz's assertion that there are no grounds for comparing the *intrinsic* merits of each activity is consistent with the Nietzschean/existentialist perspective previously outlined. Objects are not intrinsically valued via objectified value structures that rank valued objects accordingly, but instead are valued through the subjective attachments of persons who consider a range of lives and choices, and make particular commitments. A person may be faced with making two incommensurable choices that reflect different sides of that person's characteristics and identity. However, the incommensurable character of the choice, while in part based on the incomparable character of the choice or valued option as Raz states, is also, I contend, derived from recognising that an individual would become a different type of *person* by choosing one path and not another. My further contention, then, is that the choices we make and the lives we subsequently lead not only reflect who we are, but also alter who we are. Here lies the dilemma and origins of regret as previously stated – that these lives are often incomparable but only one life can be led. Therefore, the regret is not necessarily from leading a qualitatively lesser life, whatever it turns out to be, because this life may reflect the incommensurable character of the person an individual becomes, which cannot be compared with what that person *might* have become. Rather, regret occurs because quantitatively only one life can be led and so one potential life must be lost, or at least diminished, as result of choosing the other. This relationship between quantitative and qualitative considerations goes some way to addressing Haan's conclusions regarding dilemmas generally and what he calls their logical inconsistency – namely, that reason is too weak to explain dilemmas and ought is too strong (Haan, 2001, p 283). My argument is that understanding lives and choices as incommensurable in the ways just outlined sits in between reason and ought, as we have a reason to regret related to the finiteness of life, but from this we should not infer that we ought to have chosen x life rather than y. To repeat, this might seem a wasteful regret, as we are powerless to overcome these limits of the human condition, but is a regret that I believe is reasonable and objectively comprehensible. Consequently, I might reasonably regret that my life comes to an end, which means I cannot live another kind of life – even though I am glad I have lived the life I actually lived, but will certainly die and can do nothing about living the other kind of life.

Other examples of how these quantitative and qualitative considerations concerning the limits of the human condition affect how we view our lives can be found in long-term commitments to personal relationships. Choosing to live a loving monogamous life with one person could be seen as incommensurable, as well as incompatible, with living a loving monogamous life with another person. The issue is that although the quality of such relationships can often be compared with that of others, as better than, worse than, equal to or on a par with another, many cannot. Potential monogamous relationships with others could therefore be largely or even partly incomparable with the actual relationship led, if these relationships are qualitatively different in each case. However, I contend that regret for not having the potential relationship is less appropriate than in the career choice described previously. This is because regret undermines the relationship with the real-life partner, as the commitment made to love *this* person in *this* way would reasonably lead to the expectation of having no regrets that another person was committed to similarly. The specific character of love for the other person in this instance requires this expectation. This reflects Sunstein's conclusion that some forms of incommensurability exclude certain reasons being legitimately proffered to justify choices made. For example, loyalty to one's spouse would exclude the acceptance of money for infidelity (Sunstein, 1997, pp 241-2). It might be argued that the love of graphic design or animal husbandry, using Raz's example, could lead to the same expectation, and certainly a person committed to either career may live a more or less regret-free life, even if she could have authentically been a successful graphic designer or livestock farmer, but not both. Nevertheless, having some level of regret in this case I argue is less problematic than in a monogamous lifelong relationship. If, after making a career choice the person is filled with regret, one might question whether she made an authentic career choice – that is, authentically reflecting what the person wants to do at the time of choosing. But the presence of some level of regret, given that both lives cannot be lived, is considered here. I contend in this case that it is possible to make an authentic choice and still feel regret, unlike the commitment made in a monogamous lifelong relationship. The character of 'love' for a career is not equivalent to the monogamous love for a person to whom one is committed for life. This is because monogamous love involves considering how the relationship itself is defined, which, in this instance, includes having a regret-free attitude to one's partner, while the love for a career has no such attitudinal conditions attached. In the latter, I contend again that regret is a reasonable response to the unavoidable limits of the human condition, assuming it is impossible to dedicate one life to both careers, resulting in another life of a qualitatively different kind being lost. Of course, some types of love for persons need not be monogamous and so would not require a regret-free attitude to the other, such as the love for friends, siblings or children. Consequently, it is plausible and reasonable, for example, to have a quantitative type regret that I do not have more friends, siblings or children, without undermining the quality of relationships with my existing friends, siblings or children. Similarly, and as explored earlier, it is also plausible and reasonable to have a quantitative-type regret that, as a finite human being, I cannot be in two places at once, and so will lose or diminish existing friendships if I move to secure a better-paid job, again without undermining the quality of these friendships as they occur presently.

Value relativism and becoming attached

By way of concluding this chapter, the final question addressed is whether recognising value incommensurability results in value relativism – where the worth of values are considered as entirely and unequivocally subjective and so not amenable to evaluation via any universal moral criteria. My short answer is not necessarily, but provided incommensurable attachments are assumed to matter to all persons, as part of their 'basic interests' – that is, providing a platform for establishing self-respect as well as respect for others (see also Chapter One for further development of these and related themes reflecting a Rawlsian understanding of 'primary goods'). Following Amy Guttman, then, I conclude that the '… requirement of political recognition of cultural particularity – extended to all individuals – is compatible with a form of universalism that counts the culture and cultural context valued by all individuals as among their basic interests' (Guttman, 1994, p 5; see also Scanlon, 1998, pp 328-62). I further argue that the subsequent diversity of plural and often incommensurable choices and identities, both within and between lives, is also worth preserving, assuming it has the potential for enriching others as well as one's own life. In this way, it might be said again that the subjective and objective character of value are not either/or corollaries but are two sides of the same coin of human experience.

First, I will briefly highlight what is implied by the Nietzschean and existentialist non-structural perspectives explored previously regarding notions of personal identity, as this, despite appearances and claims by Nietzsche to the contrary, I believe also has an important bearing on how non-particularised or universal moral reasons might be supplied for valuing attachments. Briefly put, these perspectives promote the general view that a person's identity is not derived from essential characteristics, which are fixed in relation to intrinsically valued objects and reflect theoretical structures understood to be 'objective'. Rather, a person's identity is continually created and recreated through various subjective commitments that change over time. As already stated, I am not suggesting that these commitments are entirely explained as products of individual conscious choice. Individual choice can be an important aspect of how commitments are often made, but not always. Other commitments may reflect a more socialised understanding of identity formation, originating from sources such as parental upbringing, cultural heritage and the like. The point here is that whether commitments are seen as individually chosen, socially caused or a mixture of both, personal identity is in various states of flux, which shifts or displaces the way valued objects are viewed and responded to.

Second, this understanding of identity formation leads to a distinction between 'being', relating to existing states of individual identity shaped by present and past attachments, and 'becoming', relating to the possibility of assuming future identities, given that a person's attachments may change and develop over time. Recognising this distinction between 'being' and 'becoming' in identity formation is crucial to understanding the nature and causes of valued attachments, explaining both constancy and change in a person's identity, as well as the significant role incommensurable values can play in and across a person's life. That new attachments are not necessarily commensurable with those made previously means that incommensurable valued objects can be committed to by any one person across her life, giving a certain freedom or permission to pursue a 'new life', whatever it turns out to be (also see Finnis, 1997).

Third, I therefore reject the fixing of particular identities and promoting these identities in what might be termed 'ideal' and 'pure' forms, as found in some forms of cultural particularism and explored in Chapter One. I instead promote multiculturalism and diversity in part as a political arena for expressing what McLennan calls the '… social and personal capacity for collective reinvention' (Gregor McLennan, 2008, p 103). However, it is important to acknowledge that this 'reinvention' will happen as a matter of degree, and will considerably differ between persons and particular group members. Consequently, and again as explored in Chapter One, I do not ascribe to universally promoting 'hybrid identities', where persons are encouraged to abandon specific deeply held convictions and beliefs in favour of a more or less constantly reinvented eclectic identity (Gilroy, 1993, 2004; Bhabha, 1994).[10] Rather, the claim is that the presence of incommensurable values, while facilitating the *possibility* for social and personal reinvention, also allows individuals as group members to deeply commit to specific forms of life across their whole lives.

The further question, then, is whether this process of 'being' and 'becoming' something new, to whatever degree, alongside the promotion of a variety of lives actually led, should be promoted as a universal value. And, as a certain kind of liberal value pluralist, I would argue it should, which in turn puts constraints on how we view and behave towards others. From this, it can be concluded that much criticism of liberal universalism is therefore misdirected, as a clear distinction between universalism and value monism is often not made. The former certainly does not imply the latter, given the presence of value diversity and more specifically value incommensurability, and yet this is often implied in anti-liberal criticisms (again, see Chapter One for a further exploration of these and related issues). For example, take Iris Marion Young's argument that monism leads to an over-unified denial of difference and heterogeneity, privileging particular groups' experiences and perspectives paraded by liberals as universal (Young, 1990, pp 8-14) or the related postmodern criticism that reason and value monism over-unifies the particular experiences of individuals and groups and the values and attachments humans hold dear (see Young's exploration of Adorno, Derrida and Irigay, 1990, p 98). From my arguments presented here, none of these criticisms is of liberal universalism per se, even though they are frequently presented as such; rather, they are criticisms of over-theorised monistic value systems that seek to promote one set of commensurable values being imposed on others. My counter-claim is that promoting value incommensurability not only provides a liberal alternative that meets these criticisms head on, but also is no threat to liberal universalism, given that value incommensurability provides generalisable reasons for promoting diversity and heterogeneity – values that Young and advocates of postmodern particularism also recommend. Of course, for the full-blooded Nietzschean or existentialist, these reasons are a compromise too far as this universalism overly objectifies the character of values. But, to repeat, my argument is to accommodate *both* subjectivism and objectivism, recognising that these pull the proper consideration of values and goods in opposite directions (also see Raz, 1988, 1997, 2001; Nagel, 1989, 1995; Anderson, 1997, among others). Moreover, by curtailing value monism instead of liberalism through promoting value incommensurability, it is possible to view many of the values underpinning partial and impartial commitments as being also incommensurable (and again, see Chapter One for further exploration of these and related themes). Therefore, debates concerning the conflict between impartial and partial standpoints (see, for example, Nagel, 1989, 1991) is not resolved via either/or 'solutions', but neither can they always be ranked and prioritised. Citing Raz again:

> Personal meaning emerges through our personal and collective histories which defy two extremes. They defy the belief in immutable universal values, and they defy the dream of unfettered self-creation ...

> we tend to veer to the extreme of total immutability and independence
> of value, or to the extreme of self-creation of value, whereas the truth
> is that value is neither, and both. (Raz, 2001, pp 39-40)[11]

Following this understanding, a liberal citizen, although she may see others as 'free and equal', will not therefore be expected always to prioritise her duties as a liberal citizen over her personal goals and ambitions (see also March, 2006), given that partial and impartial commitments are often incommensurable. Whether specific liberal notions of citizenship are based on agreeing that others may lead lives that are radically different to one's own, or whether value incommensurability is promoted as a substantial liberal good, regardless of there being such an agreement, is a highly moot point (also see Lovett, 2004, who explores this conflict between these consensual and rationalist traditions of liberalism). Nevertheless, in political practice we may implement both strategies to secure and promote liberal notions of citizenship, and so recommend, using Young's phrase, an 'egalitarian politics of difference' (Young, 1990, p 157) where monism and homogeneity is rejected, but where diversity and heterogeneity is universally embraced.

In this latter context, I further contend that impartially imagining others who are different from you is more easily facilitated by persons who maintain a certain distance *within* themselves – where, to use a Nietzschean phrase (Nietzsche, 1975, p 52), individuals do not 'cleave' to their attachments, but do paradoxically commit whole-heartedly to them. Such individuals subjectively commit to their personal identities, but regard them as changeable and capable of being transformed over time, in part because of their open and reciprocal encounters with others living in a liberal community who are radically different (again, see my arguments in Chapters One, Three and Four, and Smith, 2001a, 2002a, 2002b). I believe that this understanding of being open to change but also highly committed to specific attachments also makes it easier to see why it is worth preserving the plural sense of 'person*s*' in any given community. Diversity is promoted both within and between persons partly based on acknowledging both the fluidity in the subjective character of identity formation and the possibility for mutual benefits arising from encountering radical difference. The latter reciprocity principle also directly reflects the empirical claim that experiencing plurality, both within and between persons, positively contributes to the quality of lives that are, and can potentially be, led.[12] Given this latter understanding, Sandel's criticism of Rawls (explored in Chapter One) can be both better understood and simultaneously challenged – namely, that Rawls falsely conceptualises a person as a subject 'standing always at a certain distance from the interests it has' (Sandel, 1982, p 62). According to my arguments, this distance is indeed recommended to allow for fluidity and openness in subjective identity formation, provided the experiential and highly personalised phenomenology is fully recognised fully accommodates the universal presence of deep-felt attachments to incommensurable valued objects. In short, this dual endorsement of both fluidity and fixedness in identity formation defuses Sandel's complaint that Rawlsian conceptions of selfhood are necessarily over-abstract and depersonalised, by introducing an existentialist element to the latter's philosophy, and the philosophy of liberalism more generally.[13]

To summarise and make links with the themes explored in Chapter One, having your identity positively recognised by those who are radically different from you is not necessarily derived from either a demeaning craving for status reflecting Rousseauian concerns about competitive identity formation (Gauthier, 1990, pp 83-5); from similar Sartrean concerns of being judged by others (Sartre, 1995, pp 526-8); from the desire to preserve group differences as if there is a 'pure' and 'original' culture which should remain intact (see Barry's concerns regarding the promotion of multiculturalism Barry, 2001, pp 10-11; which, as Barry claims, is recommended by Taylor, 1992, 1994); from a negative affirmation of separateness expressed as an aversion or fear of 'the other' (see Young's concerns about maintaining 'essential borders' between individuals and groups, 1990, pp 143-7); or from a deontological ethic that assumes an *a priori* and largely metaphysical separateness of persons (see Sandel's concerns about the overly abstract character of personhood committed to by Rawls and other liberal deontologists; Sandel, 1982). Rather, the positive recognition of difference is born from acknowledging that persons, in their reciprocal encounters with radically different others, can both affirm their present deeply felt subjective commitments, given the suspension of judgment between lives led derived from the definition of incommensurability offered earlier; while also allowing for the possibility of change for the future.

Finally, it is this latter type of phenomenological and existentialist claim that allows for a better understanding of, among others, Raz's and Anderson's positions explored earlier. They argue that value incommensurability is not grounded in mysterious metaphysical assumptions regarding the nature of values, but reflects what it is *be* human, subjectively attached to values, and acting beyond what reason is able to conclusively dictate. And here lies the central paradox within this process of attachment making, reflecting, I believe, many liberal intuitions concerning the value of pluralism – that we often appreciate and understand our own particular commitments and attachments better when we critically evaluate our lives through positive engagement with others who are different. To use Derek Edyvane's words in his defence of both liberal solidarity and liberal conflict, '... we embrace a degree of indeterminacy in our lives in the hope that we might come to a richer understanding of the projects to which we are devoted' (Edyvane, 2005, p 47). It is how this paradoxical understanding of attachment is manifested politically, and what is meant by the plurality of persons in relation to 'otherness', that I explore in Chapter Three, examining further the nature of agency, but recognising the limits of empathic imagination regarding other persons defined as 'disadvantaged'.

Notes

[1] Without wishing to engage in a lengthy discussion about value theory and meta-ethics, it is nevertheless important to note that claims about the subjective or objective character of value are highly controversial. However, while I argue that incommensurability is more readily found in the former rather than latter accounts, I am not making any bigger claim that all values, or even that all aspects of some values, can be accounted for subjectively. My argument is that a full account of values, whatever the starting point, should incorporate both subjective and objective elements. This, I think, is a less controversial claim, although it is certainly not trivial and so needs defending, as presented here.

[2] It is a moot point whether Isaiah Berlin is a value pluralist and incommensurabilist, as he seems to vacillate between these stronger and weaker senses of incommensurability (this issue will be explored further here and in Chapter Seven).

[3] This is not to claim that increased opportunity via an increased income cannot lead to an increased quality of life, as it often does. However, that the former need not increase the quality of a person's life indicates that increased opportunity is, initially at least, a quantitative consideration – in other words, it is about the numbers of opportunities provided for living a range of potential lives, as distinct from the quality of the one life actually led (these and related issues will be explored later).

[4] Other forms of incommensurability may, for example, include Stephen Lukes' distinction between 'sacred' and 'secular' values (Lukes, 1997).

[5] The anti-Platonic character of this understanding is reflected in, for example, Nietzsche's preface to *Beyond good and evil*, where he states that '... the worst, most wearisomely protracted and most dangerous of all errors hitherto has been the dogmatist's error, namely Plato's invention of pure spirit and the good in itself' (Nietzsche, 1975a, p 14).

[6] I am not claiming here that happiness is necessarily the same as well-being, only that there is a relationship between the two that contemporary utilitarians especially often suggest and explore.

[7] A similar point is made by Ludwig Wittgenstein, albeit more concisely and opaquely, in the latter part of the *Tractatus*: 'the world and life are one. I am the world' (Wittgenstein, 2000a, 5.621 and 5.63). Wittgenstein was also very influenced by existentialist thinking, and in turn he has profoundly affected both analytical and continental traditions of thought, providing a kind of bridge between them; see also Tanesini (2004, pp 53-88) and Chapter Seven here.

[8] This emphasis on non-rational motivation and the limits of reason also reflects the British and European Romantic Movement of the late 18th and early 19th centuries

---

(Blackburn, 1996, p 332), as well as some central themes of Nietzschean/existentialist perspective explored here.

[9] Contrary to Raz and Anderson, the will may still have 'free play', if, say, the agent is viewed as freely engaged in the difficult process of reasoned practical deliberation, exploring other questions about the commensurability of values related to the nature of 'the good' (Regan, 1997, pp 129-43; see also Millgram, 1997, pp 151-64).

[10] I am very grateful to Tariq Madood, in a conversation I had with him at the Manchester Political Theory Workshops conference in 2010, for highlighting this problem of 'hybrid' identities being promoted universally.

[11] Again, this position parts company with the full-blooded Nietzschian who would see value as *only* derived from self-creation.

[12] Admittedly, this assertion leads to a range of other problematic philosophical questions concerning the relationship between objective and subjective 'facts' that are explored in later chapters, especially in Chapters Three, Four and Seven; see also Warnock (1970, pp 1-45) for a study of how existentialism deals with these problems, and of the resulting close, but ambivalent, relationship between phenomenology and existentialism.

[13] I am not suggesting that Rawls' and Nietzsche's/existentialist's conception of personhood are similar in other respects, particularly given Rawls' Kantian influences and Nietzsche's/existentialist's rejection of Kant and other universalist/structuralist accounts of value; merely, that both traditions recommend some kind of distance is maintained between 'self' (however conceptualised) and personal attachments and interests – this recommendation being important to my account of incommensurable values and accommodating both subjectivist and objectivist perspectives so described. The relationship between Kantian and Nietzschean/existentialist understandings of selfhood is also explored in Chapter Six concerning disability identity, again in an effort to accommodate both these perspectives while recognising that they also pull in opposite directions.

THREE

Empathic imagination and its limits

Introduction

In this chapter, I explore what might is meant by the plurality and separateness of persons with regard to notions of otherness, difference and agency, and relate this to my defence in Chapters One and Two of value incommensurability, and the suspension of judgments concerning the comparative worth of people's lives and values held. For many liberal egalitarians, distributions of material resources to the disadvantaged or marginalised often presuppose a common understanding or empathic connection, eliciting, for example, the emotions of sympathy and pity for those people defined as 'worse off'. My main counter-argument here is that 'first-order' empathic imagination, which accesses objective knowledge about a person's experience, and then imagines what it is like to be that person, is a necessary but not sufficient condition for relating to others as different and separate persons, or as agents. A 'disposition of surprise' should also be encouraged responding to a person's subjective and highly unexpected engagement with her life, disrupting any epistemological settlement concerning the nature of her experiences and their imagined affects. This disposition accepts that making what I call fundamental mistakes in empathic imagination is inevitable – that is, mistakes that fail to acknowledge an agent's ability to have a qualitatively rich and valuable life beyond what is reasonably and objectively expected, given her highly subjective responses to her specific circumstances and experiences. However, recognising the fallibility of first-order empathic imagination paradoxically helps persons to identify with different others understood as separate agents. By recognising these mistakes, a person is more open to appropriately viewing and relating to 'disadvantaged others' who are agents too, remaining open to 'second-order' empathic imagination, acknowledging a person's subjective ability to have a life and to view her life as qualitatively rich and valuable – that is, contrary to expectations derived from shared 'objective knowledge' about this person and her experiences and circumstances.

Following this analysis, and the themes explored in Chapters one and two regarding identity formation, the limits of reason in explaining decision making, and the incommensurability of many valued objects, in policy and practice there exists a tension between, on the one hand, promoting social systems that redistribute resources to those objectively defined as 'worse off', reflecting the value of equality, and, on the other hand, acknowledging the ability to subjectively create a positive identity whatever disadvantage is experienced, reflecting the value of diversity. The former implies a commitment to universal principles of justice, applicable across contemporary societies or cultures, based on objectively comparing states of affairs understood to be better than, worse than, equal to or on a par with others, and therefore are understood as commensurable or comparable. The latter, meanwhile, allows for the subjective promotion of incommensurable lives, so not judging one life as qualitatively better than, worse than, equal to on a par with another life, even if the one life is objectively defined as advantaged or disadvantaged as compared with another.

Liberal egalitarian political philosophy and the perspective of others

Traditionally, liberal egalitarians commit to universal principles of redistributive justice while upholding the values of individual choice and agency (for example, Rawls, 1973, 1993, 2001; Dworkin, 1981, 2000; Sen, 1985, 1992; Raz, 1988, 2001; Cohen, 1989, 1995, 2000; Arneson, 1993, 1997, 2000; Scanlon, 1998). For most liberal egalitarians, socially just distributions accommodate the different choices and life-plans individuals make and value, but compensate for universally and objectively defined disadvantageous conditions and circumstances experienced by these individuals, particularly those conditions and circumstances that are unchosen. Defending social justice principles, liberal egalitarians also often invite persons to imagine the lives of differently situated others, especially those who are defined as 'worse off'. Imagination implies having a cognitive ability to picture what life would be like from another agent's subjective perspective and experience – what it is like from the 'inside' – simultaneously recognising that the other person's life might radically differ from one's own. Consequently, to imagine the subjective life of another as particular and other is to mentally envisage what it is like to be the other person, while maintaining what is distinctive about the actual life of the imaginer (also see Piper, 1991; Ferrell, 2008, pp 46-9). As will be explored further in Chapter Four, some liberal egalitarians also recommend that persons emotionally identify with the 'badly-off', eliciting a sympathetic engagement with suffering others, so also providing a psychological motive for prioritising this group's needs. The appeal to emotionally identify with others is traceable to Adam Smith, David Hume and Aristotle, and is promoted by contemporary thinkers such as Martha Nussbaum (Nussbaum, 1996; see also Kimball, 2001; Whitebrook, 2002).

Empathic imagination, then, can involve two capacities – the ability to cognitively imagine what life is like from another's subjective perspective being different from one's own, and the ability to emotionally identify with the plight of another's experiences and circumstances. My first claim is that acknowledging the distinction between these capacities can help us understand better some of the universal recommendations of liberal egalitarians. A cognitive ability to imagine the perspective of another *as* other permits the universal values of individual choice and agency, given that various 'conceptions of the good' (or 'valued objects') are chosen by individuals, imagined as important from the other agent's subjective perspective – recognising that these may be unimportant from the imaginer's own subjective viewpoint. For many liberal egalitarians, this willingness to see the world from another's subjective viewpoint, despite one's own very different perspective and conceptions of the good, underpins universalism. It regulates individual actions, based on an 'outside' or what might be termed an objective or impartial viewpoint, promoting a respect for others that considers the interests of all equally (see also Nagel, 1989, 1995, and Chapters One and Two of this book for a more detailed exploration of the relationship between these subjective and objective viewpoints or standpoints).

For example, John Rawls in *A theory of justice* states that respect for others is shown in '… our willingness to see the situation of others from their point of view, from the perspective of their conception of the good; and in our being prepared to give reasons for our actions whenever the interests of others are materially affected' (Rawls, 1973, pp 337-8). Rawls also argues that supplying determinate principles for regulating inequalities entails imagining the world from the standpoint of the worst-off, articulated in the 'difference principle', where inequalities are only justifiable if they support the long-term expectations of the least fortunate: 'in order to make the principle regulating inequality determinate, one looks at the system from the standpoint of the least advantaged.… Inequalities are permissible when they maximize, or at least all contribute to, the long-term expectations of the least fortunate group in society' (Rawls, 1971, p 151). Linking these complex assumptions – the capacity an individual has for imagining beyond what is distinctively her own conception of the good and personal interests, and the social obligations towards others that ensue – Rawls promotes what he sees as the universal values of individual liberty and equality. Imagining the world from another's subjective perspective or viewpoint is central to establishing impartial and universal principles of distributive justice – accommodating individual interests equally, and recognising that all individuals are free agents with plans and ambitions that matter to them.

There are, though, notorious problems making these types of move for liberal egalitarians. For example, associating cognitive imaginative capacities underpinning universal reasons for action or constraint with capacities for feeling empathy describing how persons emotionally identify with the suffering of others is far from straightforward. The difficulty, in part, derives from what many regard as question-begging assumptions found in liberal notions of individual agency, which rely on controversial conceptions of human nature and personhood (see, for example, Sandel, 1982, explored in more detail later, and Chapters One and Two of this book). In addition, there are other issues concerning the internal coherence of holding to both liberal and egalitarian principles, as these relate to particularised human experiences and emotions, and the universality or explanatory scope of reason. Some egalitarian commentators argue that experience and emotion, which is particular to persons, and universal reason, which is viewed as accessible by all, are complementary when taking the perspective of others (for example, Peters, 1973; Schwartz, 1993; Nussbaum, 1996, 1999; Mendus, 2003). The emotional capacity to identify with and *feel* for another person's circumstances and experiences is, therefore, seen as a motivating force for placing universal restrictions on inequalities. So, having sympathy and pity for the worst-off lends us towards establishing institutions that prioritise the needs or interests of the worst-off, based on reasons everyone can accept (see also Snow, 1991; Wright, 2002). Nevertheless, for others, appealing to sympathetic feelings provides shaky foundations when setting up institutions reflecting universal principles of justice. This instability is produced because the liberal commitment to the 'separateness of persons' must acknowledge that individuals are primarily self-interested, and that their life prospects usually matter to them more than the life prospects of others. Consequently, individual life prospects should not be sacrificed for the 'greater good', even if this sacrifice meets the needs or interests of the worst-off. According to Rawls, a society governed by the principle of utility, for example, would demand this sacrifice of its members, which for him is both unjust and unrealistic:

> [T]he principles of justice apply to the basic structure of the social system and to the determination of life prospects. What the principle of utility asks is precisely a sacrifice of these prospects. We are to accept the greater advantages of others as a sufficient reason for lower expectations over the whole course of our life. This is surely an extreme demand. (Rawls, 1973, p 178)

For Rawls, these kinds of demand are impossible to cultivate across large communities but explain why sympathy and benevolence towards others plays a central role in utilitarian political philosophy: 'It is evident then why utilitarians should stress the role of sympathy in moral learning and the central role of benevolence among the moral virtues. Their conception of justice is threatened with instability unless sympathy and benevolence can be widely and intensely cultivated' (Rawls, 1973, p 178). Alternatively, conceiving a system of cooperation designed to advance the good of its members must assume that all members are self-interested and separate individuals, who, from an 'original position' of equality – unaware of their particular life prospects reflecting their conceptions of the good and place in society, but aware that each individual has life prospects that subjectively matter to them – will choose a structure that is reciprocally advantageous for all. This move allows Rawls to sideline sympathy and utilitarian self-sacrifice when promoting universal principles of justice:

> Looking at the question from the standpoint of the original position, the parties ... would reject the principle of utility and adopt the more realistic idea of designing the social order on a principle of reciprocal advantage. We need not suppose, of course, that persons never make substantial sacrifices for one another, since moved by ties of affection

and sentiment they often do. But such actions are not demanded as a matter of justice by the basic structure of society. (Rawls, 1973, p 178)

The force of these Rawlsian objections to utilitarianism has led to some consensus between contemporary liberal egalitarians, limiting the efficacy of empathic imagination and emotional identification. Even those such as Martha Nussbaum, who regard the emotions of pity and compassion for 'the suffering other' as essential to establishing a civil society, acknowledge the importance of viewing persons as separate agents when identifying with the suffering of others:

> In the temporary act of identification, one is always aware of one's own *separateness* from the sufferer – it is for another, and not oneself, that one feels; and one is aware both of the bad lot of the sufferer and of the fact that it is, right now, not one's own. If one really had the experience of feeling pain in one's own body, then one would precisely have failed to comprehend the pain of another *as other*. One must also be aware of one's own *qualitative difference* from the sufferer.... For these recognitions are crucial in getting the right estimation of the meaning of the suffering. (Nussbaum, 1996, p 35; emphasis in original)

Therefore, for Nussbaum, as well as for Rawls, there is an immutable separateness between persons, relating to what might be termed the incomplete transferability of pain or suffering in empathic imagination. While emotionally aware of the pain and suffering of another, for Nussbaum a person cannot experience the pain of another as her own pain. Putting aside troubling philosophical questions concerning the existence of other minds, and the knowledge of my own mind and its dependency or otherwise on knowledge of the social world, for Nussbaum the separateness of persons allows for an appropriate response to suffering – that which does not extinguish the subjective standpoint of the empathic imaginer, allowing a response to the suffering that is reasonable and insightful (see Chapter Four for a more detailed exploration of Nussbaum's position; see also Schwartz, 1993, for a similar argument to Nussbaum's, recommending maintaining distances between persons via rational critical reflection, while also recognising the proximity of persons when acknowledging shared emotions).

To summarise so far, while the cognitive capacity for imagining the subjective perspective of others is recommended by most, if not all, liberal egalitarians, the emotional capacity for identifying with the suffering of others is viewed more ambivalently. This ambivalence relates, I have argued, to problems arising within liberal egalitarianism, where the values of individual agency and the separateness of persons risk being undermined if responses to empathic emotions do not properly account for subjective and particularised interests. The next section explores how the capacity for empathic imagination, whether related to emotional identification or not, can be more clearly conceptualised within liberal egalitarian political philosophy – that is, by better accommodating what are highly subjective responses to specific experiences and circumstances, so maintaining the separateness of persons, but by so doing, unsettling objective accounts of disadvantage and the categorisation of others comparatively defined as 'worse off'.

First- and second-order empathic imagination

I will now distinguish between first-order and second-order empathic imagination. My claim is that the former promotes the ideal that individuals should be maximally accurate regarding how they reasonably imagine another person's particular circumstances or experiences, objectively defined as better than, worse than, equal to or on a par with others. Second-order empathic imagination, meanwhile, acknowledges the possibility of making what I call fundamental mistakes in first-order empathic imagination – that is, mistakes that fail to acknowledge an agent's ability to have a qualitatively rich and valuable life beyond what is reasonably and objectively expected, given her highly subjective responses to her specific circumstances and experiences. However, recognising the fallibility of first-order empathic imagination paradoxically helps persons to identify with 'different others' understood as separate agents (contrast with Sandel, 1982, pp 62-5 and pp 133-47; Nussbaum, 1996; Whitebrook, 2002; and, again, see Chapter Four for further exploration of these and related issues).

Exercising first-order empathic imagination has as its goal the ideal of being maximally accurate regarding the subsequent identification with 'the other'. The possibility of achieving maximum accuracy implies that targets are universally fixed and objectively definable, so targets can be hit, nearly hit or not at all hit – the first being a maximal ideal, the second being a good enough rough accuracy, and the last something to avoid. This is first-order empathic imagination because, despite the acknowledgement of separate persons, it does not defer to a view of others that firmly establishes the epistemological limitations of this objectified form of empathic imagination.

At first it might seem plausible to accept an unproblematic epistemological claim about the progressive development of first-order empathic imagination, where enhancing and sharing objective knowledge about persons within a community allows for the possibility, at least in principle, of maximally accurate empathic identification with others. So, an effective empathic imaginer accesses through their cognitive and/or emotional capacities certain forms of objective knowledge, which can be variously tested for accuracy helping the imaginer becoming increasingly skilled in their empathic identification with others. For example, and as explored in Chapters One and Two, Sandel, when criticising Rawls and his understanding of separate individuated persons, emphasises how communities 'describe the subject', which allows persons to discover who they are in relation to each other, rather than, as Rawls would apparently have it, regard individuals with fixed *a priori* identities choosing their own ends (Sandel, 1982, pp 62-5). The point here is that whether derived from informal stocks of cultural knowledge, through the media for example – novels, films, television and so on – or from more formal training in, say, counselling or social work, which deliberately set out to cultivate skills in imaginative empathic engagement, these epistemological processes of intelligence gathering when relating to other lives are derived from objective understandings and universal theories of human behaviour found within these communities, which are then understood and applied accordingly (see also Wright, 2002, for a detailed account of what she calls narrative imagination, allowing us to take the perspective of others, even if others are not present in our lives).

My main counter-argument is that engaging in this form of first-order empathic imagination, accessing community-based stocks of objective knowledge, is necessary, but not sufficient, for relating to others as agents – this being especially significant when identifying with the experiences and circumstances of 'the disadvantaged'. In addition, a disposition of surprise should be encouraged, responding to a disadvantaged person's highly subjective and often unexpected engagement with her life, disrupting any epistemological settlement concerning the predictive capacity of first-order empathic imagination. Underlying first-order empathic imagination is, I believe, a question-begging epistemological assumption that the accuracy in hitting empathic targets can be unproblematically accessed and assessed universally and objectively; that is, as if this knowledge exists independently from first, the particular relational encounters between the imaginer and the imagined, and second, considerations concerning individual agency, the other's subjective perspective, and the often highly unpredictable responses to personal experiences and circumstances.

I will now explore the former contention further. However, it is important to first highlight that the ethical significance of relational encounters is also promoted by commentators explored in Chapter One, and associated with what has been called particularism and the politics of recognition. The principal assertion is that the ethical significance of my being recognised as an autonomous agent depends not only on features intrinsic to me, but also on my relations with others (for example, Young, 1990; Honneth, 1992, 2007; Frase, 1997; Fraser and Honneth, 2003; MacKenzie and Stoljar, 2000; Edyvane, 2005; see also Levinas, 1985, 1996, 2006, and compare Sandel, 1982). Take Emmanuel Levinas' position, for example; briefly put, his main assumption is that morality is born out of the concrete encounter with what he calls 'the face' of 'the other', disrupting the world of the individual self-interested person, by making demands on that person (for example, see Levinas, 1985, pp 83–92). His philosophy seems to have influenced many commentators who promote recognition politics. According to Young, '... a "moral point of view" arises not from a lonely self-legislating reason, but from the concrete encounter with others, who demand that their needs, desires, and perspectives be recognised' (Young, 1990, p 106). An anti-Kantian theme is also clearly audible in Young's attack on self-legislated reason and is explored further in Chapters One, Two and Six. The point here is that when emphasising these encounters with others, recognition-orientated proponents mainly focus on the recognition of groups rather than individuals, and so are highly critical of liberals such as Rawls, whom they claim underestimate the importance of social structure by unjustifiably elevating the self-interested individual as an agent who is immutably and universally separate to others.[1] My analysis provides an alternative exegesis of Rawlsian liberal principles that reinterprets and defends aspects of his liberalism, but accommodating certain elements of these recognition charges (for a similar strategy regarding the Rawlsian defence of justice as reciprocity, see Smith, 2002a, 2002b, 2005a).

Particular relational encounters occur in a number of ways, from relatively distant encounters with strangers, to encounters within intimate relationships. Whatever their nature, I regard them as encounters for my purposes because they disrupt the imaginer's world and unsettle her subjective perspective or viewpoint to lesser or greater degrees. They are also dynamic and relational, given that they may prompt actions that change, or at least challenge, existing relations between persons. For example, seeing the image of a starving child on television may invite the viewer to make a comparison between her life and that of the child, which then could disrupt her settled view concerning the justification of her relatively well-off position. This comparison leads her to encounter the child, who, although a stranger, is presented as a 'suffering other' who needs assistance, requiring some change in relations between the better-off viewer and the worse-off child. Intimate personal relationships can also involve relational encounters that disrupt and may change particular viewpoints within these relationships. For example, communication between two people might reveal certain subjective understandings about each person's experiences and circumstances, which disrupts their original viewpoints and so may prompt each to reassess and change their relationship.

I will now argue that these relational encounters, although they could reasonably include exercising first-order empathic imagination, accessing objective and shared knowledge about another person's condition and circumstances, ought not to include the ideal aim of being maximally accurate. Rather, there should be a second-order aim of identifying with others who are agents, requiring that the imaginer deliberately withhold the exercise of first-order empathic imagination, especially in certain contexts. Moreover, I contend that this withholding is, paradoxically, part of what it is to be emotionally and cognitively sensitive in human relations – that is, if the full force of particularist values explored in Chapters One and Two is properly acknowledged, viewing 'the other' as a separated and highly subjective agent. Consequently, it is often appropriate in relational encounters to state that you cannot empathically imagine what it would be like, or feel like, to be the other person, and that you should not even attempt to. In other words, the key to engaging in second-order empathic imagination is to withdraw from imagining how you see the other, in order to imaginatively engage with the other as *she* sees herself, fully recognising that this is precisely *not* how you see her. Developing a theme explored by Mackenzie and Scully, the resulting negative injunction is therefore to 'not try and imagine being the other from the inside. Rather, one recognises that the other is different from oneself, one imaginatively engages with her perceptions and experiences, as she represents them' (Mackenzie and Scully, 2007, p 347). My main contention, then, concerning 'disadvantage' is that a person with a radically different life to another might properly withhold judgment about the other's subjective perspective and her experience, even if on first sight it *seems* obvious to this person that the other's objective condition is universally deficient, tragic and/or pitiable. Explaining this further, I will now explore the second contention outlined earlier – that the presence of individual agency and the other's separated and subjective perspective often results in highly particularised and unpredictable responses to specific experiences and circumstances. These responses, in turn, problematise a number of liberal egalitarian accounts of disadvantage and well-being, and their subsequent recommendations for policy and practice.

The separateness of persons and objective accounts of well-being

Often principles of distributive justice are not derived from observing particular relational encounters as described in the last section, where, via first- and second-order empathic imagination, the subjective lives of persons are, when and if appropriate, compared and changed accordingly. Rather, principles of justice are founded on universal judgments concerning the quality of lives led, where priority is assigned to the worst-off, because the better-off can imagine the plight of the worst-off measured objectively – that is, without any comparisons being made between the subjective perspective of either the better or worst-off. For example, Richard Arneson claims that liberal egalitarian principles are best expressed when 'priority is assigned to aiding an individual in virtue of how badly his life is going, as measured by an objective scale of well-being, not intrinsically by any comparison between his life and that of others' (Arneson, 2000, p 343; see also Arneson, 1993, 1997). Here, the accuracy of seeing the perspective of others who are separate and different from you depends on the degree to which the lives of the badly-off correspond with certain levels of well-being that can be objectively evaluated. Maximum accuracy in empathic imagination is clearly obtainable as an ideal in Arneson's account of well-being, for an empathic judgment can be made that a person is doing badly by objectively measuring the actual life of this person against her imagined potential life universally understood as a better life.[2]

Another important step in Arneson's argument is that if, and when, objective and subjective judgments about the experience of 'bad luck' are conflicting, justice requires preferring the former over the latter. Again, according to Arneson, policy should be attentive to the bad luck experienced by persons given that they did not choose it, meaning that no reference to a person's subjective response to her bad luck is necessary. Rather, policy should respond to people's diminished 'life prospects … in favour of those who have done as well as could reasonably be expected with the cards that fate has dealt them' (Arneson, 2000, p 349). Similarly, for Nussbaum, having compassion or pity for the 'suffering other', although not required in Arneson's account, leads to policies that respond to diminished capacities for human flourishing endured by the sufferer, again considered separately from subjective and particularised responses to the suffering experienced. Indeed, according to Nussbaum, the subjective reaction of the sufferer is highly suspect because it often leads to distorted judgments, as the sufferer is likely to be in some kind of denial regarding his condition: 'the person affected does not judge that his condition is bad, however – that, indeed, is a large part of what is so terrible about it. In short: implicit in pity itself is a conception of human flourishing, the best one the pitier is able to form' (Nussbaum, 1996, pp 31-2).[3] Therefore, it is the pitier, being a member of the better-off group, who has privileged access to these objective judgments concerning the condition of others, where, despite Arneson's arguments to the contrary, lives are effectively compared as better than, worse than, equal to or on par with another. Either way, in Nussbaum's or Arneson's account, a universal yardstick for evaluating and changing social, political and economic structures is found. I will now argue that identifying this yardstick, in relation to defining well-being at least, is deeply problematic for various reasons concerning how agents relate to their lives and others, and in the highly particularised and unpredictable way disadvantaged agents respond to their specific experiences and circumstances.[4]

First, though, how does my interpretation of individual agency, and the separateness and subjectivity of persons explored in previous sections, relate more generally to liberal egalitarian political philosophy? I believe my conclusions are, to some extent, consistent with Rawls's original position, insofar as I am asking persons to reflect initially on their common or generalised capacity for agency, without making any assumptions about the particular response of others to their specific circumstances and experiences. To use Rawls's terminology regarding notions of the good (Rawls, 1973, pp 395-9), I am therefore starting from thin rather than thick conceptions of personhood to promote just policies and practices, as I am not assuming anything particular about a person's life and how she responds to it, only that, like everyone, she is an agent who has a life that matters to her. However, this Rawlsian distinction has been severely criticised by various commentators here and in Chapters One and Two, and these criticisms should, I argue, be taken seriously. Michael Sandel, for example, argues against what he sees as Rawls' broadly Kantian conception of selfhood and agency, separating the self from particular attachments and cultural circumstances, when Rawls places persons in his original position to agree on principles of justice (Sandel, 1982). For Sandel, this move is based on a profound misunderstanding of human beings and our social relations, relying on overly abstract and metaphysical definitions of individual identity and 'the subject' divorced from particular experiences, that is, despite Rawls' attempt to extract the metaphysics from Kant, offering a conception of justice that is both rights-bound (deontological and abstract) and based on what Rawls claims are individuals making substantive hypothetical contracts with each other (experiential and particular). According to Sandel, this attempt to offer Kant with a Humean face, as Sandel calls it, fails:

> ... deontological liberalism cannot be rescued from the difficulties
> associated with the Kantian subject. Deontology with a Humean
> face either fails as deontology or recreates in the original position the
> disembodied subject it resolves to avoid. Justice cannot be primary in
> the deontological sense, because we cannot coherently regard ourselves
> as the kind of beings the deontological ethic – whether Kantian or
> Rawlsian – requires us to be. (Sandel, 1982, p 14)

There is insufficient space to explore in detail this and other related objections
to Rawls and Kant. Suffice it to say, I believe they rely on a caricature of both.
It is, perhaps, easy to understand why this caricature is promoted, given how
Kant consistently argues for universal ethical objectivism that in many ways
appears entirely abstracted from particular human experiences. Simply put, he
founds morality on a duty-bound freedom to obey universalised rules that are
invoked prior to considering individual subjective preferences. Rawls directly
parallels Kant, as critically reflecting on principles of justice within the original
position deliberately excludes knowledge of particular conceptions of the good,
derived from a person's subjective preferences and/or aspirations, and instead
focuses on what individuals would reasonably agree without knowledge of these
subjective biases and partial interests. Nevertheless, despite these universal and
abstract principles of justice found in Rawls and Kant, there is a more empiricist
and experiential dimension to either which can be emphasised to both that
considerably complicates any interpretation of their respective philosophies (see
also Louden, 2000; Smith, 2002a, pp 145-9; and Chapters One and Two here).
For example, in *A theory of justice*, Rawls (1973) claims that when a person values
her own ends she depends in part on others' views of her. This could imply a
certain kind of particularised experience *of* others, based on assurances regarding
the mutual esteem and respect of associates, which, according to Rawls, in any
just society benefits all:

> ... parties in the original position ... know that in society they need
> to be assured by the esteem of their associates. Their self-respect and
> their confidence in the value of their own system of ends cannot
> withstand the indifference much less the contempt of others. Everyone
> benefits then from living in a society where the duty of mutual respect
> is honored. (Rawls, 1973, p 338)

Particular dispositions of concern and esteem, of and by others, could be based on
a Kantian-type respect or reverence for universal just law. So, we respect others and
they respect us because we all first respect universal and just principles. However,
my claim is that the Rawlsian commitment to the separateness of persons as agents
may, despite these Kantian leanings, still accommodate a more particularised and
subjective experiential and emotional disposition towards others (see Chapter One
for a further exploration of these and related issues).[5] First, it seems plausible to

suppose that attitudes of indifference and contempt, and their opposites concern and esteem, could suggest both a cognitive and emotional disposition towards 'the other', where a Rawlsian interpretation might consistently allow some level of particularised identification *with* 'the other'. Second, seeing the world from another's perspective or standpoint would, therefore, not simply be a matter of accessing a universal scheme of rational or reasonable cognition and acting accordingly, as Rawls seems to have it, but could also involve empathically engaging with particular others who are agents with ends – so engaging in second-order empathic imagination of the kind described earlier.

Following my arguments in Chapters One and Two, this understanding of second-order empathic imagination may not only be consistent with a certain interpretation of Rawlsian liberal egalitarian political philosophy, but also reflect discrete existentialist themes. For example, according to existentialists, human beings are united in their condition of freedom – as we are all free to interpret and act in the world. But this condition, for existentialists, also separates us, as individuals, from what is exterior or other, as we do not just *experience* the world – a world that includes the 'otherness' of other persons – we also interpret and respond to it *as* other. Consequently, understanding our common condition of freedom means also recognising that we are individuals who are profoundly differentiated and alone. As Sartre puts it, '... freedom is responsible for the fact of abandonment and separates us from things' (Sartre, 1980, p 509). In short, the 'us' here provides at once a deep connectedness between human beings who paradoxically, *in* this connectedness, must recognise others as entirely separated (see Sartre, 1980, 1995; see also Camus, 1982, especially pp 106-8).[6] I will now explore how second-order empathic imagination also reflects both this connectedness *and* separateness between persons, acknowledging an agent's ability to have a rich and valuable life beyond what is reasonably and objectively expected by others, given this agent's particular circumstances and experiences.

Agency and surprise

My main claim is that engaging with each other as free agents, rather than merely as experiencers of circumstance, accommodates the possibility that a person's subjective perspective and responses to her life can be, and often are, wholly surprising, that is, a surprise born from what I will call fundamental mistakes when trying to empathically imagine what it is like to be that other person. More specifically, mistakes are fundamental when they deviate from the subjective perspective and/or response of the agent, but are nevertheless either derived from socially accepted norms and practices that establish rational and reasonable criteria for objectively judging how lives are fairing, and/or go against shared expectations concerning the way an agent will view and respond to her own experiences. Fundamental mistakes therefore occur when rational and reasonable efforts have been made to ensure that first-order empathic imagination is at least roughly accurate, through accessing shared stocks of objective knowledge about persons, but the empathic imaginer still gets it very wrong, and therefore surprisingly wrong. These efforts would include, for example, making reasonable connections between the circumstances and behaviour of another and imagining the perspective and emotional response of that person. There are a number of reasons why these mistakes occur, which I will now explore.

First, standards of reasonableness are highly contingent and particular, as these standards reflect shared social meanings concerning the types of circumstances and behaviour exhibited, which often vary across time and between cultures. This is significant, raising pertinent questions about social communication and understanding, and the complex language games and political discourses individuals and groups undertake (see also Berger and Luckman, 1991; Saraga, 1998; Wittgenstein, 2000b; Foucault, 2001; Faubion, 2003). It might be argued that the so-called universality of reason and objectivity of knowledge only appear as such because many assumptions made in shared social contexts are taken for granted within these contexts, but can be questioned outside of them. Consequently, fundamental mistakes in empathic imagination could reflect what may be termed a paradigm mismatch, between dominant social expectations that are presented as universal and objective, and an agent's subjective and highly particularised response to her experiences and circumstances that may radically deviate from these expectations. For example, those within the disability rights movement (DRM) argue that supposed universal and objective representations of disabled people as tragic victims of medical deficiencies beyond their control fundamentally misrepresent the particularised subjective perspectives and experiences of disabled people (Morris, 1991; Oliver and Barnes, 1998; Swain et al, 2003; Mackenzie and Scully, 2007).[7] This is not because these medicalised representations are inaccurate as a matter of degree – and so are missing an agreed target. Rather, they are representations that belong to a radically different paradigm or perspective, reflecting non-disabled people's fundamental mistakes in their view of disabled people (see also Smith 2001a, 2001b, 2002a, 2005a, 2005b, and Chapters Four, Five and Six here). This, in turn, raises a difficult question concerning whether 'the other' is *always* in a privileged position to report on the nature of her own condition, an issue I explore further in Chapters Five and Six. However, the point here for the DRM is that the presumption at least of accuracy should lie with the disabled person. So, when she perceives herself as happy and fulfilled she is often defined by the medicalised paradigm as 'brave' and 'courageous' because she has overcome her 'tragic circumstances', which for the DRM reflects and reinforces misplaced disablist assumptions: '… for many disabled people, the tragedy view of disability is in itself disabling. It denies the experience of a disabling society, their enjoyment of life, and even their identity and self-awareness as disabled people' (Swain et al, 2003, p 71). This denial is also found in liberal egalitarian political philosophy. For example, Ronald Dworkin's analysis of disability starts with what, for the DRM, is a question-begging assumption: 'surely, all but a few of those who suffer in those ways would prefer that their handicaps were cured and that their talents were improved' (Dworkin, 2003, p

194). For the DRM, it is not necessarily individual 'cure' and 'talent improvement' that is the aim for disabled people, but rather the radical reorganisation of social structures to accommodate the different capabilities of those who are impaired, establishing equal opportunities to live a similar range of potential future lives as non-disabled people (see also Sawyer, 2010). As will be explored later, for many within the DRM, this latter aim means that social structures *can* be understood objectively as opportunities between individuals and groups are counted and compared, and as such might potentially problematise subjective assessments of personal conditions if they fail to recognise these oppressive social conditions. However, acknowledging these objective facts about social oppression for the DRM should not detract from a non-medicalised subjective account of disability identity also being promoted, which assumes that disabled people can live fulfilled and enriched lives as they engage with their experiences positively, including the experience of having an impairment (these and related issues will also be explored in Chapters Four, Five and Six; see also Smith, 2001a, 2002a).

Second, following this kind of paradigm mismatch, there are errors of empathic imagination that also occur when the imaginer is empathising with a person who is very different to her, and/or is the type of person she has not, or has rarely, encountered. Consequently, according to Mackenzie and Scully, problems of social exclusion and inequality of opportunity are reinforced 'when the other person is very different from ourselves, the danger ... [being] that we simply project onto the other our own beliefs and attitudes, fears and hopes, and desires and aversions' (Mackenzie and Scully, 2007, p 345). Young's understanding of the way certain cultures often view and respond to physical bodies shares a similar concern: 'when the dominant culture defines some groups as different, as the Other, the members of these groups are imprisoned in their bodies. Dominant discourses define them in terms of bodily characteristics, and construct these bodies as ugly, dirty, defiled, impure, contaminated, or sick' (Young, 1990, p 123). The point here is that the empathic imaginer, when she has rarely encountered the other, is more likely to rely on these shared social meanings – a reliance that may be deemed appropriate and reasonable, given the limitations of her personal encounters and the prevalence of these social meanings, but nevertheless runs a high risk of making fundamental mistakes. As Young also highlights, this risk is especially prevalent when more dominant social norms and expectations misrepresent the experiences and perspectives of minority groups. In these instances, my argument is that these mistakes in empathic imagination are often institutionalised through regulated social practices, raising political issues concerning the social construction of language and its use (Berger and Luckman, 1991; Saraga, 1998; Foucault, 2001; Faubion, 2003). My main contention is that the public use of language often defines and embodies what can be empathically imagined by others, reflecting political struggles over competing social meanings and unequal distributions of power concerning the way others are socially defined (see also Smith, 2001a, 2002b).

Third, however, my further claim is that although these kinds of institutionalised fundamental mistake in empathic imagination are common, they are not the sole cause of them. Fundamental mistakes can occur when institutional meanings have the least hold over a person's empathic imagination, and when relational encounters with relevant others are frequent and intimate. For example, within long-term personal relationships, agents often exercise empathic imagination surprisingly inaccurately. To be sure, some of these inaccuracies are derived from shared social meanings intruding and distorting the way personal encounters are interpreted. Consequently, feminist commentators have explored how publicly shared gender expectations regarding the characters and roles of men and women can have an important bearing on how private relationships are interpreted and experienced, based on misinterpretations of men and women's lives, and, within patriarchal societies at least, the undervaluing of women's subjective perspectives and experiences (for example, see Oakley, 1972; Lister, 1997; MacKenzie and Stoljar, 2000). These misinterpretations could then lead to mistakes in empathic imagination that could be remedied by a more critically reflective exercise of empathic imagination that, for example, properly takes account of women's subjective perspectives and experiences.

Nevertheless, my contention is that fundamental mistakes of empathic imagination can also occur even if publicly shared social expectations are barely, if at all, influencing empathic imagination. An empathic imaginer, through a vast personal stock of encounters with particular agents, may be able to radically challenge dominant social constructions or stereotypes concerning the so-called universal character and perspective of these agents, but still commit fundamental mistakes of the kind described earlier. The central explanation for these errors are, to repeat, centred on the capacity for agency, based on a subjective ability a person has to choose significant aspects of her life and, as importantly, an overall subjective perspective on her life that is both dynamic and unpredictable. Consequently, a free agent will often radically go against expectations regarding her individual responses to experiences and circumstances – expectations reflected not necessarily in dominant social norms and stereotypes, but gleaned from others close to her who assume to 'know her', free from these norms and stereotypes, and even from what she assumes to know about herself. For example, a person can make what is to her and others a very surprising decision – a decision that radically goes against her character and what is expected of her. It might be that this person wants to dispossess herself of a particular deeply embedded trait and replace it with another – for example, she might have wanted to take a risk in her personal life that involved doing something 'out of character'. Or, it might be impossible to fathom any reason for the decision to go against expectations – so the claim could be that the decision was made, spontaneously, as it were, without reason. In any event, what has occurred is a surprising decision for her as well as for those close to her, because it goes against expectations about who she is, even if these expectations do not conform to dominant norms and stereotypes.

But what does this going against embedded characteristics reveal about agency and empathic imagination, given the themes explored so far? One answer is that it reveals inconsistencies between what someone might imagine she is and would do, and what she actually is and does. So, when I am self-reflecting, it could be said that my first-order empathic imagination has therefore missed an objective target understood to be 'myself', leading to a mismatch between imagined expectations and what are different objectively accessible realities *about* who I am. Consequently, the problem is again an epistemological one, with the remedy being to ensure that I know myself better, through the better practice of personal introspection, individual therapy and the like. However, another answer is that the going against embedded characteristics, rather than revealing inconsistencies in imagined knowledge and objective descriptions about myself, reveals the way individual personhood changes while experience and agency occurs, including the experience of imagining different potential futures for the person I might or could become. Again, reflecting the Nietzschean and existential themes explored in Chapter Two, the self in this latter sense is not so much a fixed entity or singular 'being', but rather a more plural 'becoming' – and so is not so much known, but rather created and recreated in various forms over one life-span. My main contention in this chapter (and throughout the book) is that we need to acknowledge both these aspects of self-development, with the addition of the latter more dynamic and pluralised conception of agency and personhood, offering a more complete explanation for surprise in highly particularised human experiences and relations, and the exercise of second-order empathic imagination as defined earlier.[8] But how does this 'becoming' conception of agency and personhood apply specifically to issues explored here? I will now explore a little more closely the character of selfhood as reflecting the capacity an agent has to go against those socially shared expectations outlined previously, and as a prelude for challenging what are understood as unjust institutional policies and practices.

I invite you to empathically imagine how you, and others close to you, might react to particular experiences that would radically change your personal circumstances. I assume that these empathic imaginings, although many and varied, are certainly not difficult to engage in. Through wishful thinking or in darker contemplations of future happenings, it is relatively easy to empathically imagine changes in circumstances. The reason I make this assumption with some confidence, is because, like you, I can imagine many future circumstances in my life and my reactions to them. However, when experiences *do* radically change lives, people are often surprised by their reactions because they go against these imagined and often shared expectations. For example, empirical studies have repeatedly shown that when someone has been seriously injured and becomes disabled, the response is often very surprising for the person concerned, with quality of life indicators generally being much higher than pre-injury expectations (Cole, 2004; Mackenzie and Scully, 2007). Using arguments from the disability right movement explored earlier, explaining this surprise entails highlighting the paradigm mismatch between the personal experience of disability and dominant norms that state that acquiring a disability is unequivocally a tragic loss for the person concerned. According to one paralysed man, for example, 'I remember thinking clearly ... that if it ever happened to me I could not stand it. I would want to kill myself.... But once it did happen to me, all things I thought I would think and feel, I never felt at all' (Cole, 2004, cited in Mackenzie and Scully, 2007, p 344). It seems, then, that from his subjective perspective, the man was surprised when realising his fundamental error in what I have called first-order empathic imagination, which, although it accessed a publicly shared stock of knowledge about this type experience, was still found to be mistaken. In short, I contend that he was surprised because, as a reflecting agent, he learnt something new about both his own and socially shared expectations about what it is like to be disabled. This process of learning from oneself and others who are agents I believe has profound implications for liberal egalitarian political philosophy and policy and practice, and is explored in the concluding section to this chapter.

Learning from others who are agents: general implications for policy and practice

According to Rawls, 'the difference principle ... does seem to correspond to a natural meaning of fraternity: namely, to the idea of not wanting to have greater advantages unless this is to the benefit of others who are less well-off' (Rawls, 1973, p 105). However, following my arguments in this chapter, this is only half the story when upholding the liberal egalitarian values of individual agency and redistributive justice. Certainly, for the worst-off, the range of potential future lives that can be led is restricted by social, political and economic inequalities. This conception of inequality renders a relatively clear definition of disadvantage – it occurs when a person or group is not able to access opportunities to live the same range of valued lives as another person or group defined as advantaged (see also Cohen, 1989; Baker et al, 2004). Consequently, I argue that first-order empathic imagination, because it involves recognising this inequality as an objective social fact, allows persons to identify with those who are worse-off and so advocate redistributive policies and practices as a result. However, there are important limits to first-order empathic imagination, acknowledging that persons are agents who subjectively engage with their experiences and circumstances in often very surprising ways. I will now argue that reflecting on the limits of first-order empathic imagination in this way enables us to learn something new, not only about the general efficacy of agency, but also about the lives of particular persons, including one's own life, as well as the lives of those who are defined as disadvantaged. In turn, I recommend that the capacity and openness to learn from others should be more fully reflected in policy and practice (see also Smith, 2001a, 2002a, 2002b, and Chapters One and Two here).

Moreover, I argue that this recommendation is consistent with those made by commentators from social movements, such as the disability rights movement. The unequal position of the disadvantaged is seen as caused not only by social and economic injustice and exclusion, but also by what might be termed identity exclusion – where the diverse 'voices' of those defined as disadvantaged are ignored or marginalised in policy and practice, in favour of more dominant constructions and understandings. My main proposal, then, is that agent-based respect for persons should be upheld where capacities for empathic imagination are perceived as qualities producing a basic tension in the appropriate application of social policy and welfare practice. This tension exists between, on the one hand, encouraging a first-order imaginatively empathic response to the suffering of others, derived from shared stocks of objective knowledge about the condition of the disadvantaged other and prompting redistributive policies to the worst-off; on the other hand, encouraging a suspension of such judgments through exercising second-order empathic imagination, focusing on institutional procedures that variously allow for the expression of subjective and highly particularised responses of an agent to her experiences and circumstances, many of which may be wholly surprising to social policymakers and welfare practitioners.[9]

Contrary, then, to liberal egalitarian commentators such as Arneson and Nussbaum explored earlier, and to others such as Maureen Whitebrook, objectively knowing the other, 'calling her by name' as Whitebrook phrases it (Whitebrook, 2002, pp 542-3) is not less judgmental than maintaining distances between persons, given that there are healthy limits to what we can and should claim about what we know about 'the other'. Instead, my recommendation for second-order empathic imagination promotes a more fully-fledged distinction and separateness between persons, acknowledging the highly subjective and unpredictable responses of individual agents to their circumstances and experiences, and their encounters with others. It is this latter understanding of empathic imagination that also reflects a commitment to both universalism and particularism, explored in Chapters One and Two; that is, a commitment that is not bound by objective and universal settlements concerning the quality of lives actually led, given the highly particular exercising of agency, but that upholds the universal value of equality as related to principles of distributive justice, given that the range of lives that could potentially be led by persons may be quantitatively limited by social and economic disadvantage.

The upshot is that we should not 'lose sight of oppressions that are socially imposed' (Phillips, 2004, p 17; see also Nussbaum, 1999, 2000, 2006; Lister, 2001), but acknowledge the full force of the subjective perceptions of disadvantaged individuals and groups who may positively identify with their lives now. Certainly, the quantitative restrictions on potential lives led might be regretted as an objective social fact, but this is not necessarily because of any negative impact on the subjective responses to the quality of a life that is actually led. On the contrary, it has often been reported that the quality of life is enhanced as a result of individuals positively engaging with their various experiences, including their personal and social struggles, as identities are often affirmed and endorsed via these struggles, and are developed in solidarity with others in similar positions (Morris, 1991; Swain et al, 2003).[10] Of course, exercising agency does not necessarily yield the same welcome results – and frequently not among those defined as disadvantaged (for example, see Hoggett, 2001, pp 41-3; Galston, 2002, p 60). However, that a positive subjective response to a life led can occur to varying degrees, including the disadvantaged, leads, I believe, to a paradox in personal development. Briefly put, personal and group struggles with experiences objectively defined as bad or disadvantageous can nevertheless be subjectively incorporated into a person's life so that a person's well-being and fulfillment is enhanced as a result (see also Chapters Four, Five, Six and Seven for further exploration of these and related issues).

Following these conclusions, a radical model of agency, or second-order agency as Hoggett calls it (2001, p 51), is recommended. I contend that this model helps to explain why people seek to break out of oppressive social systems, understood as disadvantageous, while also maintaining and promoting a positive attitude to existing identities, as these are freely formed and chosen yet also subject to these disadvantageous social conditions. My main claim is that it is impossible to tell what sort of person he or she would have become without living in these disadvantageous conditions, as we do not know how that person would have chosen to respond to what would have been a different set of circumstances. Citing John Finnis, 'to choose is not only to set out into a new world: it is already to become a person … more or less different from the person … that deliberated about the goods and bads in the alternative available options' (Finnis, 1997, p 221). Or, again, using existentialist language, '… to be free is not to choose the historic world in which one arises – which would have no meaning – but to choose oneself in the world whatever this may be' (Sartre, 1980, p 521). Therefore, 'he is the self who makes himself be … whatever maybe the situation he finds himself in' (Sartre, 1980, p 533). Consequently, individual differences relate not only to the 'what' of different experiences and circumstances, but also to the 'whom' of the person she develops into. As a person responds differently to what life brings and determines, the overall trajectory of a life changes, affecting its general course and so differently shaping the actual life led. Again, following the conclusions of Chapter Two concerning value incommensurability, it is then often inappropriate to judge whether one life is better or worse than, equal to, or on a par with another. It is not that the judgment is difficult to make because it is hard to tell what the same 'being' person would have done in different circumstances. Rather, it is impossible to make, because the person herself would also have 'become' someone qualitatively and incomparably different if her circumstances and her choices were not the same. My contention is that acknowledging the presence of both 'being' and 'becoming' in personal development tends to block comparability, as lives are often led in qualitatively different 'value streams', where radically different lives are either actually led or potentially led (again, see Chapters One and Two for a further exploration of these and related issues).

Finally, how does this relate to policy and practice, the equality and diversity debate, and the conflict between universalism and particularism explored in Chapter One? Recognising the very unpredictable and highly particular and subjective responses of an individual agent to her circumstances is certainly a potent antidote to overblown claims of universalism and objectivism. More specifically, institutional relationships between persons, understood as agents, should therefore involve some kind of suspension of judgment concerning how well a person's life is going. This is because judgments concerning the well-being or state of persons, and the inequalities between them, are often impossible to decipher, given the radical variances in how particular individuals respond to their experiences – even if these experiences are objectively defined as advantageous or disadvantageous reflecting the potential future lives that may, or may not, be led by these persons. So, heeding Amartya Sen's warning, 'both well-being and inequality are broad and partly opaque concepts. Trying to reflect them in the form of totally complete and clear-cut orderings can do less than justice to the nature of these concepts. There is a real danger of over-precision here' (Sen, 1992, p 48).

However, this is not the end of it, as universal and objective principles still have normative weight within the subjectivism and particularism I have proposed, given that individual agency is a value attributable to all (again, see Chapters One and Two for further exploration of these and related issues). In short, the latter underpins a universal respect for others, recognising that persons respond to their experiences and circumstances in radically diverse ways, ways that often cannot, and should not, be second-guessed and compared in policy and practice. For example, if it is assumed that a disabled person has a tragic life, given what is objectively defined as the tragic circumstances of having an impairment, then, according to my analysis, this undermines the respect for particular disabled people who subjectively assert that their lives have not been blighted, and indeed that their lives may have been enriched as a result of experiencing their impairment. More generally, if respecting persons as equal agents is central to establishing just social relations, we should recognise two normative precepts: that social and political systems ought to redistribute resources to those objectively defined as worst off and disadvantaged given the comparably lesser opportunities they have to live a range of potential future lives than others who are better off (reflecting the value of equality); and that these systems ought to fully recognise the human capacity for creating a positive subjective identity, whatever the circumstances – an identity that often cannot be compared, or is incommensurable, with the life of another person defined as better off (reflecting the value of diversity). To summarise the arguments so far, these precepts are represented in figure 3.1 below:

Figure3.1: Equality and diversity

Opportunities for living a quantity of *potential* lives (comparable advantage where five potential lives a-e are better than two potential lives a-b)

    a   b   c   d   e

Advantage   Precept 1 (commensurability and the value of equality)

A   Better-off agent P

Quality of one life A and B *actually* led often incomparable   Precept 2 (incommensurability and the value of diversity)

                B   Worse-off agent Q

Disadvantage
that should be equalised   Precept 1 (commensurability and the

                                     value of equality)

         a   b

Opportunities for living a quantity of *potential* lives (comparable disadvantage where two potential lives a-b are worse than five potential lives a-e)

The difficult job for political philosophy and policy and practice, defining the main task of this book, is responding to both precepts while acknowledging that they often pull in opposite directions. If we fail to accommodate the former, we have failed to imagine and empathically respond to the condition of others defined as disadvantaged. But if we do not accommodate the latter fully, the values of self-creation and agency are also jeopardized, where separated persons, as agents, are less able to learn from their own lives and the lives of radically diverse others, who actively and creatively engage with their experiences and circumstances, whatever they are fated to be.[11]

In Chapter Four I explore the phenomenon of 'luck' as it concerns debates within Anglo-American political philosophy and critically evaluate what feeling compassion or pity for those who experience 'bad luck' might mean. Developing the themes from this chapter and in Chapters One and Two, my main argument is that persons understood as agents have the capacity to turn bad luck into a 'valued object', given that bad experiences can be positively incorporated into a person's life. Recognising this capacity means not only that our assumptions and ability for imagining the life of another are limited, as explored in this chapter, but also that our feelings for the suffering other are often misplaced and unnecessary, as explored in Chapter Four.

Notes

[1] For a philosophically very different but poignant exploration of Rawlsian and Sidgwickian notions of the separateness of persons, and how theories of self-interest relate to moral theory, see Parfit (1987, pp 329-30).

[2] Whether this 'seeing' also involves an *emotional* identification with badly-off others is a moot point (see Anderson, 1999; Arneson, 2000).

[3] See Nussbaum (2000) for a similar argument against the way women often adapt their preferences to accommodate unjust practices, leading to a critique, albeit not a wholesale abandonment, of existing desires and subjective and preference-based approaches to moral reasoning; see also Jaggar (2006) for a critical examination of Nussbaum's reasoning concerning well-being and her capability approach to human functioning more generally.

[4] It is also problematic for reasons concerning the way well-being is conceptualised as commensurable with other values, and whether it is a 'master value', reflecting teleological moral systems and the value of agency (see, for example, Kant, 1997, pp 51-4; Scanlon, 1998, pp 108-46; Sen, 1992, pp 56-62; Dworkin, 2002, pp 134-5; and Chapter Two here; see also Nietzsche's critique of well-being identified as a human goal in Nietzsche, 1975a, pp 135-6 and explored further in this chapter and in Chapters Four, Five and Six).

[5] It is also important to note that Rawls, in his later works (for example, 1993, 2001), partly dissociates himself from these earlier Kantian influences.

[6] For other similar paradoxes concerning the character of human relations, see Cohen's interpretation of Hegelian dialectics (Cohen, 2000, pp 46-7); Mackenzie and Stoljar's exploration of relational autonomy (Mackenzie and Stoljar, 2000, pp 22-4); Taylor's exploration of relational identity formation (Taylor, 1994, pp 32-4); Young's interpretation of heterogeneous group identities being maintained across communities (Young, 1990, pp 45-6); and Chapters Two, Six and Seven here.

[7] For a similar critique of how lone parents are often represented as 'tragic' and 'deficient', albeit for very different reasons, see Deacon and Mann (1999), and Duncan and Edwards (1999). Also, for an exploration of how poor people generally often vehemently reject being treated as tragic objects of pity or shame, see Bowring (2000, pp 313-15) and Lister (2001, pp 440-2).

[8] For example, in Chapter Two I argued that choices often, but not always, relate to subjective and changing commitments to incommensurable valued objects, which also problematises, or at least puts further strain on, the notion that there is an essential singular self underlying personal experience. Rather, within one person's life there are pluralised selves, which, although they overlap (providing continuity over time, and an explanation for long-term deep-felt attachments to, for example, religious beliefs, personal friendships, monogamous relationships and so on), can also dynamically develop through changing experiences and commitments to 'valued objects', which are often incommensurable.

[9] I believe there are many policies that reflect this basic principle, including, for example, direct payments to disabled people for social services, paid on the assumption that disabled people themselves know best how to articulate their own needs; the inclusion of 'service users' in the recruitment and education of trainee social and other care workers; and the routine inclusion of minority interests and representations on various quasi-government and non-government equality and rights-based commissions and committees.

[10] See also Chapter Two for a fuller exploration of the incommensurable character of these kinds of quantitative and qualitative 'life value', and how a person might positively view her life *now* as radically distinct from the range of lives that could be led by her in the future.

[11] There is consistency here with other political philosophers and social policy commentators, such as Guttman (1994, pp 9-10), Habermas (1994, pp 131-2), Ellison (1999, pp 80-5), Bowring (2000, pp 322-3) and Sangiovanni (2007), all of whom emphasise the importance of learning from difference and the 'otherness' of individuals and groups, including those defined as disadvantaged. See also Chapters One and Two here, Smith (2002a, 2002b) and my arguments for establishing reciprocal relations as a main plank of any just society ('Underpinning social stability through various social, cultural, political and economic exchanges').

FOUR

Critiquing compassion-based social relations

Introduction

Following the themes explored in Chapters One, Two and Three, my main argument in this chapter is that individual persons understood as responsible agents have the capacity to turn 'bad luck' into incommensurable valued objects as explored in Chapter Two, where particular conditions and characteristics objectively understood to be disadvantageous, concerning the limited opportunities a person might have to live a range of potential lives in the future, can nevertheless often be positively incorporated into the subjective life of that person as it presently occurs. That is, a life experienced as rich, valuable and unpredictable that cannot be fully compared with another that might have been led by the same person had she not experienced these conditions. Consequently, because we often fail to imagine another's life accurately, as explored in Chapter Three, so our sympathetic feelings for the 'suffering other' are frequently misplaced and inappropriate, as explored in this chapter. Moreover, acknowledging these positive subjective responses to disadvantageous conditions and characteristics unsettles any liberal egalitarian teleology that seeks to define objectively notions of well-being and disadvantage, with a view to increasing well-being for disadvantaged groups via egalitarian policies and practices.

Drawing on debates in liberal egalitarian political philosophy concerning the role of luck and choice in a person's life, I make a distinction between what I call intrinsic luck, which is a direct result of possessing a particular human condition or characteristic, so derived from features of the condition or characteristic itself, and extrinsic luck, resulting from the way social systems view and respond to certain human conditions or characteristics, so not derived from features of the condition or characteristic itself. My main claim is that intrinsic bad luck is often subjectively transformed into either intrinsic good luck, all things considered, and/or extrinsic bad luck, depending on the subjective perspective of the person who experiences the condition or characteristic and the way in which social systems view and respond to her. Therefore, although instituting collective responses to objective and universal judgments concerning what is bad luck and disadvantageous is a proper part of what justice entails, as disadvantage unfairly reduces the opportunity an unlucky person has to live a range of potential lives, normative principles must also recognise the possibility of a responsible agent responding to disadvantage, such that the objectively defined 'bad luck' is transformed and becomes a positive part of the sufferer's subjective identity through the one life actually led. Although I acknowledge that the latter certainly does not happen in all cases, or occurs often as a matter of degree, recognising these positive transformative possibilities of the agent's life allows me to use both existentialist/Nietzschean and Kantian insights within liberal egalitarian theories of justice, so better understanding the equality and diversity debate. In short, I combine an existentialist/Nietzschean emphasis on the positive transformative possibilities of a life actually led, with the Kantian emphasis on equal respect for persons recognised as agents who may legitimately seek equal opportunities to live a range of potential future lives (also see Chapters Two, Three and Six for further exploration of these and related issues).

Choice, responsibility and luck in liberal egalitarian theory

Despite accommodating the value of choice and responsibility in its negative form, so identifying what a person has not chosen or is not responsible for, my main argument in this section is that liberal egalitarian theory often does not focus sufficiently on the subjective perspective and agency of those objectively defined as disadvantaged, so devaluing what a disadvantaged person has chosen or is responsible for. My claim is that liberal egalitarianism frequently misconstrues the place of luck in a person's life, and her agency and capacity for what I will call 'reflective self-creation', revealed by two distinctions concerning how luck is constituted. First, there is the distinction made and often discussed in contemporary liberal egalitarianism between 'brute luck' and 'option luck'. Brute luck is not associated with the choices of those who experience certain conditions and characteristics, such as possessing congenital impairments, whereas option luck is choice-related, given that an individual chooses certain options that might lead to lucky or unlucky outcomes, such as the choice of a non-compulsive gambler (Dworkin, 1981, 2000, 2002, pp 139–40; Williams, 1981a, 1981b; Scheffler, 1992, 1997, 2003; Ripstein, 1994; Anderson, 1999; Arneson, 2000; Hoggett, 2001; Stoesz, 2002; Matravers, 2002, 2007). This distinction is important for liberal egalitarians delineating legitimate areas of redistribution, compensating brute luck but not option luck, and so maintaining some level of individual responsibility for choices made. There is, however, a second distinction, which although often implied in liberal egalitarian theory is frequently overlooked, between what I call 'intrinsic' and 'extrinsic' luck. Intrinsic luck directly results from having a particular human condition or characteristic, so is dependent on, or intrinsic to, possessing the condition or characteristic itself. By contrast, extrinsic luck is located in how particular societies or cultures view and respond toward these 'fated' conditions or characteristics. John Rawls, for example, famously argued that the basic structure of a fair society is deliberately shaped through human action, where it is agreed that the outcomes of each others' 'natural fates' will be shared, given that these fates are unchosen and distributed arbitrarily:

> The basic structure of ... societies incorporates the arbitrariness found in nature. But there is no necessity for men to resign themselves to these contingencies. The social system is not an unchangeable order beyond human control but a pattern of human action. In justice as fairness men agree to share one another's fate. (Rawls, 1973, p 102)

Here, the intrinsic bad luck of having a fate that is disadvantageous is alleviated by the 'good luck' of living in a social system that institutes sharing the consequences of this fate.[1] In addition, if the luck is a natural fate rather than a product of choice, it can be seen how brute luck rather than option luck is compensated by these Rawlsian redistributive principles. However, my argument also is that the presence of agency and 'reflective self-creation' allows for the possibility of subjective responses by individuals to fated conditions and characteristics, which considerably complicates the classification of luck just outlined. First, the presence of agency, as I have defined it so far and in proceeding chapters, is based on what I see as a broadly existentialist/Nietzschean claim that individual persons are responsible and creative beings, critically reflecting on their experiences and circumstances and then shaping their identity. Moreover, I also argue that, with some considerable elaboration, this general claim about persons can underpin a Kantian injunction that individuals ought to recognise separate others as persons who are responsible and reflective self-creating agents, and not therefore as merely passive and unreflective victims of disadvantageous conditions and characteristics. Second, I contend that combining these Kantian and existentialist claims provides a more robust Rawlsian account of 'justice as reciprocity' than is usually allowed, based on persons not only sharing each other's fates relating to their personal conditions and characteristics, as Rawls would have it, but also learning from each other as separate agents who may variously and positively respond to their different fated conditions. My main assertion is that a person can incorporate luck into her life such that her subjective response to this luck – which may be objectively defined as disadvantageous or 'bad' – nevertheless becomes a positive part of her identity and reflective personal narrative. Third, however, combining these existentialist and Kantian themes leads to profound tensions within any liberal egalitarian theories of justice, affecting not only judgments concerning the origins of luck, as with the brute luck/option luck distinction, but also how we view the subjective identity of a separated and responsible individual agent. I will now explore how the latter understanding of luck involves recognising 'the other' with a degree of emotional distance between the observer and the sufferer of disadvantageous fated conditions. This distance, and what might be termed its anti-pathos attitude, I believe again corresponds to an existential/Nietzschean conception of reflective self-creation, and so rejecting key aspects of compassion- or pity-based theories of justice found in many versions of contemporary liberal egalitarianism.

The role of compassion and pity in theories of redistributive justice

For many liberal egalitarian commentators, experiencing the emotion of compassion or pity is integral to what motivates social action and how the conditions of others are identified with impartially. Risking over-simplification, there is also some agreement between these commentators that compassion and pity is similar to other related emotional states, such as sympathy and mercy, being all supposedly other regarding, reflecting a person's emotional identification with a negatively conditioned 'object' being a named 'sufferer' (Snow, 1991; Nussbaum, 1996; Wright, 2002). The subsequent identification between 'myself' and the 'suffering other' also prompts collective action, placing equal weight on the other's interests, based on an impartial consideration of the other's good. This argument, linking compassion or pity with impartiality is traceable to Adam Smith, David Hume and Aristotle, and is supported by contemporary liberal egalitarians such as Martha Nussbaum and Maureen Whitebrook (Nussbaum, 1996; Whitebrook, 2002; see also Snow, 1991; Mendus, 2003). Their main contention is that experiencing the emotions of compassion or pity is central to how we reason and impartially engage with others, providing a rational justification and motivational explanation for creating civil society.

There is, though, disagreement over what may, or may not, distinguish these emotions, and the more nuanced relationship between different cognitive and behavioural responses resulting from a person's emotional phenomenology – that is, a person's conscious awareness of experiencing a particular emotional state.[2] For example, Nussbaum assumes that the emotional phenomenology of pity is indistinguishable from compassion: 'when I use the words "pity" and "compassion", I am really speaking about a single emotion' (Nussbaum, 1996, p 29). According to Nussbaum, this assumption is consistent with ordinary definitional usage, where 'the terms are frequently heard as translations of one another, and are thus pulled toward one another in meaning' (Nussbaum, 1996, p 29). Consequently, for Nussbaum, naming a single emotion as either pity or compassion is unimportant, as a similar meaning is given to the same emotional engagement felt by one person for another. For brevity, I will call this understanding of emotional phenomenology the 'emotion-led' model, as the focus, initially at least, is on the emotional experience of feeling for another.

However, there are other understandings of emotional phenomenology that more sharply distinguish pity from compassion. For example, rather than stressing the similarity between the emotional experiences of pity and compassion, as with the emotion-led model, the focus instead could be on the differences in what is believed when consciously reflecting on these similar emotional states. The assumption is that these differences in turn will influence the expression, interpreting and naming of these emotional states, leading to significant distinctions concerning the holding of different beliefs as reflecting particular emotional experiences. So, the emotion of pity could signify not only a feeling of compassion for the sufferer, but also the belief, held by the pitier, that she stands in some kind of superior position to the pitied because she is not suffering (also see Young, 1990, pp 5-6; Piper, 1991, pp 734-5; Snow, 1991, p 196; Kimball, 2001, pp 330-43). Here, emotional empathic engagement, while sympathising with the negative condition of the other person, is also shaped via a hierarchical belief structure, with those in superior positions pitying the condition of those who are 'less fortunate' (also see Anderson, 1999, explored in more detail later). In effect, the judgment made, implicitly or explicitly by the pitier, is that she prefers, all things considered, that she is not leading the life of the sufferer as compared with her own life, because of the sufferer's diminished quality of life – that is, her diminished well-being, capacity for experiencing happiness, human flourishing and so on. Again, for brevity, I will call this understanding of emotional phenomenology the 'belief-led' model, as the focus is not on what a person feels for another, but what a person believes *about* the other person whom she feels for.

Following this distinction, I will now argue that those who seem to initially adhere to the emotion-led model, although they acknowledge the role of belief in discussions concerning pity and compassion, nevertheless underestimate the specific content of these beliefs as these affect the judgment of the pitier as she views 'the sufferer'. For Nussbaum, rational thought and belief, based on what she calls standards of 'truth' and 'appropriateness', are central to ensuring a just response to suffering: 'compassion is ... not merely impulsive, but [involves] thought and belief ... [it is] suffused with thought, and thought that should be held to high standards of truth and appropriateness' (Nussbaum, 1996, pp 30-1). Consequently, despite her claims that the emotions of pity and compassion are identical, thought and belief informs this initial emotional-led response to suffering, with the information supposedly connecting the single emotion with an objective truth-filled and appropriate understanding of those who suffer. My contention here is that lying behind these standards of truth and appropriateness, there are often question-begging assumptions regarding the diminished condition of a pitied person's life which for that person inform beliefs about her which are often profoundly mistaken. In addition, these assumptions, I argue, undermine our respect for this person, who should instead be viewed as a responsible agent, reflecting on and responding to her adverse circumstances in highly unpredictable and often life-enhancing ways. According to Kimball, 'when people say they don't want to be pitied or don't want us to feel sorry for them ... they don't want us to think of their lives as completely ruined' (Kimball, 2001, p 337). Mirroring this response, my main claim is that the reflective self-creative capacities of the person who is pitied can positively incorporate her experiences and conditions into her personal narrative – so acknowledging the surprising and paradoxical manner in which persons often respond to their objectively defined disadvantaged conditions, in ways that can be described as life-enhancing (see also Chapters Three and Seven for further exploration of this and related themes).

However, before exploring the last claim further, I will outline how the interchangeability of pity and compassion in the emotion-led model often derives from a liberal egalitarian teleology found within many compassion or pity-based theories of justice. In short, a broadly teleological account of human flourishing is often used by liberal egalitarians that focuses on achieving well-being as an intrinsically valuable goal, but is defined again as an objective category of experience and/or state of consciousness. This, I contend, ignoring the highly subjective and unpredictable responses of persons as reflective self-creating agents.

Liberal egalitarian teleology and well-being

Liberal egalitarian teleology promotes equality, not because equality is regarded as an intrinsically valuable goal, but because it is seen as a means to the end of enhancing some other good said to have worth, such as human well-being. For example, Richard Arneson defends a version of prioritarianism that he calls a form of 'liberal egalitarian teleology' (Arneson, 2000). Priority is given to the worse-off, not because disparities between persons should be equalised after comparing them, but because in so doing we aspire to attain higher objective levels of well-being for those who are doing badly: 'prioritarianism is egalitarian in tilting in favour of those who are badly-off. But priority is assigned to aiding an individual in virtue of how badly his life is going, as measured by an objective scale of well-being, not intrinsically by any comparison between his life and that of others' (Arneson, 2000, p 343; see also Chapter Three for further exploration of this and related themes).

In addition, according to Arneson, prioritarianism should be 'responsibility-catering' in the negative sense, where well-being is maximised for those who are badly off, and if persons are not significantly responsible for their condition as a result of previous behaviour: 'roughly stated, the idea is that justice requires us to maximize a function of human well-being that gives priority to improving the well-being of those who are badly-off and of those who, if badly-off, are not substantially responsible for their condition in virtue of their prior conduct' (Arneson, 2000, p 340). Consequently, the role luck plays in producing well-being is important when promoting equality, as assessing the impact of luck helps decide the priority given to responsible worse-off persons who have done as well as could be expected, given life's misfortunes: 'the point of equality I would say is to improve people's life-prospects, tilting in favour of those who are worse-off, and in favour of those who have done as well as could reasonably be expected with the cards that fate has dealt them' (Arneson, 2000, p 349).

Arneson also provides a counter-argument to one part of Elizabeth Anderson's critique of what she calls 'luck egalitarianism' that is very relevant here – namely, her analysis of pity and compassion within egalitarian theories of justice (Anderson, 1999). Anderson argues that the liberal egalitarian focus on luck leads to pity being directed toward those defined as less fortunate. The problem for Anderson is that certain beliefs associated with pity, also for her being a type of compassion, are anti-egalitarian, reflecting the conclusions of those who might adhere to the belief-led model of emotional phenomenology identified earlier.[3] Briefly put, when pity is fostered within luck egalitarianism, according to Anderson, it undermines principles '… that express equal respect for all citizens … it evokes the pathos of distance, a consciousness of the better-off's own superiority to the objects of their compassion' (Anderson, 1999, p 301).[4]

However, Arneson's response to Anderson is that if this criticism is aimed at prioritarianism, being a form of luck egalitarianism, it misfires. As previously stated, prioritarianism distributes according to how badly a life is going as measured against an objective scale of well-being, not by any comparison between that person's life and those of others. For Arneson, if this measurement of well-being does not depend on any comparisons between persons, there is no reason to associate prioritarianism 'with a psychology of pity' (Arneson, 2000, p 343) – assuming pity relies on comparing persons in the way Anderson describes. Moreover, there is no claim that the pitier is superior to the pitied in Arneson's account, as the good luck of the former and the bad luck of the latter is undeserved (Arneson, 2000, p 343). Finally, Anderson's notion that equal respect for persons is a basis for deciding issues of justice is rejected, as it could not do 'any work in selecting principles of justice, or in determining that some candidate principles are driven by unseemly motives' (Arneson, 2000, p 344). For Arneson, the commonly shared injunction that we should have respect for persons is derived from reasoned and substantial principles of justice, not the other way around.

> One expresses due respect for persons and treats them respectfully by acting toward persons in accordance with the moral principles that are best supported by reasons. In this sense respect for persons looks to be an unobjectionable but purely formal idea, neither a clue to what principles are best supported by moral reasons nor a constraint on what principles might be chosen. (Arneson, 2000, p 344)

I will now examine Arneson's claims regarding his objective accounts of well-being and egalitarian justice, by way of responding to some of his criticisms of Anderson. In any given society, it might be argued that some of the better-off could be in this condition despite their bad luck not because of their good luck, and the worse-off likewise in their condition because they are responsible for their prior conduct. But if this is so, the difficult question for Arneson is where does his responsibility-catering prioritarianism go? Does he take from the worse-off to give to the better-off in the name of responsibility, or vice versa in the name of prioritarianism? I will not dwell on this problem in too much detail. Suffice it to say, Arneson partly bases his argument on what could be a controversial empirical assumption that there is a direct correlation between the condition of worse-off persons relating to their well-being, and their diminished choices and deservedness relating to their 'bad fates'. In an earlier publication exploring understandings of responsibility and deservedness, Arneson argues precisely this empirical point.

> Even though many factors determine the distribution of poverty, on average we would expect that impoverished members of society tend to be cursed with choice-making and choice-following deficits, so even if their conformity to accepted standards is less than average, one cannot infer that their deseveringness, all things considered, is less than average. (Arneson, 1997, p 332)

We may concede that this sociological claim is plausible and even likely, given, for example, the presence of structural disadvantage. Indeed, the political position I defend here, and identified in previous chapters, promotes such an understanding of disadvantage, focusing on those disadvantaged individuals and group members who have limited opportunities to live a range of potential future lives. My additional claim, though, regarding the character of responsibility, is that attention should be paid not only to how people are often not responsible for their bad fated conditions, as emphasised by Arneson – and so rightly leading to institutional responses that compensate or alleviate these conditions – but also to how individuals are also responsible agents who often subjectively and positively engage with these same conditions. This exercising of agency, in turn, may have a surprisingly positive effect on a person's well-being, and is often discussed in liberal egalitarian literature.[5] For example, Ronald Dworkin, in defending his resourcist conception of equality and critiquing 'welfare egalitarianism', explores how well-being does not often track personal circumstances because the responses of the badly-off can often be surprisingly positive, such that their well-being is enhanced (Dworkin, 1981, 2000, 2002, pp 139-40; see also Chapter Three here).[6] For my part, these responses are explainable via the broadly existentialist conception of responsibility and reflective self-creation offered here, accommodating the subjective and unpredictable engagement of an agent with the luck she experiences – an accommodation that both Arneson and Nussbaum, I believe, mistakenly minimise within their theories of justice. I will now explore and defend this claim in more detail.

Well-being and luck revisited

It might seem implausible in any egalitarian theory of justice to hold a person positively responsible for the way she actively engages with and perceives the misfortune she experiences. Consequently, alongside liberal egalitarian teleologists, it could be argued that just systems respond to the objective worse-off conditions of disadvantaged persons or groups, rather than to a particular person's subjective reaction to her worse-off condition, precisely because the latter's reaction is unpredictable and therefore cannot generate consistent universal rules to be followed. Someone might be made miserable by, or be indifferent about, or even positively accepting of, the bad luck she experiences. But, whatever her response, a just society cannot base its rules on these subjective reactions, as justice requires that universal rules are applied that rectify, or at least alleviate, the objective misfortune people experience. For example, according to Arneson, there is a social imperative to act justly because of the bad luck experienced by persons given they did not choose it, meaning no reference need be made to any person's subjective response to her bad luck. Rather, to repeat, the wider community should respond to diminished 'life-prospects ... in favour of those who have done as well as could reasonably be expected with the cards that fate has dealt them' (Arneson, 2000, p 349). Or, following Nussbaum, emotionally identifying with the suffering of others through pity requires the wider community to respond justly to the diminished capacity for human flourishing endured by the sufferer, again considered separately from the subjective reaction of the pitied to their own pain and suffering. Moreover, for Nussbaum, the subjective reaction of the sufferer is highly suspect as the suffering person often fails to recognise the seriousness of his condition, so leaving any judgment concerning the content of human flourishing explicitly with the pitier and not the pitied. This judgment, for Nussbaum, is implied within pity itself : 'the person affected does not judge that his condition is bad, however – that, indeed, is a large part of what is so terrible about it. In short: implicit in pity itself is a conception of human flourishing, the best one the pitier is able to form' (Nussbaum, 1996, pp 30-1). Personal viewpoints and preferences may have been adapted by the sufferer to accommodate his poor condition, but for Nussbaum this should have no bearing on the requirement of justice to compensate the objective disadvantage experienced (see also her later work, 1999, 2000, 2006, for similar arguments regarding the adaptive preferences of women and disabled people; and see Stein, 2006, and Chapters Three, Five and Six here for a more detailed exploration of subjective preferences as related to disabled people and others defined as disadvantaged).

For Arneson and Nussbaum, then, the goal of well-being, whether reflecting life prospects or human flourishing is considered independently from the subjective responses and adaptability of those who experience and suffer bad luck, allowing objective judgments concerning the quality of the lives led to be made by those defined as 'better-off'. More generally, the objectified character of well-being is accommodated within the teleological aspirations of both theories of justice, where equality is valued in each as a means to the end of enhancing well-being, through prioritising redistributions towards those who are in an objectively defined worse-off condition, either because the bad condition occurs through no fault of those who experience it (Arneson), or via compassion motivated social action that emotionally empathises with those who suffer the most (Nussbaum). My counter-assertion is that this instrumental egalitarian case made by both theorists promotes redistributive principles of justice that undermine equal respect for others who are considered positively responsible agents.

First, though, it is important to acknowledge that Nussbaum, at least, seeks to defend 'a form of liberalism ... [which] begins from the idea of the equal worth of human beings ... in virtue of their basic capacity for choice and reasoning' (Nussbaum, 1999, p 10). Regarding my position, these capacities may include the subjective ability to reflect on and positively incorporate adverse circumstances and conditions into personal narratives and so 'overcome' life's obstacles. However, significantly, for Nussbaum, this ability is irrelevant to implementing universal principles of justice that seek to eradicate obstacles to agency: 'no human being should be expected to overcome all potential life obstacles, and people who have to fight for the most basic things are precluded by that struggle from exercising their agency in other more fulfilling and socially fruitful ways' (Nussbaum, 1999, p 19). Certainly, I concur with Nussbaum that if life's obstacles prevent a person from exercising her agency, these obstacles should be alleviated via redistributive policies and practices – that is, given the diminished opportunities to live a variety of potential lives. This conclusion also reflects Amartya Sen's capability equality, where capability is understood as a 'set of vectors of functionings, reflecting the person's freedom to lead one type of life *or another*' (Sen, 1992, p 40; emphasis added). Nussbaum, especially in her later work (2000, 2006), has explicitly defended and developed Sen's capability approach to equality. In addition, I acknowledge that experiencing disadvantageous conditions and circumstances can diminish a person's well-being as well as other positive endorsements of her life. We should therefore, through institutional mechanisms, share the burden of these outcomes to facilitate a more egalitarian distribution of opportunities, so enhancing the various capabilities of living different and potentially fulfilling lives (see also Chapters Two and Three for further development of these arguments).

Nevertheless, I also maintain that, despite the implications of Nussbaum's and Arneson's positions, the imperative to respect others as equal and responsible agents can, in many circumstances, sharply contrast with these redistributive arguments. Even if, for some people, well-being and the positive endorsement of their lives are reduced as a result of disadvantage, this is certainly not the case for all. Consequently, the actual life led by a disadvantaged person may be surprisingly enriched and enriching, despite the diminished opportunities for living a range of other potentially fulfilling lives.[7] The main problem with both Arneson's and Nussbaum's account of well-being and human flourishing is that an implicit question-begging judgment is made by the better-off person that the life of the sufferer that is actually lived is, all things considered, qualitatively 'lesser than' her own life, being inevitably tainted by objectively defined disadvantageous conditions. I will now explore this problem further by elucidating a distinction regarding the kinds of fate or luck people experience.

As outlined previously, in contemporary liberal egalitarian debate much has been discussed concerning the brute luck and option luck distinction (Dworkin, 1981, 2000, pp 287-99; Williams, 1981a, 1981b; Scheffler, 1992, 1997, 2003; Ripstein, 1994; Anderson, 1999; Arneson, 2000; Hoggett, 2001; Matravers, 2002, 2007; Stoesz, 2002). Brute luck is caused by fated conditions outside the individual's control – such as congenital impairments – whereas option luck directly reflects individual choice – such as the choice of a non-compulsive gambler. The main argument often defended, derived from this distinction, is that compensation for the bad luck of the former should usually take priority over providing compensation, if at all, for the bad luck of the latter. However, there are considerable disagreements between liberal egalitarians, and between social policy analysts, concerning the precise role and meaning of choice and responsibility in these instances, and the ways in which people's actual fates are likely to be derived from a complex mix of both types of luck (see, for example, Williams, 1981a, 1981b; Scheffler, 1992, 1997, 2003; Ripstein, 1994; Dwyer, 2002; Deacon and Mann, 1999; Hoggett, 2001; Matravers, 2002, 2007; Stoesz, 2002).

In addition to distinguishing brute luck and option luck, there is, though, another luck distinction, shedding, I believe, some light on these controversies by exposing variances in the types of claim made by liberal egalitarians and others concerning responsible agency. First, there is what I call 'intrinsic luck', being the bad luck directly resulting from the consequences of possessing a particular condition or characteristic – that is, luck conceived as dependent on having the condition itself. Second, there is what I call 'extrinsic luck', being the bad luck indirectly resulting from the consequences of possessing a particular condition or characteristic – that is, luck conceived as existing independently from the condition itself, instead reflecting the various social responses *to* that condition or characteristic. For example, being struck by lightning is usually uncontroversially regarded as intrinsic bad luck, at least in the first instance (see arguments later). The bad luck experienced is dependent on the condition of being struck by lightning, as this particular condition is, so to speak, carrying with it the bad luck. But other conditions are not so easily associated with the condition itself, and are therefore more like extrinsic luck. For example, proponents within social movements would not argue that being, say, black, a woman, gay or even disabled is unlucky because of a particular condition reflecting the specific characteristics of race, gender, homosexuality or disability. Rather, these conditions and characteristics are freely and positively incorporated into a person's identity, where a person is glad to possess them, and so are not thought of as intrinsically *unlucky* at all.[8] Instead, the unlucky character of these conditions relates to the way a person possessing them, while choosing to positively incorporate and identify with these characteristics, does not choose to be born into a society dominated by white, male, heterosexual or non-disabled norms and interests – thereby reinforcing the structural inequalities and disadvantage she experiences as they relate to these characteristics (see also note one).

Using this distinction between intrinsic and extrinsic luck, I will now argue for a more dynamic understanding of identity formation than is often implied in liberal egalitarian teleology, based on a broadly existentialist conception of freedom and identity identified and explored here, and in Chapters Two and Three. According to Jean-Paul Sartre, for example, 'to be free is not to choose the historic world in which one arises – which would have no meaning – but to choose oneself in the world whatever this may be' (Sartre, 1995, p 521). Put another way, 'he is the self who makes himself be ... whatever may be the situation he finds himself in' (Sartre, 1995, p 553).[9] Certainly, many persons are still unlucky to live in a society that happens to unfairly discriminate against them. Nevertheless, it is a mistake to view this type of bad brute luck as an intrinsic feature of the condition itself; rather, it is derived from the extrinsic functions of unjust social relations.

These extrinsic functionings are, I believe, philosophically and politically significant for other reasons too, because if extrinsic luck occurs separately from brute luck or option luck, Arneson's criticism of Anderson can be turned against him. To be sure, the brute luck/option luck distinction has bite, given that the latter can accommodate substantial notions of individual choice and responsibility. However, if the distinction between intrinsic and extrinsic luck is also recognised, Arneson's injunctions concerning luck, and what should be compensated, can also appear as purely formal. For example, when extrinsic bad luck is also bad brute luck, the injunction that we should compensate the brute luck people experience is derived from principles of justice, and not the other way around. This is because extrinsic luck relates not to the condition itself, but to how social systems respond to persons with these conditions, raising important questions about what makes luck intrinsic and how it overlaps or can be turned into extrinsic luck, with these questions not readily answered by appeals to distinctions between brute luck and option luck. An individual might have bad brute luck because she was unlucky to be born into a social system that unfairly disadvantages her. However, the luck is extrinsic to her *even if* social systems might define or socially construct it as intrinsic bad luck. The significant point here is that these social construction processes effectively disguise how social structures of human cooperation and the subsequent collective responsibility for changing social circumstances *are* within human control and so are not subject to chance or random occurrences. In short, Arneson's and other liberal egalitarians' focus on 'luck' and the distinction between option luck and brute luck, seem, therefore, to be missing the point about what is *not* unlucky about living in an unjust society (see also Chapter Six for an exploration of how the social model of disability variously deals with this and related issues).

Given this conclusion, there is another objection to the kind of liberal egalitarian teleology proposed by Arneson and Nussbaum that I believe goes to the heart of their liberal egalitarian credentials, assuming the importance attached to notions of individual and collective responsibility within these and other forms of liberal egalitarianism. In liberal egalitarianism there are two distinct claims – one for the separateness of persons and the other for collective notions of social cooperation. Developing Sidgwick's earlier work, the separateness or distinctiveness of persons was famously articulated by John Rawls (1973) as central to his critique of utilitarianism and its view of social cooperation (see also Chapter Three here). Briefly put, for Rawls,

> [the utilitarian] view of social cooperation is the consequence of extending to society the principle of choice for one [person], and then, to make this extension work, conflating all persons into one through the imaginative acts of the impartial sympathetic spectator.

> Utilitarianism does not take seriously the distinction between persons.
> (Rawls, 1973, p 27)

My criticism of compassion-based theories of justice and liberal egalitarian teleology parallel these criticisms of utilitarianism. These theries also do not take seriously the separateness of persons, given my understanding of individual agency and responsibility – this understanding also being used to defend a recast Rawlsian conception of collective responsibility and 'justice as reciprocity'. Moreover, I contend that this criticism and general defence are broadly consistent with both the Kantian and existentialist/Nietzschean understandings of equality and identity formation so far outlined.

Luck, agency, separate persons and justice as reciprocity

As Arneson highlights, one difference between his position and that of compassion-based theorists like Nussbaum is that Arneson he does not hierarchically compare the pitier and the pitied. This is because the good luck of the pitier, for Arneson, is no reason for feeling superior, as it is undeserved. However, from my arguments so far, we can see that Arneson's prioritarianism is still vulnerable to Anderson's critique of luck egalitarianism. This is because Arneson may still elicit other condescending attitudes via a belief structure that makes assumptions about the better-off's viewpoint regarding the worse-off's 'objective state'. For example, both Arneson and Nussbaum focus on subjective experience insofar as a person is said to experience suffering, but the subjective perspective of the sufferer, critically reflecting and responding to her *own* experiences, is largely ignored as she is judged by others to be in a diminished condition measured against an objective scale of well-being or human flourishing. One of my main arguments is that this scale can be condescending towards this person, as assuming such a diminished condition fails to fully acknowledge the agency and separateness of persons, including the person who is defined as disadvantaged. Developing themes explored in Chapter Three, I will now defend this latter contention further.

It is plausible to suppose that most, if not all, human experiences and conditions lead to responses of various kinds, either from others and/or from the person concerned. However, given these responses, intrinsic luck may contain at least some elements of extrinsic luck, even in the supposedly uncontroversial case of being struck by lightning. This experiencing certainly contains lots of intrinsic bad luck at least initially, but it might be, assuming a person survives the experience, that she positively reflects on and responds to her life in ways that were difficult or impossible for her to achieve, and even comprehend, before the experience occurred. For example, the physical vulnerability experienced might prompt that person to more urgently make the best of her remaining life, to use her resources and personal talents more productively, to give and receive more from her personal relationships, and so on. Consequently, in the long term, she could be grateful for having this experience and so not consider it unlucky, all things considered

– that is, when she reflects on and evaluates her life overall, albeit that when the lightning struck she may have felt overwhelmingly that she had suffered bad intrinsic luck. More generally, then, it might be said that a person who rationally reflects on her life with some time distance from the emotional impact of certain types of experience may be able to self-creatively incorporate the luck of these experiences positively into her life; that is, her subjective response to this luck, which is now seen as an identity transforming event, becomes a positive part of her personal narrative and identity (similar arguments can be made with respect to acquired disabilities; see Chapters Three, Five and Six). This understanding of identity formation parallels Schwartz's conclusions regarding the dramatist who expects the audience to maintain proximity and distance when responding to the dramatic events portrayed. Audiences are asked to both feel for characters and give space for rational and critical reflection, in order to learn something new about the human condition (Schwartz, 1993). Analogously, I have argued here that individuals often, in effect, become an audience to their own lives, critically reflecting on personal circumstances and conditions rather than merely experiencing or feeling them, and so often unpredictably responding to their lives as it unfolds and develops (again, see Chapters Two and Three for further exploration of these and related themes). But what of compassion- or pity-based social relations, given these complications in identity formation and the self-transforming possibilities when experiencing these different types of luck?

Compassion- or pity-based egalitarian theorists, like Nussbaum, for example, do not deny that human beings who suffer can, in many unpredictable ways, overcome adversity (see also Kimball, 2001, pp 343-4). Rather, her claim, outlined previously, is that the perspective of the sufferer is likely to be distorted, so leading, among other things, to the false adaption of personal reflections and preferences that are modified according to unjust and inegalitarian expectations. Principles of justice should therefore be formulated independently of subjective perspectives and these adapted personal preferences. For example, in *Sex and social justice*, Nussbaum states: 'women do overcome the greatest of obstacles, showing an amazing courage and resourcefulness.... But this is no reason not to change the conditions that placed these obstacles in their way, especially when the conditions are unequally experienced by women just because they are women' (Nussbaum 1999, pp 18-19; see also Nussbaum, 2000, 2006, and for a similar argument see Lister, 1997, 2001; Phillips, 2004). However, I will now argue that the sharp disjunction made here by Nussbaum, shared by Arneson, between subjective responses to adversity and the conditions of adversity, can be misleading in matters relating to justice. These egalitarian theorists, mistakenly in my view, attend mainly to the conditions of adversity as a matter of social justice – thereby underestimating the normative significance of an agent's reflective response to adverse circumstances, and the separateness or distance that ought to also be maintained between persons as a result.

Certainly, Nussbaum acknowledges the separateness between persons that might, on first blush, look similar to the position I have so far defended:

> In the temporary act of identification, one is always aware of one's own *separateness* from the sufferer – it is for another, and not oneself, that one feels; and one is aware both of the bad lot of the sufferer and of the fact that it is, right now, not one's own. If one really had the experience of feeling pain in one's own body, then one would precisely have failed to comprehend the pain of another *as other*. One must also be aware of one's own *qualitative difference* from the sufferer.... For these recognitions are crucial in getting the right estimation of the meaning of the suffering. (Nussbaum, 1996, p 35; emphasis in original; again, see Chapter Three for further exploration of these and related issues)

Consequently, this qualitative difference and separateness between persons, for Nussbaum, reflects what might be termed the incomplete transferability of pain or suffering, given that a person cannot experience the pain of another as her own pain. She is not claiming here that experiencing pain is an entirely private affair, as this would imply the absence of any degree of empathic imagination and emotional identification. Concurring with Nussbaum, it seems very difficult to comprehend what any human relations would be like without the presence of some degree of empathic imagination – given that, without this capacity, persons would not be able to detect relevant similarities between the behaviour of others and their own (see also Piper, 1991, pp 726-57, especially pp 730-1, and Chapter Three here for a fuller exploration and defence of this claim). Rather, the public nature of 'sharing pain' via empathic imagination and emotional identification, for Nussbaum cannot, and should not, extinguish the differences between one's own pain as distinct from another person's. However, despite her commitment to the irreducible character of individual experience, this is not, I believe, sufficient to promote the separateness between persons as I have understood this here. My understanding is derived from assuming not only that a person cannot experience *being* another, but also that persons actively reflect and respond *to* their experiences – reflections and responses that can be radically different, even between those who share similar experiences. Consequently, I heed Mackenzie and Scully's warning that:

> ... imagining oneself differently situated, or even imagining oneself in the other's shoes, is not morally engaging with the other; rather, it is projecting one's own perspective onto the other.... Furthermore, thinking that it is possible leads to morally relevant differences and particularities being obscured. (Mackenzie and Scully, 2007, pp 345-6; again, see Chapters Two and Three for further exploration of these and related issues)

I will now argue that as well as this stress on separateness, difference and agency being reminiscent of a Kantian/Rawlsian epistemology concerning the knowledge possessed by human beings about their agency, there is an existentialist/Nietzschean interpretation of identity formation that can also be emphasised, relating to a highly particular and personalised conception of reflective self-creation that further reinforces the distinctiveness and separateness of persons just described. For example, in *Gay science*, Nietzsche claims that:

> ... our personal and profoundest suffering is incomprehensible and inaccessible to almost everyone; here we remain hidden from our neighbour even if we eat from the same pot. But whenever people notice that we suffer they interpret our suffering superficially. It is the very essence of the emotion of pity that it strips away from the suffering of others what is distinctly personal. (Cited in Conolly, 1998, p 284)

The point here is that this Nietzschean perspective on the incomprehensible and inaccessible character of another's pain directly opposes claims made by commentators who promote compassion-based theories of social justice, such as Nussbaum, Snow and Whitebrook, as these stress the ability persons have to identify with others who suffer and, in the process, seek to recognise and identify with what is common, and *not* distinct, between them. According to Snow, for example, '... feeling compassion for another presupposes the ability to identify with the other. Persons' ability to identify with others is enhanced by recognising similarities between others and themselves' (Snow, 1991, p 204). Following a similar theme, for Whitebook, 'the compassionate actor is less judgmental than "loving" – knowing the other "calling by name"' (Whitebrook, 2002, p 542). In stark contrast, Nietzsche sees the exercising of this kind of pity and compassion as deeply harmful to both the pitier and pitied. So, in *Thus spoke Zarathustra*, he proclaims: 'for I saw the sufferer suffer, and because I saw it I was ashamed on account of his shame; and when I helped him I sorely injured his pride' (Nietzsche, 1975b, p 113). In *Beyond good and evil*, he attacks acts of charity as being motivated by pity and a duplicitous desire to help, which on first impressions might seem enabling, but for him seeks to manipulate others, based on the desire to provoke gratefulness and submissiveness, and to 'possess' those who are helped:

> Among helpful and charitable people one almost always finds that clumsy deceitfulness which first adjusts and adapts him who is to be helped: as if, for example, he 'deserved' help, desired precisely *their* help, and would prove profoundly grateful, faithful and submissive to them in return for all the help he had received – with these imaginings they dispose of those in need as if they were possessions, and are charitable and helpful at all only from a desire for possessions. (Nietzsche, 1975a, p 99; emphasis in original)

It is pertinent to observe the similarity between this criticism of pity and charity and the disability rights movement's slogan 'piss on pity', central to its campaign against the UK TV charity fundraiser Telethon and other charity events of this kind broadcast during the 1980s and 1990s. These events were considered profoundly patronising and disempowering for disabled people, based on what was seen as false representations of disabled people as tragic victims of circumstances beyond their control, designed to produce piteous responses from the audience and so prompting donations to charities.[10] Again, this contrasts starkly with those assumptions made by Nussbaum and others who promote compassion-based theories of social justice. For example, according to Whitebrook, '... pity and compassion include an element of equality, by way of the sense of fellow feeling involved, a sense of suffering with *rather than* having power over' (Whitebrook, 2002, p 539; emphasis added).

Finally in this section, I will explore some implications of keeping faith with these criticisms of compassion, pity and charity, reflecting the Rawlsian neo-Kantian premise that reciprocity or mutual exchange ought to be an integral feature of just distribution and notions of collective responsibility (see also Chapters One, Three and Six for further development of this theme).[11] John Rawls argues that the principle of reciprocity should be central to any understanding of justice and fairness. According to Rawls, justice expresses a commitment to reciprocity, recognising that mutual benefits between persons take place within any just society through acts of cooperation and exchange. For Rawls, the importance of this commitment is based on a Kantian injunction that there be equal respect for persons, which for Rawls 'heightens the operation of the reciprocity principle' (Rawls, 1973, p 499). The value of mutuality is derived from maintaining both self-respect and respect for others, and what he calls a human 'tendency to answer in kind', without which, he claims, 'fruitful social cooperation [is made] fragile if not impossible' (Rawls, 1973, pp 494-5).

Inevitably, many criticisms have been made of the Rawlsian position that cannot be explored in detail here (for example, see Barry, 1995, pp 28-51; Cohen, 1995, pp 187-98 and pp 224-56; Arneson, 1997, pp 339-40). However, I have argued elsewhere that political philosophers, defending what on the face of it might seem like more radical political causes, have moved too swiftly in criticism of the Rawlsian defence of justice as reciprocity (for example, see Smith 2001a, 2002a, 2002b). Briefly put, my counter-claim is that there is much more to reciprocity than first meets the eye, when examining how productivity, understood as the production of valuable 'objects', is managed and structured through cooperation and mutual exchange. Whether through individual or collective forms, mutual acts of giving and receiving between persons while characterising reciprocal relations do not, I argue, solely depend on the production of valuable objects that can then be used by others. Certainly, a principle aspect of establishing reciprocal relations concerns the value of things produced for mutual exchange, but this value cannot be assessed independently from what I call the 'ontological stance' of givers and receivers. It is how people *are* with others, not only what they produce *for* others, that defines and shapes reciprocal relations. For example, if a person is open to receiving a wide variety of benefits from what another person has to offer, reciprocal exchange is more likely than if that person is less able or willing to receive, even if the giver has the same to offer in both cases. Moreover, if a person defines herself, or is defined by others, as having little or nothing to contribute in mutual exchanges, the possibilities of both acknowledging and developing reciprocal relations are diminished. First, contributions that might already be made by this person are likely to go unrecognised, and second, potential contributions will often be resisted or prevented on the possibly false assumption that the person's lack of productive capacity, whether this relates to her condition and/or behaviour, renders mutual exchange impossible.[12]

Following my argument and the analysis here, establishing reciprocal relations, therefore, in large part relies on a collective or social responsibility to foster an attitude of mutual self-worth derived from a positive general assessment of what one person can offer another, and what the other can contribute for the benefit of the first person. It is within this context that, paradoxically, the differences and separateness between people explored earlier can, I contend, be more readily promoted within these social relations, anticipating that these differences and separateness will produce multiple and varied arenas in which reciprocal exchanges can occur. Consequently, any normative political philosophy fostering the politics of recognition and difference must emphasise the importance of establishing a certain kind of community; that is, a community that expects enriching and multi-dimensional relational experiences between persons who recognise their differences and separateness as profound, even between those who share the same or similar experiences. This recognition, in turn, provides collective arenas for mutual exchange and reciprocation, as these persons are more able to learn from others who are radically different.

Developing these arguments, it can be seen that underpinning this commitment to diversity promotion is a dual normative principle for collective responsibility, reflecting a tension between the egalitarian universalism of Kant and the diversity and particularism of Nietzsche, explored and defended earlier. First, we have a collective responsibility to share the objective outcomes of each other's fates, given the unjust consequences of disadvantaged circumstances – circumstances that diminish the range of opportunities to live a variety of potential future lives. Second, we also have a responsibility to learn from each other's fates, given the diversity of particular lives actually lived and the way persons subjectively but often positively reflect on and respond to their circumstances, including those circumstances objectively defined as disadvantaged (see also Chapters Two and Three for further exploration of these and related themes).[13] This dual principle underpinning collective responsibility therefore rejects the individual solitude embraced by an uncompromised Nietzsche: 'for solitude is with us a virtue: it is a sublime urge and inclination for cleanliness which divines that all contact between man and man [sic] – "in society" – must inevitably be unclean' (Nietzsche, 1975b, p 195). However, it also rejects the opposite claim that the emotional proximity of persons, achieved via pity and compassion, and as recommended by Nussbaum, Whitebrook and others, is central to any collective responsibility exercised toward the 'the suffering other'. Instead, I acknowledge the paradoxical character of my having deep connections with others who, like me, are reflective self-creating agents, but recognise, too, the profound otherness between myself and the highly particularised and subjective character of 'the other' who is different and separate to me (see also Chapters Two, Three and Seven for further exploration of these and related issues).

The main point here is that when recognising persons this way, I can engage in new and creative understandings of myself and others in wider social relations. In short, I am able to more fully recognise that the deep differences that may exist between individuals and groups can also be mutually enriching (see also Taylor, 1992, 1994; Guttman, 1994; Habermas, 1994; Ellison, 1999; Parekh, 2000; Galston, 2002; Edyvane, 2005, 2007). By way of conclusion, I will now examine further how acknowledging the limits of empathic imagination, as explored in Chapter Three, and the limits of compassion-based social relations, as explored in this Chapter, involves a substantive commitment to respecting others as individually responsible self-creating agents.

Keeping our distance in compassion-based social relations

My arguments in this chapter support a nuanced and paradoxical conception of compassion and agency, where capacities for compassion and agency are perceived as qualities producing a fundamental tension within human relations. This tension exists between, on the one hand, encouraging a compassionate and collective response to those who experience what is objectively defined as disadvantage – given the diminished range of lives that might be potentially led as a result of bad luck or bad-fated conditions – and, on the other hand, suspending such an objective judgment, recognising that the human qualities of individual agency and reflective self-creation possessed by 'the disadvantaged' mean that the initial bad luck can be positively integrated within the disadvantaged person's subjective identity, at least as a matter of degree. I believe the difficult job of promoting the values of equality and diversity is to respond to both injunctions, recognising that they pull in opposite directions and cannot be reduced to each other.

I have also argued that these claims reflect the Kantian imperative that respect ought to be afforded to others as persons, derived from the assumption that individuals are equally free and positively responsible agents. However, this emphasis on agency and equality does not entail replacing compassion-based social relations entirely. Rather, the invitation is to compassionately empathise first with the person who, like you, is a positively responsible subject, but who in the second place might expect a redistribution of resources, rectifying the disadvantage of diminished opportunities to live a range of potential future lives resulting from bad luck. However, this second expectation regarding just distributions should not diminish the first act of empathic engagement with the other agent – who, despite the diminished range of opportunities to live a range of lives is still living the *one* life that may well be experienced as rich, valuable and unpredictable and cannot be fully compared with another life that might have been led by the same person had she not experienced these disadvantaged conditions. Briefly put, this lack of comparability is derived from her living in the present and singular, with her life being necessarily bounded and finite, which in turn affects her subjective motives, reasons and values, which become peculiar and important to her. It is in this latter context that I have argued that a critically reflective person is able also to stand back from these motives, reasons and values, and then freely and positively accept them as hers and hers alone. The point is that this subjective endorsement then profoundly influences her choices about what she does and who she becomes, even if we acknowledge the presence of objectively defined obstacles to her choice making. Citing Thomas Nagel to illustrate further my argument:

> ... we all want external freedom, of course: the absence of obstacles to doing what we want. We don't want to be locked or tied-up, or closed off from opportunities, or too poor or weak to do what we would like. But reflective human beings want something more. They want to be able to stand back from the motives, reasons and values that influence their choices, and submit to them only if they are acceptable. (Nagel, 1989, p 127; see also Chapters Two, Three and Five here for further exploration of these and related issues)

My principal claim, then, is that if the latter process of acceptance is not recognised fully in our collective responsibility to each other, there is a danger of not sufficiently considering how individually responsible self-creating agents might positively, and paradoxically, identify with personal characteristics associated with 'being disadvantaged'.

Finally, using both these Kantian and Nietzschean emphases on equality, human agency and reflective self-creation signifies a commitment to positive notions of collective and individual responsibility that are both unbound by contingency and uphold the value of equality related to principles of justice. Respecting persons as free and equal agents is therefore seen as foundational, acknowledging the profound separateness between persons and giving full expression to the values of individual freedom, self-creation and responsibility. However, it is also centrally important to acknowledge the collective responsibility for establishing equal opportunities to live a range of potential lives that disadvantaged individuals and group members are presently less able to access. I have argued here and in the proceeding chapters that the latter objective state of affairs can be compared with other states that are more fair or just, and so should be rectified according to principles of equality, while the former commitment is based on an assumption that subjective lives that are actually led are often incomparable or incommensurable. The next two chapters start to apply these philosophical arguments in more detail to disability issues. Disabled people are often regarded as archetypal victims of circumstances beyond their control, and so primary candidates for redistribution based on some kind of egalitarian principle of justice. However, my counter-claim is that emphasising the value of equality in relation to this group again exposes the tensions and paradoxes, highlighted in this chapter and previously, concerning the character of individual human experience and agency, and the highly subjective, dynamic and unpredictable development of personal and group-member identities.

Notes

[1] Some may object that using the term 'luck' for the latter is misleading, as social responses of this kind are within our collective control and are not therefore subject to chance or random occurrence (I am grateful to Phillip Cole for raising this objection to a paper I gave to a bio-ethics workshop organised by the Social Ethics Research Group at the University of Wales, Newport in 2010). While I have some sympathy with this objection, given that it highlights the social or collective responsibility we have for each other through 'human action', as Rawls calls it (and see my arguments later), I defend the use of the term here for two main reasons. The first is for consistency in language, as liberal egalitarians often refer to luck in contemporary debate in the ways just outlined, but the second, and more substantial reason, is because the luck of an individual is that she does not have a choice about what society she is born into, even if social systems are within human control and are changeable. Consequently, individuals are indeed lucky or unlucky to live in a society that either disadvantages or advantages them, reflecting certain natural and/or other fates.

[2] How a person's conscious state is affected by a person's choices or options is also highly controversial but is not examined in detail here (see Chapters Two and Three for further exploration of these and related issues), although the various answers to this controversy do affect understandings of how beliefs generally relate to emotions, explored extensively in this chapter.

[3] These beliefs are also anti-Rawlsian, as he argues that pity and compassion could not be nurtured sufficiently enough to ensure a stable society given the presence of self-interest (Rawls, 1973, pp 118-94); again, see Chapter Three for a fuller discussion of these and related issues.

[4] Of course, there are many different conceptions of distance. For example, a Kantian conception of distance, as I use the term here, universally recognises others as equal and separate agents who respond to their experiences differently, whereas the existentialist/ Nietzschean conception of distance, again as I use the term here, acknowledges that a person subjectively and reflectively creates herself differently as a result of living a radically different life from others. There is, though, another conception of distance that Anderson refers to and critiques, namely a hierarchical distance derived from recognising that one life, being 'better off', is of a superior quality to another life, the life of the 'suffering other' who is 'worse off'. My response, with Anderson, is to reject the last conception of distance, but to accept elements of the first two. Both these former conceptions, I argue, are in tension, but can be combined in new ways to understand better the equality and diversity debate, that is, emphasising the intrinsic value of equality between persons respecting

each other as reflective self-creating agents and 'subjects' with ends and so not viewing the other as an 'object' of pity or compassion (see also Chapters Three, Six and Seven).

[5] It is worth noting that just as the worse-off do not necessarily engage negatively with their fated conditions, neither do the better-off necessarily engage positively with theirs, so the latter are not guaranteed increased well-being purely by virtue of having more opportunities.

[6] For a different, but related conclusion, T.M. Scanlon argues against the teleological claim that well-being is a 'master value' (Scanlon, 1998, pp 108-46; see also Sen, 1992, pp 56-7).

[7] Given these differences between people who may have similar conditions and experiences, one obvious policy and practice recommendation would be to ensure that these people communicate meaningfully in self-help support groups and the like. That many people have in practice managed to positively transform their experiences in the ways described here, I think, in large part explains the popularity of such groups and how they enable group members to learn from different and positive responses to adverse circumstances and conditions. Certainly, this is an insufficient policy response to the objective conditions of disadvantage discussed throughout this chapter and in Chapters Two and Three. However, it does provide some kind of individualised response to trauma and adverse circumstances that resists defining the person as 'passive victim' in the way critiqued in this chapter. There is a growing body of literature in fields such as psychology, social work and counselling that focuses on the power of 'personal resilience' in overcoming difficult circumstances, which also provides some empirical evidence for the arguments presented here (for example, see Lishman, 2007; Cyrulnik, 2009; Neenan, 2009).

[8] This positive incorporation is perhaps more straightforwardly appreciated in respect of race, gender and homosexuality, although I argue here and in Chapters Three, Five and Six that disability can be reasonably viewed this way.

[9] See also Sartre (1995, pp 508-9) for an account of how freedom separates us from the world, but allows us to give it and our own lives meaning – and again see Chapters Two and Three for further exploration of these and related themes.

[10] Similar objections from other economically disadvantaged groups being represented as powerless 'objects of pity' have been found in various empirical studies (for example, see Bowring, 2000, pp 313-14).

[11] It is also important to note that, despite other philosophical differences between Kant and Nietzsche, the former too is highly critical of the claim that pity and compassion are central to establishing healthy social relations (see also Nussbaum, 1996, pp 27-9 for an exploration of the anti-pity tradition including Kant and Nietzsche; Schwartz, 1993, pp 281-7; Kimball, 2001; and my arguments in Chapter Three concerning Rawls's contention that pity and compassion is an unreliable foundation for establishing just

societies). In addition, it is interesting to note Nietzsche's uncompromising attack on the main assumption of liberal egalitarian teleology in *Beyond good and evil*: 'Well-being as you understand it – that is no goal, that seems to us an *end*! A state which soon renders man ludicrous and contemptible – which makes it *desirable* that he should perish! The discipline of suffering, of *great* suffering – do you not know it is *this* discipline alone which has created every elevation of mankind hitherto?' (Nietzsche, 1975a, p 136; emphasis in original). It is a highly moot point as to whether the latter rhetorical question from Nietzsche reveals a form of teleology in his own position, based on the goal of human perfectibility, individual strength and creativity (Appel, 1999; Devigne, 1999), but the point here is that it is certainly not the teleology promoted by many contemporary liberal egalitarians critiqued earlier. In short, my main argument, although it tempers the Nietzschean polemic for reasons concerning his anti-egalitarianism and lack of attention to collective responsibility for alleviating objective disadvantage, acknowledges, alongside the disability rights movement, the force of his antagonism toward teleological accounts of well-being, that is, as related to his other critiques of compassion and pity (see also Chapters Five and Six for a more detailed exploration of the disability rights movement's position and how it reflects both Nietzschean and Kantian philosophies).

[12] In relation to the first, I have argued elsewhere that this view is especially prevalent concerning lone parents (Smith, 1999); and in relation to the second, I have argued that this view permeates medical model understandings of disability (for example, see Smith, 2001a, 2002a, 2002b).

[13] For the view that a new and radical set of norms can be developed based on the idea that we can learn from 'the disadvantaged', see Bowring (2000, p 323).

FIVE

Egalitarianism, disability and monistic ideals

Introduction

In this chapter, I argue that the medical and social models of disability, while establishing clearly located poles for understanding competing interpretations of disablement, allow for a range of interpretations between these two extremes. In this light, the chapter outlines these various interpretations, to help clarify the different types of claim made by the disability rights movement (DRM) as related to the equality and diversity debate explored in previous chapters.

Briefly put, the medical model is commonly regarded by the DRM as an inaccurate interpretation of disablement, reflecting and reinforcing the oppression, exclusion and exploitation of disabled people by non-disabled people. First, the medical model is seen to incorrectly define disablement as a fixed condition relating to the severity of a medical impairment; consequently, there is no distinction between impairment and disability when viewing a disabled person. Second, it incorrectly assumes that it is this medical condition, often defined as 'handicap', that inevitably causes the dependency of the disabled person, thereby legitimating dependent relations being formed between the disabled person as 'cared for' and the non-disabled as 'carer'. Third, it falsely locates disability with an individual deficiency, so leading to persistent and chronic levels of dependency; therefore, the medical model links the term 'handicapped' with 'individually-based functional limitations', which in turn falsely implies that 'the impairment is permanent and that [the disabled person] will almost certainly remain dependent throughout their lives' (Barnes, 1991, p 2).

For the DRM, the social model is a radically alternative paradigm for understanding disability, identifying the causes of disablement within various social, political and economic arenas. Therefore, the experience of disability is not a fixed medical state relating to the severity of an individual's medical impairment, but rather reflects how society is organised and structured in respect of particular medical conditions. From this social perspective, the focus for the DRM is on the 'politics of disablement', where citizenship, inclusion and problems of accessibility are central to the struggle of 'being disabled', rather than on individual functional limitations requiring treatment, care, personal adjustment or 'cure', as defined by the medical model (Liachowitz, 1988; Oliver, 1990, 1996; Barnes, 1991; Morris, 1991; Swain et al, 2003; Vehmas and Makela, 2009).

However, these two models of disability can be variously interpreted. Theoretical modelling, after all, although it may provide useful generalisations concerning the understanding of human experience, is necessarily an abstract process requiring further substantive interpretation relevant to specific policy and practice (see also Heredia, 2007, pp 123-39; Smith, 2007a, 2007b). Therefore, I start by outlining two interpretations of the medical model, with one mixing elements of the medical and social models, plus two interpretations of the social model. My main argument is that, while these interpretations are not exhaustive, each has distinct implications for the way disabled people are viewed and treated. Consequently, when following particular interpretations of the medial model, disabled people are often viewed and recognised by non-disabled people as loss bearers and archetypal victims of tragic circumstances beyond their control, and so are ideal beneficiaries of resources redistributed under egalitarian principles. However, these interpretations, I contend, risk ignoring the various issues and complexities explored in Chapters Two, Three and Four concerning the character of human experience and agency, and the subjective and particularised development of personal identity. For example, in Chapter Four I argued that bad luck or misfortune could often be subjectively transformed into good luck or fortune by the person concerned. These transformative possibilities, when exercised by disabled people, require us to view disabled people as reflective self-creating agents actively engaging with their experiences who positively affirm their identity, including 'being impaired', despite unjust social conditions that frequently diminish disabled people's opportunities to live a range of potential future lives.

Following these themes, I argue in this chapter that values associated with the condition of being impaired are subsequently often conflicting and incommensurable. On the one hand, these relatively limited opportunities to live a range of potential future lives can be objectively compared with the experiences of non-disabled people – my claim being that this state of affairs ought to be remedied by egalitarian policies and practices designed to equalise these opportunities. On the other hand, the one actual life subjectively led by a disabled person often cannot be wholly compared with another life that might have been led by that person if she were not impaired, or cannot be compared with the life of another person who is not impaired. My central claim is that this lack of comparability is derived from the absence of a singular and/or monistic value structure or set of ideals that measures the worth of these lives. Nevertheless, as I also explore in this chapter aspects of both the medical and social models that do promote a singular value structure or monistic ideal to be pursued by all, notably the value of independence considered an 'ideal state of being' for both disabled and non-disabled people. In short, this state is recommended and pursued as much as possible for disabled people via medical intervention, as prompted by the medical model, or via social, economic and political restructuring, as prompted by the social model. My main contention is that this elevated ideal of independence, being based on misplaced essentialist understandings of the human condition, fixes human identity to objectified states of being understood as 'best' and 'normal', thereby excluding other valuable forms of life that might also be maintained and promoted, and characterised as either 'dependent' or 'interdependent'. I counter that promoting the plural and often conflicting values of independence, dependence and interdependence provides greater opportunities to live a range of potentially fulfilling lives, derived from a richer, more complex and multi-dimensional understanding of human identity and social relations than is otherwise allowed.

Finally in this chapter, I develop arguments concerning the incommensurability or incomparability of lives led, by exploring the positive role pain and suffering can play in a person's life – arguing that although it might be reasonable when pursuing a pain-free happy life not to want a painful life, it is also reasonable not to want a painless life either, given the other values we often legitimately pursue but that are incommensurate with a happy and pain-free life. More specifically, while a disabled person may regret the presence of pain in her life in some respects, in other respects she may welcome it, as a way of, for example, furthering her personal growth and reflexive capacities, her solidarity and commitment to others in a similar position, and so on, regardless of whether the pain is medically and/or socially caused. Following this understanding, I recommend what I call a 'pain-incorporating perspective' to human identity and experience that views pain and suffering, or certain levels of it at least, as a valuable characteristic of a life led. Therefore, the classic monistic utilitarian response to the problem of disability and equality, often implied in the medical model, is inadequate, as the increase of welfare or happiness, and the commensurate reduction of pain and suffering, is promoted as a primary value.[1] My main counter-argument is that this response fails to capture important aspects of the human condition that reflect, in turn, the incommensurable values of pursuing pain-free happiness and positively accepting pain and suffering as both being legitimate aims of a valuable life led.

Reinterpretations of the medical model

One of the primary objections of the DRM to the medical model is that it is based on essentialist understandings of disability (Saraga, 1998; Swain et al, 2003, pp 98-102; Heredia, 2007; Vehmas and Makela, 2009). These understandings associate disability with fixed, medically measurable conditions and objectively defined characteristics viewed as essentially 'deficient' or 'dysfunctional'. Consequently, possessing these medical conditions, leading to a personalised tragic loss in a disabled person's life, makes her an object of pity and/or fear for non-disabled people. I will call this interpretation of the medical model the full essentialist individual deficiency (FEID) interpretation. The principal result is that policies and practices based on FEID render disabled people passive and powerless 'victims' who become targets of intervention through non-disabled medicalised expertise. For the DRM, this targeting reduces the identity of a disabled person and her experience to an essentially 'abnormal' and 'lesser than' medical condition, as compared with the 'normal' and 'ideal' condition of non-disability. The FEID interpretation is reflected in legislation throughout the industrialised world, and defines people with impairments as medically 'subnormal', 'invalids', 'handicapped' and the like. Policies of segregation, alongside highly evasive forms of medical treatment, are also justified in the FEID interpretation, with disabled people categorised as unable to function normally and so requiring separated and special 'care' (Hevey, 1992; Oliver, 1996; Heredia, 2007). At its most extreme, FEID is found in the eugenics movement and fascist ideology of the late 19th and early 20th centuries, where the essential deficiencies of disabled people were feared and seen as a threat to establishing a 'pure' race. This not only led to impaired people being segregated from the essentially 'normal' and 'ideal' population, but also to the recommendation and practice of genetic eradication, and even the systematic murder of people with impairments (Hevey, 1992; Reeve, 2009).

However, the FEID, in its most unadulterated form at least, has been rejected by most contemporary policymakers and replaced by more social and integrated interpretations of impairment. For example, disability can in part be seen as caused by medically deficient bodily structures or dysfunction, reflecting FEID, but these in turn are viewed as deficiencies relating to complex social functionings, reflecting more social interpretations of disablement. Therefore, an impaired person may be defined as medically deficient because they cannot walk, but the complex social activity of mobility can accommodate for this deficiency if the environment is made accessible to wheelchair users. Assuming this interface between medical and social functionings leads to an interpretation of disability that moves away from FEID, recognising that an impaired person could potentially participate in mainstream society, albeit as a matter of degree. This latter understanding of impairment I will call the part essentialist individual deficiency (PEID) interpretation. Briefly put, this interpretation assumes that an impaired person is able to participate, at least to some extent, in 'normal' social activity, despite her individual medical deficiencies, and if the social and physical environment is changed to accommodate these deficiencies. Consequently, as with FEID, PEID assumes that there are essential differences between the disabled and the non-disabled person, but these differences do not mean a disabled person cannot 'function normally', at least in certain limited social contexts.

The PEID interpretation, synthesising elements of the medical and social model of disability, can be found in various policies and practices, and is used implicitly by the World Health Organization (WHO) in its Second International Classification of Functioning (ICF) (WHO, 2001). The 2001 ICF classification revises the WHO's earlier definition of impairment and disability, responding to criticisms by Disabled People's International (DPI) of its first classification. The earlier classification was eventually published as an official WHO document in 1980, but was criticised by the DPI for focusing almost exclusively on the problems of possessing certain medical conditions, rather than on problems of inaccessible and discriminatory social environments. The second ICF classification addresses some of these criticisms, recognising that deficient bodily function can be accommodated, facilitating a more active participation of people with impairments in mainstream society.

However, this synthesis of the two models is still seen as inadequate by many within the DRM. For example, although the second, more socially minded, PEID interpretation moves away from the FEID understanding of individual deficiency, given that the social environment is seen as part of the problem, it relies on a medicalised understanding of disability and so cannot avoid an essentialist interpretation of normality. Therefore, disabled people are still defined as problematic because they are unable to conform to standards of normality, which in turn are standards associated with what is seen as 'ideal' or 'best'. This understanding informs policy instigated by non-disabled professionals who, as guardians of this normalisation process, are assumed to be experts with privileged knowledge regarding the facilitation of social functioning. Consequently, elements of the FEID interpretation are found within PEID and are reflected in contemporary policies and practices. According to Jenny Morris:

> Someone who is blind is thus viewed as experiencing a 'personal tragedy' and it is the role of the professional to mitigate the difficulties caused by not being able to see ... the medical and 'personal tragedy' models of disability and the attitudes which go with them are a very important part of the powerlessness experienced by disabled people in their relationship with those professions whose role is so important to the quality and nature of our daily lives. (Morris, 1991, p 180; see also Oliver, 1996; Swain et al, 2003; Heredia, 2007)

Often underpinning these policies and practices is the PEID interpretation of impairment, involving non-disabled experts changing the individual's deficient or tragic condition through medical intervention, and/or providing rehabilitation programmes for making individual adjustments to that condition. The point for the DRM is that these policies and practices, despite their social leanings, usually serve to reinforce the oppression and exclusion of disabled people – even if these policies involve considerable resources being redistributed to meet the so-called 'special needs' of disabled people (see also Oliver, 1996, pp 62-77; Heredia, 2007). Consequently, intervention strategies that meet those needs defined by non-disabled experts, while justified on the grounds of providing care and enhancing participation, in fact function as mechanisms for exerting power and social control, serving to undermine the autonomy and decision-making power of disabled people. For example, according to Michael Oliver, UK community care policy has made:

> ... needs led assessment the linchpin of service delivery ... however, above all else assessment of need is an exercise of power, as even the language we use to talk about the exercise shows.... The professional assesses the need of the client or 'user', as they have now come to be

called....[Yet] various studies show that professionals have distorted or defined their needs....The new reforms do not change this balance of power at all. (Oliver, 1996, p 70; see also Heredia, 2007; Brown, 2009; and Chapter Six here for further exploration of these and related issues)

Reinterpretations of the social model

What, then, of the different interpretations of the social model? Many within the DRM promote an understanding of the social model that I will term the politics of disablement (POD) interpretation.[2] Instead of recommending medical or rehabilitation policies, via the FEID or PEID interpretations, attention is directed by the POD interpretation solely toward changing social and political institutions and organisations. Consequently, this interpretation offers a structural, as distinct from an individual, account of disability, in effect bracketing the personal experience of disability, other than what an impaired person might experience when living in discriminatory and inaccessible social and political environments. Via the POD interpretation, the DRM, as a result, makes a clear distinction between impairment and disability. Impairment is associated with a particular medical condition, which may, or may not, lead to a disability, and disability is associated with various social and political restrictions, often, but not always, imposed on people with impairments. For example, according to the Union of the Physically Impaired Against Segregation (UPIAS), 'impairment is the functional limitation within the individual caused by physical, mental or sensory impairment. Disability is the loss or limitation of opportunities to take part in the normal life of the community on an equal level with others due to physical and social barriers' (cited in Bickenbach, 1999, p 1173). Following this distinction, disability is consequently seen by many within the DRM as a thoroughgoing social and political concept, having no medical or individualised import whatsoever. Therefore, according to Liachowitz, '... disability exemplifies a continuous relationship between physically impaired individuals and their social environments, so that they are disabled at some times and under some conditions, but are able to function as ordinary citizens at other times and other conditions' (Liachowitz, 1988, p 2).

However, my argument is that POD, although in many ways it radically challenges the two medical model interpretations, adheres to the same essentialist myth of 'ordinary' or 'normal' living, because it too relies on fixed assumptions concerning what is objectively defined as 'normal' and 'abnormal' as related to ideal and non-ideal 'states of being'. Briefly put, my claim is that the value of independent functionality, reflected in notions of ordinary citizenship, is elevated by the POD interpretation, as a fixed and monistic ideal or value – that is, as one paramount value, based on a normalised, shared social goal of attaining independence for all, including people with impairments. Certainly, understandings of independence and normality are conceptualised differently by the POD compared with the medicalised interpretations explored earlier, as

POD refers solely to the social rather than medical origins of dependence. Also, the specific meaning of independence may vary, as notions of 'self-reliance', being a defining feature of independent living, will change as the definition of need varies, relating, say, to a person's physical or cognitive capabilities, financial resources, geographic environment and so on. However, my point is that whatever substantive interpretation of independence is used, FEID, PEID and POD define this deficiency as a social problem, with the ideal condition of ordinary citizenship reflecting the value of independence and promoted as the main aim of each. Consequently, although according to the POD interpretation a disabled person's inability to achieve the goal of independence is derived from social causes, the shared axiom between this interpretation and PEID and FEID is that an essential and objectively defined deficiency still occurs if the goal of independence remains unachieved. Consequently, the POD interpretation often portrays disabled people as looking forward to, and struggling for, a future where they can participate in the same 'ideal' and 'normal state' as non-disabled people are already supposedly enjoying. In this context, the ideal of independent living is often promoted by the DRM as the best state for disabled people to be in, epitomised by what has been called the Independent Living Movement (ILM), a highly influential wing of the DRM.

Relating to the wider issues explored throughout the book, my main contention here is that pursuing such a goal as a monistic ideal excludes the possibility of promoting various and incommensurable values reflecting radically different 'forms of life' – these being many, conflicting and often incomparable (see also Berlin, 1969; Raz, 1988, 2001; Galston, 2002; and Chapters One and Two here). More specifically, for those issues concerning disability, if the ILM promotes independent living as the ideal, other very different values – and the opportunities to live a range of lives reflecting this diversity – risk being restricted or obscured. Therefore, even if it were agreed that independent living is a desirable state of being for some people, or even for all people in certain contexts, this should not imply that it is the *only* desirable state of being or form of life worth promoting. Other states, such as dependence or interdependence, where the responsibility for meeting, say, personal needs is shared or even given over to another person, may also have value for those engaged in these relationships. However, my contention is that the quality of these relationships becomes marginalised and more difficult to recommend, or even perhaps to understand, if independence as '*the* ideal' is promoted instead (see also Smith, 2001b).[3]

With all the interpretations of disability examined so far, my claim, then, is that deficiency is fixed reflecting essential and objectively defined 'facts' concerning dependence, whether these are social facts, medical facts or a mixture of both. These facts are seen as causing the problem of dependence, which is remedied through strategies promoting ordinary or normalised citizenship – whether via social and/or medical adjustment, as with PEID and POD, or, as with the FEID interpretation, via segregating or even systematically eradicating people with impairments. These interpretations in turn, I have argued, reduce the opportunities of promoting incommensurable values relating to radically diverse states of being or forms of life, such as those lives characterised as being independent, dependent or interdependent, or some combination of all three.

There is, though, one other interpretation of the social model that I believe complicates any exegesis of the DRM's position. My main contention is that disabled people are unfairly discriminated against via two types of social processes. First, and reflecting the POD interpretation, structural environments unjustly exclude individuals with certain medical conditions. Second, social discourses use exclusionary binary descriptions of individual and group-member characteristics, by defining them as, for example, *either* 'talented' *or* 'handicapped'. In this latter interpretation, disability and dependence are not only socially caused by inaccessible and discriminatory social environments, but also socially constructed. In other words, the definition and social meaning given to individual deficiency or dysfunction and their opposites, talent and capability, are derived from particular social and political discourses that oppressively describe disability and disabled people as essentially deficient, dysfunctional, subnormal, dependent and so on. I will now explore this second type of social process, underpinning what I call the social construction of disablement (SCOD) interpretation of the social model.

With the SCOD interpretation, the DRM focuses not only on issues of inaccessibility and social inequality, but also on the negative and devaluing social construction of disabled people's individual and group characteristics and identities. For example, the medicalised assumption that experiencing impairment is necessarily tragic is wholeheartedly rejected by the DRM, partly for structural reasons regarding the unequal power relations between disabled and non-disabled people highlighted by POD, but also because a disabled person's subjective identity, *as* a disabled person, is undermined as a result. According to Swain and colleagues, '... for many disabled people, the tragedy view of disability is in itself disabling. It denies the experience of a disabling society, their enjoyment of life, and even their identity and self-awareness as disabled people' (Swain et al, 2003, p 71). Linking this view to the discussions here, and in Chapters Two, Three and Four, the social construction of deficiency or dysfunction, and what is seen as their opposites, talent and capability, leads therefore to a lack of recognition concerning what might be positive aspects of a disabled person's identity reflecting their subjective

Table 5.1: Interpretation of the medical and social models

Medical model	Interpretation	Understanding of disability
	1. Full essentialist individual deficiency (FEID) interpretation	Disability caused by measurable and objectively defined medical characteristics based on essential or fixed understandings of 'deficiency' and 'dependence'.
	2. Part essentialist individual deficiency (PEID) interpretation	While disability is caused by medical characteristics, it can be partially alleviated by changing social environments, enabling some degree of 'independent living' seen as a monistic ideal.
Social Model	Interpretation	Understanding of disability
	3. Politics of disablement (POD) interpretation	Disability caused by social practices that systematically exclude impaired people from 'ordinary citizenship' and the monistic ideal of 'independent living'.
	4. Social construction of disablement (SCOD) interpretation	Disability caused by the way impairments are defined or described – such as 'being dependent', 'incapable', 'lack of talents' – these assumptions often, but not always, have a negative impact on the subjective identity of disabled people.

experience of being impaired. The four interpretations of the medical and social models are summarised in Table 5.1.

I will now explore how this lack of recognition, identofied in SCOD, is manifested in other ways, reflecting the various social constructions that might be made of 'talent' and 'capability'.

First, aspects of a disabled person's identity that could be defined as talented but occur separately to an individual impairment are often ignored when the social construction of deficiencies and dysfunction are linked to disablement. This lack of recognition, though, is relatively easy to comprehend once the distinction between talent and impairment is acknowledged, as promoted by the DRM and POD interpretation outlined earlier. For example, Professor Stephen Hawking has severe physical impairments that, according to the POD interpretation of disablement, may or may not lead to a disability, depending on the social environment's accessibility. Nevertheless, whatever the impact of the social environment on Hawking's life as a disabled person, his physical impairments are separate to his talent for understanding maths and physics. However, for the DRM, because disabled people's talents are often obscured by dominant medical interpretations of their impaired conditions, as reflected in FEID and PEID, this often leads to misjudgments about a particular disabled person's other talents or capabilities. More formally, a fallacy of composition has occurred, where a false conclusion is drawn about the whole person based on features of some of her constituent parts. Indeed, recognising this as a fallacy has now been accepted by mainstream policymakers and governments that have, for example, sought to encourage and even ensure that employers view disabled people as possessors of talent – despite their medical impairments – through implementing various forms of anti-discrimination legislation (see also Chapter Six for further exploration of how disability policy has been influenced by an increased awareness of this fallacy).

However, there is a second, much stronger, claim about the talent possessed by impaired people that is also implied in the SCOD interpretation of the social model. A particular medical condition, considered an impairment in some respects, may be viewed as an unrecognised talent in other respects. The problem, according to this claim, is that the individual deficiency axiom, found in FEID and PEID, starts with an unquestioned assumption about the relationship between impairment and talent, namely that medical impairments in *all* respects necessarily signify a reduction of talents for the individual who possesses them. But following those within the DRM who promote the SCOD interpretation, this assumption is only deemed true through discriminatory social construction processes. According to SCOD, defining certain medical conditions as deficient in all respects is itself disabling. Consequently, the portrayal of disabled people as tragic victims leading less fulfilled and independent lives than non-disabled people tends not only to reinforce limited expectations and opportunities of what disabled people might do and achieve through the exercise of talents occurring separately to their impairments, but also to undermine any positive subjective evaluation that might be made about possessing particular 'impairments' so defined. The crux is that medical interpretations of impairment exclude the latter evaluation, as they effectively reduce the individual and her condition to disabling definitional categories that view impairment as deficient in every sense, leading to dependency, dysfunction and so on. Alternatively, the SCOD interpretation of disability encourages a disabled person to have a positive attitude to her own subjective state of being that can include 'having an impairment'. Consequently, a person with an impairment experiences a state of being, all things considered, that this person can positively affirm, which implies that having the impairment is not disadvantageous in every sense, even if it is conceded that certain aspects of her impairment may lead to other deficiencies. I argue in the next section that once this more complex and nuanced response to disability and impairment is accepted, possibilities for understanding impairments in new and enabling forms are allowed, as the monistic ideal of independence is again rejected. More generally, I argue that these possibilities also encourage the promotion of radically diverse forms of life, reflecting the incommensurable values of pursuing not only both independence and dependence (as explored earlier), but also both belonging and exclusion, and both pain-free happiness and a pain incorporating perspective within and across any valued life.

Impairment as talent, and pain as disvalue and value

It is important to first highlight that talents, however these are identified substantially, are qualities or characteristics that can only be talents if not everyone possesses them to the same degree. Therefore, talent is associated with the differences between human beings rather than their similarities (see also Smith, 2001a; 2002a, pp 79-112). One of the central questions in this chapter, and throughout the book, is how we value these differences, including those relating to physical and mental characteristics. For example, physical and mental differences between individuals might indicate the existence of talent, if these differences have the potential of producing various valuable forms of life – which would be difficult, or even impossible to produce, if there were no such diversity. If this point is conceded, a particular medical condition, although it might be regarded as an impairment in some respects, could potentially be viewed as a talent in others.

I contend that this latter conception of medical impairment is often promoted implicitly within the DRM. For example, Jenny Morris in her book *Pride against prejudice* cites disabled interviewees who see their medical condition as a source of personal strength, insight and positive self-development, which, for them, could not be achieved without the condition. According to one disabled women, 'not all of us view our disability as the unmitigated disaster and diminishment that seems expected of us…. [For me] it has brought spiritual, philosophical and psychological benefits' (cited in Morris, 1991, p 187). The interviewee continues:

> If we can appreciate that to be an outsider is a gift, we will find that we are disabled only in the eyes of other people, and insofar as we choose to emulate and pursue society's standards and seek its approval…. Once we cease to judge ourselves by society's narrow standards we can cease to judge everything and everyone by those same limitations. When we no longer feel comfortable identifying with the aspirations of the normal majority we can transform the imposed role of outsider into the life-enhancing and liberated state of an independent thinking, constantly doubting Outsider who never needs to fight the physical condition but who embraces it. And by doing so ceases to be disabled by it. (cited in Morris, 1991, p 187)

There are four points requiring emphasis here that relate to my previous arguments concerning how the medical and social models of disability are variously interpreted. First, underlying her the interviewee's claims is the assertion that the talent is not the ability to produce these characteristics *despite* the medical and/or social conditions of disability and impairment (as with the FEID, PEID and POD interpretations), but rather because of these conditions. In other words, the conditions are not necessarily a deficiency, all things considered, but an exploitable talent, given that they can lead to these characteristics and life insights. Second, these qualities anticipate, by the interviewee's standards at least, a much richer and more diverse society than exists presently. For example, this society would construct the concepts of normality and abnormality as merely statistical trends, precluding erroneous value judgments about the essentially diminished capabilities of persons with characteristics outside the normal range. Third, using the SCOD interpretation of disability, certain physical and mental conditions, otherwise objectively defined as impairments, can be subjectively redefined as talents because they can be beneficial for the individual concerned, and even for those without the condition. Regarding the latter, the capacity non-disabled people have for being liberated from conventional norms and ideals could be enhanced by insights gained from disabled people, who through their more immediate subjective experience of being defined as outsiders, can convey new possibilities for living, unconstrained by these norms and ideals.[4] Fourth, the possibility of living an unconstrained life in the ways just outlined is philosophically, as well as politically, defensible, if it is assumed that the resulting lives led are also incommensurable or incomparable. In short, my main claim is that although objective comparisons can be made concerning the lack of opportunity to live a range of potential future lives – a state of affairs that ought to be remedied by egalitarian policies and practices – what often cannot be fully compared is the quality of lives actually led by disabled and non-disabled people, given the subjectively complex and nuanced way disabled people respond to and experience their medical condition and social disablement. I will now explore these points further by examining the SCOD interpretation in more detail to make better sense of its claims, my main argument being that despite its promising anti-essentialist credentials and more empowering interpretation of the social model, there is danger of it losing plausibilityin terms of its understanding of the experience of possessing some impairments. This danger, in turn, has other important implications for understanding the value incommensurability and, more specifically, the value of talent and handicap, as well as for broader understandings of the value of pursuing a life with or without pain or suffering.

Certainly, having a physical condition outside of a statistical norm does not sufficiently determine whether that condition is defined as a handicap (disvalue) or a talent (value). For example, being unusually tall might signify a handicap to an aspiring jockey or ballerina, but an advantage to a basketball player or supermodel. Social construction processes therefore define this abnormal characteristic as a handicap or disvalue in certain social contexts but a talent or value in others. However, the social transformability, as it might be called, from handicap to talent, is less possible for Jenny Morris's disabled interviewee. Her abnormal characteristics are regarded as less than ideal because they are defined by others as handicaps across all domains. This means that although she can exploit her abnormal 'gift' as a value for her own benefit to become a more liberated person and independent thinker from her subjective perspective, this aspect of her personal experience would not usually be appreciated as valuable by non-disabled people. Such devaluing is derived from wider social construction processes that objectively define certain disabled conditions as handicaps in all social contexts, thereby disregarding those subjective perspectives that assert otherwise. Therefore, using the SCOD interpretation, the claim is that disabling social construction processes allow others, namely non-disabled people, to disvalue physical characteristics defined as essentially unqualified handicaps (for a further exploration of how this kind of disvaluing social construction process relates to other excluded groups, see, for example, Young, 1990, pp 58-59; Honneth, 1992, 2007; Parekh, 2000; and Chapter One here).

However, one objection from liberal egalitarians, among others, to the SCOD interpretation is that there are bound to be abnormal medical conditions, defined as deficiencies, that are inherently not prone to this type of SCOD transformability of handicaps to talents. For example, chronic incontinence might be considered a deficiency or disvalue across various social and cultural domains, thus undermining the SCOD interpretation so far outlined. Similarly, having a severe learning impairment in any society possessing more than a basic level of technology may be considered a handicap or disvalue, regardless of how this impairment is variously social constructed between specific communities. Nevertheless, even with these cases, objections to SCOD are, I believe, proceeding too quickly. I have argued elsewhere (Smith, 2001a, 2002a, 2002b; Smith and O'Neill, 1997), and here in Chapters Three and Four, that liberal egalitarians often make over-hasty generalisations concerning disabled people's experiences and subjective perspectives. Ronald Dworkin, for example, assumes 'all but a few who suffer [as disabled people] would prefer that their handicaps were cured and that their talents were improved' (Dworkin, 2003, p 194). Following the arguments presented so far, my response is that this assumption fails properly to recognise the positive subjective responses that can be made to human experiences, despite the wholly negative views that might be held by others of these experiences, as highlighted by SCOD (see also Chapters Three and Four, which develop and explore these and related themes).

Nevertheless, by conceding to some of the liberal egalitarian arguments, there are, I believe, hidden ambiguities concerning what the SCOD interpretation is asserting, which leads to questions concerning the plausibility and coherency of the DRM case when promoting both the POD and SCOD interpretations. These questions in turn have a profound bearing on how the experience of pain and suffering is generally perceived. I will now explore the contention that pain and suffering are both a disvalue and value, whether a person is disabled or not. My main claim is that while we should not ignore the possible debilitating effects of pain and suffering on any person's life, we should maintain a certain amount of ambivalence, regardless of whether the pain and suffering is rooted in medical or social causes. My principal argument is that, whether we are referring to physical or emotional pain, reflecting the FEID and PEID interpretations, or pain and suffering derived from experiencing social oppression and exclusion, reflecting the POD and SCOD interpretations, there are often both negative and positive aspects to pain and suffering that help shape, overall, the quality of any life led.

Certainly, a person may pursue a life of happiness without pain, but experience pain and suffering as an inevitable outcome of practical living, which might then be traded off against the levels of happiness experienced. However, the inevitability of living this mix in real life is a separate consideration to the way our lives are variously and qualitatively shaped by what I argue are two radically different notions of value. These differences, I contend, underlie the choices we often make in our everyday lives, which, on the one hand, endorse the pursuit of pain-free happiness, and yet, on the other, also positively accept the value of experiencing some level of pain and suffering. First, I assert that it is consistent with our moral intuitions regarding what is a valuable life not to want a painful life, but neither to want a painless life. Second, these intuitions in turn, I argue, endorse two incommensurable 'forms of life', namely one that pursues painless happiness – and so a life free from pain and suffering – and another that positively accepts experiencing pain and suffering, as it helps to facilitate self-development and reflects our healthy relations with others. For example, I explored in Chapter Two how our deep-felt commitments to other people assumes a state of interdependency – related to the mutual fulfillment of emotional and physical needs, and so on – but often requires us to accept some level of pain as an inevitable part of our lives, whether this pain is derived from the various costs of these commitments during the relationship,[5] or from the psychological rupture experienced when the relationship ends, through break-up or death. The point here is that accepting the presence of pain in one's life, alongside the finitude of life, can be seen as a positive value, insofar as it reflects the meaningfulness of these deep-felt commitments, as without these types of pain, it could be reasonably assumed that relationships are neither deep-felt nor committed.

But although experiencing pain diminishes the level of happiness experienced by a person, at the same time I acknowledge that a person might also legitimately pursue a life of pain-free happiness, exposing the conflict between two incommensurable values reflected in these different forms of life. Briefly put, and following my arguments in Chapter Two, my main claim is that it is missing the point about living a valuable life to ask whether a life of pain-free happiness is better than, worse than, equal to, or on a par with another life that experiences at least some level of pain or suffering, as such lives are incomparable or incommensurable. This is because imagining a pain-free life must include imagining a life without deep-felt and meaningful commitments to others, which I believe is difficult to achieve given the kind of persons we are, or usually will become. Certainly, some persons might find value from becoming hermits, free from these types of relationship, but this is very much the exception rather than the rule. For most of us, living a valuable life involves acknowledging the finiteness of the human condition, which cannot experience both deep-felt commitments and pain-free happiness across the whole of a person's life, despite what is seen as the legitimate pursuit of pain-free happiness.

But why, then, is it legitimate to pursue a life of pain-free happiness, given these limits of the human condition and our common understandings of valuable relationships? My response is that value incommensurability, where values pursued are conflicting and incomparable, while in part a product of being unable to transcend the limits and finitude of the human condition just outlined, also permit human beings to pursue permanence and stability in their personal relationships – paradoxically, these latter characteristics being also important to the pursuit of meaningful and fulfilling long-term commitments with others. In short, seeking after permanence and stability – while incommensurable with the positive acceptance of pain and suffering reflecting the changing character of relationships and the limits and finitude of life – is nevertheless consistent with the legitimate pursuit of pain-free happiness across the whole of a person's life, given that the latter, by definition, pursues a clearly identifiable good for that person and their relationships, goods which are persued as both permanent and stable. The paradox and subsequent dilemma is that the pursuit of pain-free happiness is a goal for individuals affirming the permanence and stability of relationships enjoyed, while experiencing pain reflects the value of this relationship as it develops and matures, and eventually ends.[6] Consequently, positively accepting the experience of pain as part of a valuable life led, and reflecting a commitment to healthy relations, seems incomparable with what is also the value of pursuing a life of pain-free happiness – both are coherent and comprehensible and yet seem to be in qualitatively different 'value streams'. Both can be pursued, in other words, but have no common reference point or yardstick for measuring the relative worth of pursuing one type of life *over* the other (see also Chapter Two for a fuller exploration of these and related issues).[7]

Following these conclusions, I therefore recommend what might be called a 'pain-incorporating perspective' to human life, which views pain and suffering, or certain levels of them at least, as valuable, in that they generally reflect who we are as human beings, and the value of our significant relations with others.[8] My argument, then, although accepting that pursuing a pain-free, happy life is consistent with the legitimate pursuit of permanence and stability in personal relations, recognises how other values worth pursuing often conflict with this pursuit, including the positive role pain and suffering can play in and across a person's life. I will now argue that this role not only reflects the establishment of healthy personal relations as explored in this section, but also, as explored in the next section, relates more specifically to disabled people's experience of suffering the pain of social discrimination and oppression. My main claim is that the experience of social and political struggle in the lives of disabled people again produces various dilemmas and paradoxes concerning the character of pain and suffering – again acknowledging the presence of human agency, and the positive affirmation of oppressed identities, with both needing to be fully addressed in any theory of justice.

Identity, human agency, struggle and oppression

From what has been explored so far, there are important philosophical questions raised for the DRM concerning the nature of values pursued – most notably, how to positively embrace and assert existing disabled identities, reflecting SCOD, but recognising the presence of disabling social and political structures, reflecting POD. The central issue is that the correlate to the value of eradicating inequalities and partly oppression, as promoted by POD, is that positive and valued identities formed *out of* social and political struggle and promoted by SCOD will inevitably change and even disappear as a result. The subsequent dilemma for radical politics was articulated well by Aristotle: 'no-one chooses to possess the whole world if he first has to become someone else ... he wishes for this only on condition of being whatever he is' (cited in Stocker, 1997, p 210; see also Chapter One). Consequently, it seems that promoting structural transformation, and so changing valued existing identities, produces a paradox and political dilemma for the DRM and radical politics more generally, that is, between, on the one hand, promoting disabled and oppressed identities as these presently exist, within a world that, by definition, is in some ways painful, and, on the other hand, promoting future non-oppressed painless identities as these would exist after radical social and political transformations have taken place. More specifically, the paradox for disabled people is that positive self-awareness and personal and group-member identities are lived out of and worked through what are, according to POD, disabling social and political environments. In other words, according to SCOD, these identities are valued attributes that are, in part at least, shaped by these environments, and so *include* the pain and struggle of experiencing inequality and oppression.[9]

I will now examine the horn of this paradox and dilemma further, as related to experiencing the pain of 'deficiency', whether viewed as medically or socially caused, by separating out two claims that could be made by proponents of the SCOD interpretation, and then exploring the various implications of this distinction for my arguments presented so far. The first claim is that an individual medical condition when defined as deficient is socially constructed in every sense, and the second, that medical model interpretations of disability socially construct incorrectly medical impairments as deficient in every sense.

A SCOD interpretation of the social model may make both claims, but this is not logically necessary. So, when maintaining a distinction between these two claims, it is possible to concede some limited ground to the medical model, through rejecting the first claim, and therefore admit that having certain medical impairments at least in some respects involves the pain of deficiency in a non-social sense (albeit deficiencies or pains reinforced by discriminatory social practices). Nevertheless, via the second claim, it is possible to argue from the SCOD interpretation that possessing even a severe impairment is not unambiguously deficient. This is because value too might be gained from possessing the condition, which in turn contributes to a disabled person's positive sense of her own subjective identity, including any pain experienced whether medically or socially caused.

I argue that this latter move, combining the second social constructionist claim of SCOD with the social structuralism of POD, is broadly consistent with the UPIAS distinction highlighted earlier, between impairment – defined as a *limiting* medical condition – and disability or handicap – defined as a socially imposed restriction on the impairment. The pain of impairment might therefore be that it is limiting, according to UPIAS, but without this necessarily having a detrimental effect overall on a disabled person's subjective affirmation of her identity, when all things are considered, and even if this pain is experienced alongside socially imposed restrictions.

But despite the appeal of theoretical elegance, is logical coherence between these various interpretations of disability what we want, either normatively or politically? I have so far argued that my interpretation is consistent with two main claims from the DRM. First, the objectively defined disadvantage of disabled people is that they have less opportunity to live a range of potential future lives compared with non-disabled people, reflecting structural oppression and injustice. Second, the positive affirmation of lives actually led by the disadvantaged are effectively ignored or marginalised in favour of more dominant social constructions, which leads to what might be termed identity exclusion. I will now outline how implicit within either of these claims is a particular conception of human agency, found in the POD and SCOD interpretations but often ignored or downplayed. My main assertion, explored in Chapters Two, Three and Four, is that the capacity for human agency provides a person with the possibility at least of dynamically engaging with her experiences. This engagement would involve that person stepping back from, and freely interacting with, her social and other circumstances, so reflecting and responding *to* them, often in very surprising and life-enhancing ways. Consequently, she can develop a capacity for choice, including a choice of perspective on her life, that is subjectively and reflectively 'self-creating', and so therefore not wholly amenable to objectified interpretation and epistemological prediction concerning her well-being, happiness, human flourishing and so on. As a result, she is also able to radically go against objective expectations regarding her responses to disadvantaged conditions – expectations reflected not only via dominant social norms, but also from others close to her, and even perhaps from herself. Certainly, recognising this capacity does not result in positive outcomes every time, and, furthermore, it could well be that some experiences correlate with a reduction, rather than an increase, in this kind of agency. However, even after recognising these possibilities, and if the dynamic engagement with experiences is asserted as a matter of degree, there is still, I contend, considerable room left for a subjective response to objectively defined disadvantage that is both dynamic and life-enhancing. This response has profound implications for how the phenomenon of 'disability' is subsequently viewed and responded to, and directly informs the arguments presented here.

For example, take the experience of pain, understood in the widest sense defined earlier, and caused by medical and/or social circumstances beyond a person's control. There can be many subjective responses to this pain. A person might wholly regret the experience and the circumstances that cause it, so leading to an unqualified deficiency or disvalue in her life. Using the language of the SCOD interpretation, the suffering therefore produces a deficiency or disvalue in every sense. It may be that some disabled people respond to their impairment in precisely this way, and consequently conform entirely to the expectations of the FEID interpretation of the medical model – namely, that having an impairment leads to a life that is essentially deficient. However, according to the DRM, many disabled people do not confirm to these expectations, and so, following SCOD, will reject the FEID interpretation. Indeed, there has been fierce debate within the DRM as to whether the former subjective perspective of disability, which views particular impairments as deficient in every sense, should be seen as merely a product of dominant medical constructions of disability that define being disabled as necessarily tragic, or whether it is a perspective that should be taken more seriously as a legitimate response to certain impaired conditions (Morris, 1991; Shakespeare, 2006; Vehmas and Makela, 2009). Although I do not have space to explore these debates in detail here, it is important to emphasise that my preference for the second claim of the SCOD interpretation identified earlier would allow disabled people to legitimately regret aspects of their experience of impairment and disability, without necessarily concluding that they are entirely capitulating to medicalised constructions of disability. This is because the regret may be compensated for by other gains in a disabled person's life as a result of possessing an impairment.

I will now explore how, in the latter context especially, my other claims about human agency can be better understood. First, it might be argued that pain and suffering defined in a narrow medical sense, albeit a reality for some disabled people, is certainly not the case for all, so allowing for a regret-free impairment even for someone pursuing a life of pain-free happiness. Second, following my previous arguments, I also contend that the experience of pain and suffering, whether medically or socially caused, is not, in any event, straightforwardly deficient for reasons concerning the complex and paradoxical way human beings value their lives, and as this reflects their capacity for agency. Consequently, a person often dynamically responds to her experiences, which may include experiencing some level of pain and suffering but lead to a more enriched and capable life, all things considered – as this person, for example, learns and positively appreciates her own vulnerability, facilitating her capacity to positively engage in solidarity and interdependent relations with others, and so on (again, for various personal accounts of disability consistent with these outcomes, see Morris, 1991; Swain et al, 2003; Mackenzie and Scully, 2007). Given the *possibility* at least of this enrichment, while it might be thought reasonable that no-one would want a painful life, a painless life could also quite plausibly be seen as deficient or disvalued – not only for the various reasons explored earlier concerning the value of deep-felt committed relationships, but also because highly subjective responses to pain and suffering may in certain respects be life-enhancing (see also Chapters Three and Four for further exploration of these and related issues).[10]

My further contention, though, is that this understanding of pain and suffering, whether medically or socially caused, allows for a more nuanced interpretation of human experience than is usually allowed in the interpretations of disability so far explored. It clearly blocks any essentialist interpretations of disability, that having impairments necessarily preludes a life seen as essentially tragic in the FEID and PEID interpretations. However, it also prevents tendencies in certain SCOD interpretations of disability, namely those that make the first claim identified earlier, that deny the possibly diminishing experience of pain and suffering for disabled people, at least some of the time and in some circumstances. Nevertheless, acknowledging the force of SCOD in accepting the second claim recognises that experiencing pain or suffering derived from being impaired and/or disabled is not necessarily an unqualified deficiency or disvalue for the individual concerned. This is because advantages too might be gained from these experiences, which in turn contribute to a disabled person's positive sense of her own subjective identity as this exists presently, within the disabling social and political environments highlighted by the POD interpretation.

Selfhood, utilitarianism, value conflict and disability

But where do these claims about disability, human agency and experience more generally take us in respect to the equality and diversity debate explored in this book? By way of concluding this chapter, I will now pay further attention to the subjective notion of selfhood and agency so far outlined, for both disabled and non-disabled people, relating to the capacity individuals have to go against objective expectations regarding their responses to experiences, and the nature of value as reflecting their experience of pain and suffering. As explored in Chapter Three, when we experience radical change in our lives, we are often surprised by our reactions and responses because these go against our imagined expectations. However, I also explored the meaning of 'going against' in this context. One meaning is that the going against reveals inconsistencies between what a person imagines she would do and/or be, and what she actually ends up doing and/or being. Therefore, the going against is an epistemological problem, with the remedy being to ensure that a person, as a critically reflective agent, knows herself better through personal introspection, individual therapy and the like. But another menaing of 'going against' is that – rather than revealing inconsistencies in the imagined knowledge and actual knowledge of a person – it reflects how subjective personhood is itself in a state of flux, and so changes while experiences are occurring and through the exercise of agency. To borrow the language of existential philosophy, 'the self' is therefore not so much a fixed objective entity or essential 'being' that is 'back there' waiting to be discovered, but rather is a non-essential and subjective 'becoming' that is subjectively created and *re*created through an agent who dynamically engages with her experiences. The notion of agency explored and defended in this chapter and throughout the book acknowledges the force of both conceptions of selfhood, but recognises that the latter opens up various possibilities for how we understand better the positive affirmation of subjective identities and the promotion of incommensurable values.

To recall the SCOD interpretation of the social model, the oppression of disabled people is not only caused by the social disadvantage of having fewer opportunities to live a range of potential future lives compared with non-disabled people, as the POD interpretation would have it. It is also derived from what might be termed identity exclusion, which devalues the lives actually led by disabled people in the present who experience oppression. Reflecting the existentialist conception of identity and agency defended here, this exclusion process occurs when highly diverse and dynamic responses to the experiences of those defined as disadvantaged are effectively ignored or marginalised in favour of more dominant constructions. Agent-based respect has consequently been sidelined, where a person with conditions associated with suffering and disadvantage is essentially defined as a tragic and passive victim of circumstances and experiences beyond her control, so undermining her agency and subsequently her own self-created identity.

Following this analysis, I support a dual conception of agency and identity that produces a certain kind of normative paradox when promoting socially just relations (see also Chapters Three, Four and Seven for further exploration of these and related issues). In short, I recommend that individuals imagine and identify with others who are self-creating responsible agents, engaging with their existing, often incomparable, subjectively lived-out experiences in highly unpredictable and often positive ways. However, I also recommend the structural transformation of social and political environments, alleviating the objectively predictable and comparable disadvantage of having restricted opportunities to live a range of potential lives in the future. My claim is that holding these recommendations in tension means that highly diverse and particularised 'forms of life' can be celebrated and affirmed, so rejecting monistic ideals for living while also providing universal reasons for changing social and political practices to equalise opportunities for those who are disadvantaged. Regarding disability, monistic ideals such as independence are therefore rejected, not because independence itself is seen as a disvalue, but rather because other incommensurable forms of life that are, for example, highly dependent or interdependent, could also be regarded as a legitimate source of value for particular persons. Similarly, the monistic, teleological ideal of securing a happy and painless life is also rejected in favour of a more ambivalent attitude to pain – again, not because the pursuit of a painless life is seen as a disvalue or as illegitimate, but rather because facilitating a positive acceptance of pain is also viewed as an integral part of what it is to live a valued life engaged in meaningful relationships, including wider political struggles. I will now explore further how this anti-monist and anti-utilitarian attitude to values can be reflected in policy and practice.

Utilitarianism on the face of it is a quick-fix policy solution to the conflicts and dilemmas presented so far. It promotes one principle as the most important, allowing for systematic adjudication between other lower or secondary policy aims. In relation to social policy, maximising human welfare, however this is defined substantially, for many contemporary utilitarians is the common yardstick for deciding which policy ought to be implemented. Other goals, such as the reduction of inequalities, only act as a means to the end of serving this utilitarian principle. However, I have argued elsewhere that although utilitarianism might appear superficially attractive in providing a 'solution' of sorts to decision making, it is an inadequate normative response to policy and practice debate for a number of reasons (for exmaple, see Smith, 1997, pp 92-3; 1998, pp 214-62; 2007c). Consequently, utilitarianism is notably unhelpful when articulating and addressing specific questions pertinent to the justification of particular policy and practice. For example, fulfilling the principle 'maximising human welfare is desirable' fails to address the question of who is responsible for delivering certain welfare outcomes. Here, an important distinction has been made within political philosophy between states of affairs and moral agency (Parfit, 1987, p 430). Consequently, bringing about x state of affairs is not necessarily the same question as who is responsible for bringing x about, and most ethical positions need to account for both domains to make proper sense of the moral claims being made. Reflecting what has been explored in this chapter and throughout the book, I believe that these these ethical questions are partly addressed in the way values are properly seen to be many and conflicting.[11] My claim has been that there is no monistic solution to this conflict, so suggesting values pluralism.

However, value pluralism can come in many different forms. At one end of the spectrum – the least insoluble – conflicting values are placed in a lexicographic ordering, exemplified in John Rawls's *A theory of justice* (1973, pp 42-5 and pp 541-54). More specifically, the value of individual freedom is understood as conflicting with the value of distributive equality. However, Rawls addresses this conflict by guaranteeing certain freedoms, acting as a first principle, after which, when fulfilled, a further distributive principle comes into play, acting as a second principle but without having to refer to the first. At the other end of the spectrum – the least soluble – and as defended here, conflicting values are viewed as often being incommensurable or incomparable. As explored in Chapters Two and Three, according to Joseph Raz: 'A and B are incommensurate if it is neither true that one is better than the other nor true that they are of equal value' (Raz, 1988, p 332). Therefore, it is not possible to lexically rank values, given that they are not comparable. Instead, qualitatively different losses and gains are experienced depending on what choices are made. Somewhere in the middle of the spectrum, it is possible to trade off values, suggested by Brian Barry, for example (Barry, 1990, pp 5-7). Here, one value is diminished for the sake of the other but without entirely sacrificing the first. A certain balance of conflicting values is achieved that is intended to reflect our moral intuitions about what comparative balance or weighting is ethically appropriate, given individual and/or wider political and social circumstances.

I have argued elsewhere that engaging in these debates concerning value conflict can throw considerable light on how social policy is variously justified, although in political discourses these conflicts are often obfuscated (Smith, 1998, pp 234-42;

2007c; see also Cohen and Ben-Ari, 1993 for a sociological account of why this obfuscation occurs). Moreover, I have argued in this chapter and throughout the book that we need to consider not only the different ways values conflict, among a set of ethical commitments held by particular positions, but also how persons as agents variously and subjectively view and respond to their social environments and personal circumstances. Recognising the latter as a dynamic and unpredictable process gives an account of why disabled people who are objectively categorised as tragic victims by the medical model often militantly reject being categorised or socially constructed in this way. Instead, disabled people are keen to assert their ability to both survive *and* thrive through their subjective experience of particular conditions and circumstances, regardless of how these conditions and circumstances are objectively defined and/or caused, and even if these produce certain degrees of pain and suffering. Applying this latter understanding to my claims regarding value pluralism and value incommensurability requires us also to acknowledge two qualitatively distinct moral concerns. First, we must acknowledge that the positively affirmed identities of those who belong to disadvantaged groups are derived from the moral significance of *being* one person who is often incomparably different to another, given the highly subjective or particular exercising of agency in dynamic and reflective self-creation, whatever circumstances are experienced. Second, we must also acknowledge the unfair treatment of disadvantaged group members derived from the moral significance of *claiming* just distributions – that is, requiring social, political and economic restructuring so that the opportunities for those who are in disadvantaged groups to live a range of potential future lives are made more equal to those in advantaged groups.

In Chapter Six, I explore these and other related themes further and argue that, consistent with social work codes of ethics and mainstream social policy objectives, the DRM promotes the universal values of equal rights and individual autonomy, drawing heavily from Kantian philosophy. However, an anti-universalised Nietzschean perspective is also promoted via the social model of disability, challenging the political orthodoxy of rights-based social movements, and the aspirations of social workers to empower disabled people. I argue that these Kantian and Nietzschean strands within the DRM are also incommensurable, but again, when held in tension, permit a radical assertion of disability identity – that is, without conceding to the uncriticality of value relativism and postmodern particularism, but allowing a thoroughgoing 'celebration of difference' through establishing and promoting reciprocal and interdependent social relations with others who are radically different.

Notes

[1] It could be that well-being provides another kind of non-classical utilitarian measurement or yardstick for evaluating the whole of person's life that is overarching and comparable, while also promoting incommensurable values as part of what it is to live a valued life in the ways just stated. This possibility leads to an interesting question as to whether promoting incommensurable values necessarily makes incoherent or empty the meaning

of well-being as a coherent, overarching and comparative value, or whether promoting a certain range of incommensurable values is compatible with promoting substantive forms of well-being, despite first appearances (see also Sen, 1985; Griffin, 1986; Raz, 1988, pp 288-320; Scanlon, 1998, pp 108-43).

[2] The phrase 'politics of disablement' alongside the classification of the medical and social models of disability, was used by Michael Oliver in his 1990 publication, *The politics of disablement: Critical texts in social work and the welfare state*.

[3] Parallel arguments are found in Mackenzie and Stoljar, 2000; they also critique independent living and the value of individual autonomy, often promoted as a masculanised patriarchal norm.

[4] Similar conclusions are reached by Finn Bowring, who demonstrates how poor people are often more able than rich people to positively disengage from dominant and oppressive consumerist norms (Bowring, 2000, pp 313-14; see also Levitas, 2001, pp 449-50).

[5] These costs could include the sharing of material resources, the use of time dedicated to maintaining the relationship, or the emotional costs of sharing the psychological burdens of the other person in various relational contexts.

[6] Given these limitations of the human condition, and the subsequent inevitability of experiencing some level of pain as a result, it could be said that at least part of the motivation for pursuing a life of pain-free happiness – despite its modern and secular resonance – is based on a more ancient and non-secular yearning for an eternal pain-free life, promised in many religious traditions.

[7] Again, interesting questions are also raised concerning the pursuit of well-being, and whether, or the extent to which, this allows for the incommensurable pursuit of both pain-free happiness and the maintenance of deep-felt commitments.

[8] I am partly endorsing the Nietzschean perspective of pain and suffering explored in Chapter Four, which sees pain as a basis for 'elevating mankind', as Nietzsche calls it – this being profoundly distinct from pursuing happiness and/or well-being as a teleological goal. While in Chapter Four I temper the Nietzschean perspective on pain and suffering by recognising the independent value of pursuing happiness and/or well-being, I follow Nietzsche's critique of pity, and his challenge to establishing happiness and/or well-being as an *all* important teleological goal. Endorsing other Nietzschean concerns explored in Chapter Four, and reflecting the SCOD interpretation of disability outlined here, pursuing happiness may also encourage a patronising attitude of pity towards those who suffer, seeking to oppressively change the lives of the 'pitiable' according to preconceived and objectified understandings of happiness and well-being (see Nietzsche, 1975a, pp 71-7, pp 91-9, pp 135-6; Chapter Six here; and my critique of Arneson's liberal egalitarian teleology and Nussbaum's understanding of pity as a 'basic social emotion' in Chapter Four.)

[9] The resulting vexed question of whether to preserve positive identities, formed in part from experiencing oppressive social environments, was also explored in Chapter One, most particularly in relation to Nancy Fraser's position (especially but not exclusively in relation to her earlier work; Fraser, 1997).

[10] This conclusion is also reminiscent of the themes explored in Aldous Huxley's insightful novel *Brave new world*, where personal relations and critical self-development are rendered shallow and superficial as a result of lives led that are painless.

[11] According to those ethical positions I have sympathy with, what these different domains produce is a *pro tanto* moral dilemma – that is, a dilemma that is not solved by any single philosophical system (see also Chapters One and Two for further exploration of these and related issues). This insolubility can be contrasted with *prima facie* dilemmas that are solvable by reference to, for example, monistic philosophical systems such as utilitarianism – leading to either one choice being made, or a number of choices being allowed but without producing a moral dilemma or conflict (see also Gowans, 1987; Smith, 1998, pp 214-62).

SIX

Equality, identity and disability

Introduction

Consistent with social work codes of ethics and mainstream social policy objectives, the disability rights movement (DRM) promotes the universal values of equal rights and individual autonomy, drawing heavily on Kantian philosophy. However, I argue here that an anti-universalised Nietzschean perspective is also promoted via specific interpretations of the social model of disability, explored in Chapter Five, that challenge the political orthodoxy of rights-based social movements and the aspirations of social workers to empower disabled people. Developing and applying the philosophical themes explored in previous chapters, my main claim here is that these Kantian and Nietzschean strands within the DRM, albeit conflicting and incommensurable, permit a radical assertion of disability identity, that is, without conceding to the value relativism of some forms of postmodern particularism, and providing a philosophical justification for 'celebrating difference' across diverse communities through promoting reciprocal social relations.

As explored in Chapter Five, the DRM has had considerable political success promoting the social model of disability, based on principles that contrast starkly with the medical model, with the latter underpinning, in its various applications, oppressive social policies and practices (Oliver and Barnes, 1998; Swain et al, 2003; Heredia, 2007; Vehmas and Makela, 2009). Contemporary policy and practice has certainly synthesised elements of both models and has conceded to some main tenets of the social understanding of disability. Rather than viewing disabled people as medically deficient requiring 'cure' or 'treatment', following the medical model, mainstream policy and practice has variously incorporated the social model, which seeks to remedy systemic institutional inadequacies that fail to include disabled people. Historically, these inadequacies have occurred across numerous social and economic domains – labour markets, educational and training facilities, housing and health provision, transport, private and public services, and so on. Consequently, the DRM has vigorously campaigned for equal rights to access, enabling equal participation and inclusion across these domains, as opposed to 'special needs' provision delivered via segregated welfare state or charity services (Barnes, 1991; Barton, 1996; Oliver and Barnes, 1998; Swain et al, 2003; Heredia, 2007). Despite initial resistance, governments worldwide have responded by introducing variety of legislation reflecting the social model, outlawing what are now generally regarded as unjustifiable forms of institutional exclusion and discrimination (for example, see the 1990 Americans with Disabilities Act in the US; the 1992 Disability Discrimination Act in Australia; the 1995 Disability Discrimination Act in the UK).

However, although there have been significant advances promoting the social model, representatives of the DRM and others sympathetic with its cause are keen to remind policymakers and practitioners that progress is at best patchy (Morris, 1991; Oliver, 1996; Swain et al, 2003; Brown, 2009). Some of the patchiness reflects the slow rate at which physical environments previously only catering for non-disabled needs are adapted for disabled people. Nevertheless, there are other limitations relating to what might be called discourse or value landscapes, shaping how non-disabled people view disabled people as possessing a necessarily or essentially diminished condition of disablement (Liachowitz 1988; Barton 1996; Heredia, 2007; Edwards, 2009; Ikaheimo, 2009). Consequently, the DRM focuses not only on issues of inaccessibility and social inequality, but also on questions concerning the detrimental social construction of individual and group-member identity (Hughes and Lewis, 1998; Saraga, 1998; Heredia, 2007). As explored in Chapter Five, this stress on social constructionism reflects a particular interpretation of the social model, highlighting the social meaning given to disability and the subsequent devaluing of 'being disabled' – this being distinct from other interpretations emphasising the social causation of disability through institutional practices that structurally exclude people with impairments. My argument is that both these interpretations are promoted by the DRM but produce tensions and difficulties concerning the philosophical bases of its claims, and the political demands that ensue.

For example, the medicalised assumption that the experience of impairment is always diminishing and is a tragic personal loss is wholeheartedly rejected by the DRM: '... for many disabled people, the tragedy view of disability is in itself disabling. It denies the experience of a disabling society, their enjoyment of life, and even their identity and self-awareness as disabled people' (Swain et al, 2003, p 71). However, following this assertion, the difficult philosophical and political question for the DRM is how to fully affirm existing identities given the presence of disabling social structures. The main issue, explored in Chapter Five, is that positive self-awareness is often worked out *within* and *through* disabling social practices. Consequently, even if particular environments are viewed as unjust and discriminatory, struggling and living a life in these environments form part of a disabled person's subjective narrative, developing what might be for her a positive identity and self-awareness, facilitated by comradeship and solidarity with other disabled people who share similar experiences. In addition, I explored how disabled people also often speak of how their outsider or excluded status – being externally imposed by discriminatory social practices – paradoxically can provide a platform for liberating them from pervading dominant norms, and so be subjectively enriching and beneficial (for example, see Morris, 1991, pp 187-90; Mackenzie and Scully, 2007).[1] As discussed in Chapter Five, and also explored in Chapters Three and Four, this is not to ignore the disadvantages that many disabled people face when living in discriminatory environments that often severely restrict the range of potential lives that may be led by disabled people compared with non-disabled people. Nevertheless, recognising the possibility of experiencing liberated 'states of being', as a direct reflection of disabled people's excluded status, exposes the highly ambivalent character of discriminatory environments, as these relate to the creative and positive shaping of personal identities.

Therefore, for the DRM, there is a complex and nuanced interface between providing a critique of existing social structures that fail to include disabled people, simultaneously promoting a radicalised, positive assertion of disabled people's 'other-like' and excluded identities. My contention in this chapter, developing the themes explored throughout the book, is that both aspirations – a future looking forward to a more just and inclusive society; and a present affirming existing identities born out of personal and political struggles – often pull in opposite directions, reflecting a philosophical tension within the DRM, drawn, in part, from two distinct and incommensurable traditions of thought. On the one hand, the DRM appeals to the universal and Kantian values of equal rights and individual autonomy, providing a robust normative foundation for challenging existing institutional practices. My principal argument here is that this appeal is based on a future orientating objective perspective – looking forward to what is universally understood as a better world of just practices, equalising the opportunities for disabled people to live a range of potential future lives. On the other hand, the DRM also appeals to an anti-universalised Nietzschean view of values, challenging the political orthodoxy of rights-based social movements. This is based on a full-blooded, present-orientating subjective perspective that views all universal standards and values as oppressive, even those standards and values associated with the demands of egalitarian politics. I argue that both the philosophical and political tensions between these traditions of thought should be more openly acknowledged within the DRM, to understand better its recommendations for policy and practice, as well as to inform the wider debates explored in this book concerning the conflict between promoting values associated with equality and diversity principles.

Kantian ethics: needs, rights and citizenship in policy and practice

Reflecting the ethics of Immanuel Kant, many contemporary political philosophers recommend that social and political institutions should establish individual rights to autonomy, affording equal respect for persons as agents or choosers (Kaufman, 1999; Louden, 2000; Reath, 2006; see also Chapter One for further exploration of these and related issues). However, this recommendation is interpreted in various ways. For example, some Kantian commentators justify the state meeting people's needs, where state intervention is seen as a requisite for exercising individual autonomy, underpinning the individual's ability to formulate and implement life-plans. The main claim is that many people would find it impossible to exercise this autonomy, given the presence of unconstrained economic markets (Rawls, 1973;

Van der Linden, 1988; Hill, 2002). For example, John Rawls establishes individual liberty as a first principle of justice, so that persons can exercise freedom and choice, while also instituting a mechanism for redistributing resources from the better-off to the worse-off operating as a second principle of justice (Rawls, 1973, 1993, 2001). In contrast, other Kantian commentators have argued that guaranteeing rights to exercise autonomy and freedom implies that individuals should not have legitimately earned resources taken from them via a compulsory tax system, intent on redistributing from the better-off to the worse-off (Nozick, 1974; Hayek, 1993). For example, Robert Nozick claims that a welfare state would undermine Kant's second formulation of the categorical imperative that we should not treat others '… simply as a means, but always at the same time as an end' (Nozick, 1974, p 32). The problem for Nozick is that the compulsory character of a redistributive tax system funding a welfare state does treat people, the better-off, 'simply as a means', given that members of this group are forced to support the interests of the worst-off (Nozick, 1974, pp 32-3). Friedrich Hayek, in justifying a negative conception of liberty, also refers to Kant's second formulation of the categorical imperative, to make a similar case against the welfare state:

> Our definition of the meaning of liberty depends upon the meaning of the concept of coercion … by coercion we mean such control of the environment or circumstances of a person by another that … he is forced to act not according to a coherent plan of his own but to serve the ends of another … coercion is evil precisely because it thus eliminates an individual as a thinking and valuing person and makes him a bare tool in the achievement of the ends of another. (Hayek, 1993, pp 20-1)

More generally, it seems then that the relationship between abstract ethical principles and their practical implementation is not straightforwardly delineated. I have argued elsewhere that ethical principles often at best provide only a very broad framework for evaluating policy and practice, and that while such a framework may rule out certain policies and practices out, it does not necessarily rule in specific recommendations (for exmaple, see Smith, 1997; 2007b, pp 1-18). So, within welfare practices such as social work, Kantian ethics provides a philosophical basis for respecting the clients' or users' rights to autonomy and choice, found within various professional codes of practice. However, again there is considerable dispute concerning how these rights are substantially interpreted (Hugman and Smith, 1995, pp 36-7; Banks, 2001, pp 24-30). Some commentators amalgamate Kantian ethics and utilitarian commitments to increasing welfare, arguing that commitments to the former lead to the latter. For others, meanwhile, this hybrid solution glosses the substantial conflicts between Kantian ethics, establishing individual autonomy as an 'end in itself', as distinct from utilitarian ethics promoting autonomy 'merely as a means' to enhancing happiness and/or well-being (Banks, 2001, p 35).[2]

But how are these various debates reflected in the DRM's position and its promotion of equality and rights? One move of the DRM is to promote individual rights to choice making as a separate category to the state meeting individual needs, as meeting 'special needs' in policy and practice is often found to override disabled people's capacity for decision making (Morris, 1991; Stainton, 1994; Oliver, 1996; Oliver and Barnes, 1998; Heredia, 2007; Hull, 2009). Substantial conceptions of need are defined by non-disabled professionals who exert power over disabled people by imposing state definitions of need on their clients or users. Therefore, meeting individual needs, while it may appear benign, is paternalistic and invasive, undermining a disabled person's autonomy and rights to self-determination. For example, according to Michael Oliver:

> Professionalised service provision within a needs-based system of welfare has added to existing forms of discrimination ... based upon invasions of privacy as well as creating a language of paternalism which can only enhance discriminatory practices ... institutional discrimination is embedded in the work of welfare institutions when they deny disabled people the right to live autonomously. (Oliver, 1996, pp 75-7)

The link Oliver makes between anti-paternalism and a disabled person's right to live autonomously is audibly Kantian. Kant was also deeply antagonistic towards paternalistic policies that ground morality, and subsequent social relations, in predefined values being imposed on individuals (Kaufman, 1999, pp 38-9). Instead, he argued that morality must be grounded in human will and the capacity persons have to choose. Briefly put, the will is undetermined, and therefore free, providing the foundation for any subsequent moral values being chosen by individuals. So, according to Kant, '... to be independent of determination by causes in the sensible world ... is to be free ... when we think of ourselves as free, we ... recognise the autonomy of will' (Kant, 1998, pp 120-1). More abstractly, '... now we have a will ... the principles of empirically unconditioned causality must come first ... the law of causality from freedom ... constitutes the unavoidable beginning and determines the objects to which alone it can be referred' (Kant, 1997, p 13; see also 1997, pp 105-6; 1993b, pp 50-4). Consequently: 'A subject of ends, namely a rational human, being an individual, must be the ground of all maxims of action' (Kant, 1998 (1996), p 105).

However, as already highlighted, Kant's philosophical commitment to autonomy and free will can be variously interpreted, especially in relation to the recommendation or otherwise of state redistributive policies. A Kantian ethic might consistently advocate meeting needs via state provision, if state representatives show they first respect rights to individual autonomy and self-determination. Rights to autonomously define one's own needs could be established, rather than having needs defined by social workers, but as a prelude to these needs being met by the state. Indeed, this is allowed in Oliver's position, despite his initial anti-state-meeting-needs polemic: 'It is nonetheless right to appropriate welfare services to meet their own self-defined needs that disabled people are demanding, [but] not to have their needs defined and met by others' (Oliver, 1996, p 7). Consequently, the anti-paternalist Kantian who is sympathetic to state provision establishes the right to choose as foundational to state provision, thus squaring the circle between rights relating to needs-based resource distribution – which can be implemented without respecting the user's choice and autonomy – and rights reflecting individual autonomy, so meeting a person's needs consistent with her choices or wishes. This conclusion also has implications for how notions of citizenship are understood, as it is from the latter that, what Oliver calls, active as opposed to passive conceptions of citizenship are promoted. For Oliver, passive conceptions of citizenship are rooted in traditional Fabian justifications of welfare state provision, which often assume that a welfare recipient is a passive receiver of goods and services (Oliver, 1996, pp 63-77). Active conceptions of citizenship, however, assert that the beneficiary is an agent, derived from what are, as argued here, Kantian notions of individual rights to autonomy – where disabled people are perceived as choosers who may actively negotiate with their providers the way services are designed and delivered.[3]

Moreover, according to Oliver, passive conceptions of citizenship are reinforced in medical model justifications of welfare state provision, viewing disabled people as victims of medical deficiencies leading to dependency and further passivity (Oliver, 1996, pp 63-77). Active conceptions of citizenship, by contrast, are found in social model justifications of rights, participation and equal access, providing disabled people with opportunities to shape the way their needs are defined and met. Oliver cites the political philosopher Michael Ignatieff, who also associates active conceptions of citizenship with the values of rights, freedom and liberty, and passive conceptions with the values of therapy and having compassion for 'the needy'. According to Ignatieff: 'As a political question, welfare is about rights, not caring, and the history of citizenship has been the struggle to make freedom real, not to tie us all in to the leading strings of therapeutic good intentions' (Ignatieff cited in Oliver, 1996, p 71). He then claims that: 'The language of citizenship is not properly about compassion at all, since compassion is a private virtue which cannot be legislated or enforced. The practice of citizenship is about ensuring everyone the entitlements necessary to the exercise of their liberty' (Ignatieff cited in Oliver, 1996, p 71; see also Chapters Three, Four and Five here).

The point is that Ignatieff's position is again audibly Kantian, insofar as he divorces feelings and emotions from reasoning, emphasising the importance of establishing individual rights and freedoms. My argument in Chapter Four, while not separating emotion and reason so completely, also provides a criticism of the claim – often made by liberal egalitarian political philosophers – that committing to principles of social justice is properly motivated by compassion or pity. My central claim is that the motivation derived from these feelings for the 'suffering other', while often well intentioned, is frequently misplaced. It often leads the pitier to view persons who suffer as passive victims of circumstances beyond their control, so ignoring the subjective capacity a person has to positively respond to her experiences, even those experiences objectively defined as disadvantageous. It is in this context I argued that a subjective capacity to positively affirm a life that is actually led in disadvantageous conditions often cannot be compared with a life that might have been led without these conditions. Consequently, this subjective capacity, reflecting a highly particularist and incommensurable perspective, should be considered independently from any universal demands for equal opportunity, rights and access, that explicitly set out to compare the lives of 'the advantaged' with 'the disadvantaged' and alleviate the conditions of the latter accordingly (see also Chapters One, Two and Four for further exploration of these and related issues). Developing these themes in this chapter, I argue that the DRM, despite its universalism, also draws from an anti-universalist tradition founded on a Nietzschean subjectivist or particularist philosophy. Nevertheless, I also explore how this conflict between Kantian and Nietzschean themes within the DRM can help to explain more fully its political demands, which both positively affirms the present subjective identities of disabled people, alongside recommending the radical transformation of objective social conditions for the future.

Nietzsche as a surprising ally of the disability rights movement

There are many aspects of Friedrich Nietzsche's philosophy that seem deeply antagonistic toward the DRM. The latter promotes the universal and inclusive values of equal rights to individual autonomy and participation, which, as previously explored, can be understood in broadly Kantian terms. These values are general moral principles applicable to all persons and cultures and are seen as truths that can be accessed by all rational human beings. The universal value of equality is readily committed to by the DRM as a correlate to establishing these rights, reflecting universal descriptions of the human condition and what it is to be an autonomous person, which includes persons with disabilities.[4] In marked contrast, for Nietzsche, the Kantian association between reason and 'truth', and the values of equality and rights, require an oppressive obedience and conformity to universal rules, stultifying individual assertiveness and subjective capacities for 'self-creation' (Nietzsche, 1956, pp 70–3 and pp 169–70; 1975a, pp 53–5 and pp 121–2; see also Copleston, 1994, pp 390–406; May, 1999, pp 13–15). According to Nietzsche, demands for equal rights, however these rights are conceptualised, emasculate individuals and individuality as human goals are universally endorsed by, what he calls, a common herd. For example, in *Beyond good and evil*, Nietzsche states that '… the diminution of man to the perfect herd animal (or, as they say, to the man of the "free society") [is the] … animalization of man to the pygmy animal of equal rights and equal pretensions' (Nietzsche, 1975a, p 109 and pp 175–85).

However, I will now argue that there are Nietzschean themes found within the DRM, despite the latter's commitment to equal rights and individual autonomy. There are four main planks of the Nietzschean position that explain further his anti-universalist perspective: his anti-essentialism; his critique of pity and compassion; his critique of ideals and dualism; and his eternal recurrence thesis – all these I believe reflecting a specific particularist understanding of individual empowerment and identity assertion that is also promoted within the DRM (see also Chapter One for a detailed exploration of the conflict between universalism and particularism and how this relates, in turn, to the wider equality and diversity debate).

Philosophical essentialism claims that certain characteristics of any 'object' are essential, and therefore not incidental to its existence (Blackburn, 1996, p 125). Unsurprisingly perhaps, there is considerable dispute over what constitutes essential human qualities or characteristics. However, that these qualities or characteristics ought to be identified still has considerable intuitive appeal, one that is often unquestioned by disputants who subsequently promote, for example, universal rights reflecting these qualities or characteristics. For Nietzsche, though, this type of essentialism is fundamentally flawed, as it mistakenly assumes that it is possible to objectively identify these traits via rational reflection and/or scientific method – promising an underlying explanation of who we are as human beings, subsequently giving an essential meaning to human lives (for example, see Nietzsche, 1975a, pp 15-36). This is an empty promise for Nietzsche, distracting us from addressing what he sees as our completely unexplainable and meaningless existence (Copleston, 1994, pp 397-8). There is no essential objective reality that is understandable and purposeful. Rather, human beings invent and create explanation and meaning, derived from particular perspectives or 'species of life', as Nietzsche calls it, that radically vary according to each person's instinctively and highly particularised lived experience (Nietzsche, 1975a, p 17; and related themes explored in Chapter Two).[5] Although there is disagreement among Nietzschean scholars concerning both the coherence and centrality of Nietzsche's anti-essentialism (Berkowitz, 1997; Appel, 1999; Devigne, 1999), the claim from Nietzsche, at least, is that it offers a new way of understanding philosophical pursuit, where essentialism's pretension for finding 'truth' and 'meaning' is seen as a disguise for what are merely instinctive prejudicial assertions. For example, in *Beyond good and evil* Nietzsche claims:

> Most of a philosopher's conscious thinking is secretly directed and compelled into definite channels by his instincts. Behind all logic too and its apparent autonomy stands evaluations, in plainer terms physiological demands for the preservation of a certain species of life … for the most part [philosophers] are no better than cunning pleaders for their prejudices, which they baptise 'truths'. (Nietzsche, 1975a, pp 17-18)

But how is this anti-essentialist Nietzschean theme reflected in the DRM? As explored in Chapter Five, the main objection of the DRM to the medical model is that it is based on an essentialist philosophy of disability (Swain et al, 2003, pp

98-102; Heredia, 2007; Vehmas and Makela, 2009).[6] The medical model associates disability with fixed essential characteristics, defined by non-disabled medical experts, that necessarily signify a life of personal loss or tragedy. According to my arguments here, for the DRM these essentialist interpretations of disability effectively allow non-disabled experts to assert their prejudicial understanding of disablement as being essentially deficient – thus ignoring the possibility of disabled people positively endorsing their identities, including possessing their impairments (for example, see Swain et al, 2003, pp 54-6).[7] The Nietzschean claim from the DRM is that there is no one essential truth to 'being disabled' that is fixed across time and cultures, but rather a series of perspectives on disability that variously affect disabled people's lives as these relate to particular social conditions. Personal loss or tragedy is therefore not an inevitable characteristic of impairment possession, despite particular cultural and social prejudices that assume these characteristics are essential to the disabled condition.

The second Nietzschean theme is a critique of pity. As explored extensively in Chapter Four, Nietzsche views this emotion as a drain on the energies of those who experience it, and as condescending to those who are pitied (Nietzsche, 1975a, pp 102-3, pp 132-6 and pp 188-90). Pity also generates feelings of guilt and obligation on the part of the pitier, which for Nietzsche diminish the individual's capacity for self-creation and positive assertiveness. Moreover, being the object of pity denies the separateness of persons, ignoring differences in how people respond to and experience personal suffering (see also Conolly, 1998; Fraser, 2002; and Chapters Three and Four here). Consequently, for Nietzsche, pity, for all concerned, is the antithesis to what he calls 'the energy of the feeling of life' and renders human suffering overwhelming, undermining the individual's ability to overcome life's obstacles. For example, he states in *The anti-Christ*:

> Pity stands in antithesis to the tonic emotions which enhance the energy of the feeling of life: it has depressive effects. One loses force when one pities. The loss of force which life has already sustained through suffering is increased and multiplied even further by pity ... it gives life itself a gloomy and questionable aspect ... which inscribes *Denial of Life* on its escutcheon. (Nietzsche, 1968, p 118, emphasis in original; see also Conolly, 1998, pp 280-4)

In a similar vein, the DRM has often campaigned using anti-pity slogans. For example, in the UK a demonstration by disabled people against TV's Telethon charity fundraiser during the 1980s and 1990s used placards with the injunction 'Piss on pity!'. The DRM objected to disability charities eliciting the emotion of pity as a motivator for prompting donations from the public, as this reinforced the view that disabled people are passive and tragic victims of their impairment.[8] For the DRM, universal generalisations are made about the experience of impairment that override or marginalise the subjective perspective of disabled people that having an impairment may, contrary to expectations contained within these generalisations, contribute positively to a person's life. As explored in Chapter Five, the DRM acknowledges that some, but certainly not all, impairments cause pain and suffering, but this should not detract from the capacity disabled people have to incorporate the experience of their impairment in ways that are positive and life-enhancing.

The third Nietzschean theme is anti-idealism and anti-dualism (also see May, 1999, pp 64-5 and pp 88-91). Ideals imply the classification of opposites or dualities. For example, moral ideals imply the duality of good and evil, and aesthetic ideals imply the duality of beauty and ugliness. For Nietzsche, organised social and cultural systems impose dualities and ideals on individuals, leading to what he calls 'bad conscience' and the 'internalisation of man' (Nietzsche, 1956, pp 189-230). For example, ideals operate as templates for individual repression, where understandings of goodness and beauty – being derived from external sources, such as religious institutions, the family, popular culture and so on – are then internally endorsed by individuals who conform to dominant social norms and values associated with these ideals. Ironically for Nietzsche, internalisation often involves considerable self-discipline where the individual through her bad conscience imposes on herself these externally sourced values, which in turn fuels a self-loathing and contradiction within the self, diminishing the creative energies of a life that could be led free from conventional moralities and norms. For example, in *The genealogy of morals* Nietzsche states:

> Bad conscience is nothing other than the instinct of freedom forced to become latent, driven underground, and forced to vent its energy upon itself.... This secret violation of the self, this artist's cruelty ... impose[s] on recalcitrant matter a form, a will, a distinction, a feeling of contradiction and contempt. (Nietzsche, 1956, pp 220-1; see also May, 1999, pp 64-5 and pp 88-91)

In response, Nietzsche invites individuals who are strong and defiant to reject dualistic categories such as good and evil and beauty and ugliness, as these reflect externally imposed and objective categories, and instead freely invent and create particularised and subjective identities and values (see also Nietzsche, 1975a, pp 17-18). My claim is that this Nietzschean theme is also found in the DRM, and similarly emphasises the oppressive character of non-disabled ideals and dualities that explicitly associate 'less than' ideal characteristics with being disabled. Consequently, idealism imposes norms and standards that, according to the DRM, devalue a disabled person's subjective evaluation of her life, with non-disabled objectified categories of beauty, well-being, goodness and personal fulfillment oppressively dominating.[9] Alternatively, positively asserting disability identity involves rejecting these non-disabled ideals, substituting them with self-created standards that affirm and celebrate being 'abnormal'. Echoing these Nietzschean themes, this kind of subjective self-creation for many disabled people becomes the hallmark of a liberated life – being free from externally imposed ideals and norms. According to one disabled woman:

> If we can appreciate that to be an outsider is a gift, we will find that we are disabled only in the eyes of other people, and insofar as we choose to emulate and pursue society's standards and seek its approval.... Once we cease to judge ourselves by society's narrow standards we can cease to judge everything and everyone by those same limitations. When we no longer feel comfortable identifying with the aspirations of the normal majority we can transform the imposed role of outsider into the life-enhancing and liberated state of an independent thinking, constantly doubting Outsider who never needs to fight the physical condition but who embraces it. And by doing so ceases to be disabled by it. (cited in Morris, 1991, p 187; see also Chapter Five for further exploration of these and related issues)

The outsider who asserts her highly particularised identity in this kind of life-affirming way directs us to the fourth and final Nietzschean theme found within the DRM, namely the thesis of eternal recurrence (for example, Nietzsche, 1975b, pp 330-2). Nietzsche advocates a test for evaluating the strength of the individual where a person is asked to subjectively embrace her life in its entirety, including her personal suffering and struggle, as an eternal recurring event, while also recognising the meaningless content of that life, understood objectively. If she can say a joyful 'yes' to her life being lived for eternity in this way, she has overcome what, for Nietzsche, is the objective meaninglessness of human circumstance and experience (also see Solomon, 2001, pp 136-7). This test further reinforces his critique of pity, as those who pity 'the sufferer' effectively ignore the latter's capacity to be strengthened by this most positive subjective endorsement of a person's life.

Nevertheless, it is important to highlight an equivocation within the eternal recurrence thesis that is sometimes explored by Nietzschean scholars, and relates to the arguments presented here and in proceeding chapters. Is Nietzsche claiming that suffering changes form when a person endorses eternal recurrence, so it cannot properly be called suffering as a result? Or is he claiming that suffering remains, with the endorsement of eternal recurrence prompting a new attitude to it (see also Fraser, 2002, pp 72-153)? Pertinent to my arguments throughout this book, the DRM addresses a similar ambiguity within its critique of the medical model of disability. For example, as explored in Chapter Five, one of the main objections from the DRM to the medical model is that it mistakenly associates having an impairment with suffering and loss. I have argued in this chapter that this association is rejected by the DRM on the broadly Nietzschean grounds that impairment possession, despite non-disabled people's expectations to the contrary, can prelude an enhanced affirmation of life. However, as with Nietzsche's explication of the eternal recurrence thesis, this particular understanding of impairment possession can be interpreted in at least two ways. First, that the life enhancement subjectively experienced eradicates personal suffering – this perspective being ignored by those who promote the medical model of disability and define being disabled as necessarily tragic and deficient. Second, that a person who possesses an impairment can subjectively lead a life that is enhanced, all things considered, *even though* this impairment can sometimes/often cause suffering objectively understood. I argued in Chapter Five that the DRM promotes both interpretations of impairment possession, but that the second is probably a more plausible experiential account of disablement in its various forms – especially if the meaning of suffering includes the pain of social discrimination. However, disabled people, even via the second interpretation, can still refuse to be defined *merely* as tragic victims of circumstances beyond their control, and still therefore endorse 'eternal recurrence' as recommended by Nietzsche. This is because having an impairment can be fully affirmed, comprising a positive part of the disabled person's identity as she subjectively understands and interprets her life – even if having that impairment can cause suffering at least some of the time, whether derived from medical and/or social sources.

From Kant to Nietzsche in more than one uneasy move

But where do these arguments concerning the Kantian and Nietzschean themes found within the DRM take us regarding social policy and welfare practice? There are, I believe, three broad responses to the simultaneous promotion of these themes. The first would be to combine elements of these Kantian and Nietzschean philosophies, producing a coherent synthesis of both. This can be called the eclectic response, and holds attractions for policymakers and practitioners who often have to respond to competing demands and interests. However, there are serious difficulties concerning both the philosophical coherence and political plausibility of this eclecticism. It is not clear, for example, how a Kantian commitment to individual autonomy allows for self-creation and individual empowerment of the kind promoted in broadly Nietzschean terms. Exercising individual autonomy, within a Kantian ethical framework, involves first conforming to moral laws based on universal duty-bound obligations to others. These moral laws are, according to Kant, self-imposed, therefore preserving individual autonomy, but as we have seen, this is a very different conception of self-creation and empowerment from that envisaged by Nietzsche, who places the empowered individual outside of universal moral laws – including those derived from Kantian ethics. Some scholars argue that there is a philosophical lineage traceable from Kant to Nietzsche, and later existentialist thinkers, based on what has been called Kant's Copernican revolution, which centralises human perspective and individual free will within epistemology and ethics (Pippin, 1991; Solomon, 2001). Consequently, it is possible to interpret Nietzsche with this Kantian influence, if Nietzsche's stress on the subjective reformulation of value is emphasised – that is, where the meaning of value is redefined by individuals, as distinct from his more radical perspectivism that rejects all values outright.[10] However, even if the former interpretation is granted, this need not concede that Nietzschean conceptions of individual autonomy, self-creation and empowerment are entirely derivative of Kant – albeit they might be in some way related.

For example, in general terms, empowerment and autonomy is associated with expanding freedom of choice and action, increasing a person's control over the resources and decisions affecting her life. If people exercise choice, so the argument goes, they are empowered, being able to devise and put into practice their life-plans (also see Dworkin, 1988; Stainton, 1994). However, there is considerable conflict between the DRM and social work practitioners over how disabled people should be viewed and treated when promoting individual empowerment. I contend that much of this conflict can be explained by the tensions between the Kantian and Nietzschean conceptions and themes so far explored. Consequently, the DRM's Nietzschean leanings are a source of great anger often directed towards social workers and other welfare practitioners who are seen to profoundly misunderstand disabled people's demands and expectations. For example, Oliver and Barnes severely criticise the pretence of voluntary and social workers who aim to empower disabled people:

> There are numerous texts advising on how to empower … and conferences where the powerful talk endlessly about how to empower the disempowered. The contradiction in all this is that empowerment is only something that people can do for themselves because, ultimately, deciding to empower someone else, whether they want it or not, is the most disempowering thing that can be done to them. (Oliver and Barnes, 1998, p 10)

In other words, empowerment is not about conforming to an objective set of universal rules, accessible by anyone, including non-disabled professionals, which then can be implemented accordingly. Rather, it is about a person creating for herself a subjective perspective on personal empowerment, to be used against those who seek to impose universal sets of rules, including and especially, those rules that purport to empower. As explored earlier, Nietzsche accuses philosophers, and Kant in particular, of similar manoeuvres to social workers in respect of promoting individual autonomy and free will. Kantian values seemingly underpin personal choice and empowerment, but for Nietzsche, and reflecting the DRM critique, these are guises so as to impose universal values on people that, through this imposition, disempower them.[11]

However, given this Nietzschean critique found in the DRM, what happens to the DRM's other commitments to universal values, reflected in the Kantianesque slogan 'equal rights for all'? This awkward question prompts a second response to the Kantian and Nietzschean themes found within the DRM – that the differences between these two philosophies are irreconcilable and incommensurable, exposing a deep incoherence at the heart of the DRM's position, as moral and political theory is unable to solve the contradictions between these themes. This can be called the incoherent incommensurable response, which, I will now argue, has more philosophical plausibility than the eclectic response, because it does not try to artificially combine or synthesise two conflicting perspectives, but is inadequate both for philosophical and political reasons. As explored extensively in Chapters Two, Three, Four and Five, according to Joseph Raz, 'A and B are incommensurate if it is neither true that one is better than the other nor true that they are of equal value' (Raz, 1988, p 332). When valued objects are not equal to or on a par with each other, but neither is one better than the other, they are not comparable and therefore incommensurable. My point here is that the conflict between the Kantian and Nietzschean themes found within the DRM might indeed be incommensurable. I will now defend the assertion that the commitment to a Nietzschean perspective of personal empowerment, involving a rejection of externally imposed objective values or 'ideals', does not readily compare with the Kantian promotion of equal rights to individual autonomy, derived from a commitment to follow universal moral rules.

I argued in Chapter Two that lack of comparability blocks the possibility of two conflicting values being weighted and traded off against each other, or from being placed in some kind of lexicographic ordering, with one value taking priority over the other. Instead, lack of comparability reflects a paradigmatic conflict over radically different perspectives concerning the relationship between values and the lives of persons that are incommensurable. Trade-offs between conflicting values reflect the assumption that the relationship between values and the person making ethical decisions is comparable for each value. For example, the value of negative freedom (as related to freedom from government constraint) and the value of economic equality (as related to resources being coercively transferred from the better-off to the worse-off through a tax system) have often been traded off to justify maintaining welfare states within a free-market economy. Those who argue for this trade-off assert that, despite the conflict between negative freedom and economic equality, both should be promoted. More specifically, trading off involves maintaining a balance between these values, recognising that as one value diminishes it is possible to compensate for this loss through the corresponding increase of the other, assuming both values are appropriately compared and weighted; without this comparative assumption, it would be impossible to measure corresponding increases and decreases in conflicting values (for further exploration of these issues, see my arguments in Smith, 1998, pp 214–45; and Chapter Two here). Consequently, when two equally weighted values are traded off, one unit of p will always be equivalent to one unit of q. So, if there is more of p compared with q, some of p might be traded off allowing for more q, until an appropriate balance is reached – in this case an equal balance. Alternatively, when radically different paradigms or perspectives concerning the relationship between values and persons are at stake, there are, in effect, qualitatively different objects that cannot be measured or compared. Therefore, x amount of value p cannot be weighed against y amount of value q, as there is no like for like being traded off as x of p and y of q are not equivalent in any way. Again, following the terminology in

Chapter Two, this is because these values exist in two qualitatively different 'value streams', and so the loss of one cannot compensate for the increase of the other, and, where one value is not lexically prior to the other, they cannot be ranked either – instead, they are incomparable and so incommensurable.

However, if the Kantian and Nietzschean themes found within the DRM are so qualitatively different that they are in two incomparable value streams, this could lead to the claim that its case is incoherent. Either there is a commitment to Kantian universal moral rules and rights, or to a Nietzschean anti-universalist conception of self-creation and empowerment, but there cannot be a rational commitment to both, as they are based on different assumptions concerning the relationship between values and persons. I believe, though, that there is a third response to this conflict consistent with arguments for incommensurability – that is, promoting equal rights and social justice understood in broadly Kantian terms, alongside a Nietzschean type subjective affirmation of individual identity and empowerment. This response does not depend on synthesising the two perspectives as with the eclectic response, or on making trade-offs between them, leading to some kind of measured settlement regarding a 'right' balance between the two. Rather, it asserts that recognising this conflict as incommensurable produces irresolvable philosophical and political tensions – but that accepting this irresolvability leads to a better understanding of the DRM's position, as well as of the wider debates about the conflict between equality and diversity principles.

First, the claim that committing to incommensurable values is incoherent begs a question about the outcome of rational deliberation concerning conflicting values. It assumes that rational deliberation necessarily resolves value conflict through applying a philosophical principle, theory or method. However, as explored in Chapters One and Two, this assumption is controversial, given that there are different philosophical claims that can be made about the efficacy of rational deliberation in these circumstances (see, for example, Raz, 1988, pp 321-68). Constraining the efficacy of rational deliberation is therefore philosophically plausible, but is often not countenanced by theorists who argue that committing to incomparable or incommensurable values is incoherent. Again, according to Raz:

> Theories which provide general recipes for comparing values ... begin by establishing people's actual judgements on the relative value of options, and extrapolate principles which can be applied generally and without restriction to any pair of alternatives. Unrestricted generality is built into the theory forming process as a theoretical desideratum. The question of incommensurability is begged without argument. (Raz, 1988, p 335)

Second, and as explored in Chapter Two, providing philosophical 'solutions' to value conflict masks the complexities of lives enmeshed in networks of competing obligations and personal aspirations, relating to, for example, career choice, financial opportunity, the competing demands of family and work, responsibilities to friends and strangers, and so on. However, those who argue that these values and choices are often incommensurable recognise that these complexities lead to various conflicts that are held in some kind of unresolved tension, compounded by individual choices and values that often change over time. The point is that these conflicts or tensions may be at the bottom of philosophical enquiry, where further philosophical digging is neither required nor possible to explain completely and perfectly the truth of rational deliberation reflecting those choices made. Again, to quote Raz:

> There is a strong temptation to think of incommensurability as an imperfection, an incompleteness ... the mistake in this thought is that it assumes that there is a true value behind the ranking of options.... Values may change, but such a change is not the discovery of some deeper truth. It is simply a change of value. Therefore, where there is incommensurability it is the ultimate truth. There is nothing further behind it, nor is it a sign of imperfection. (Raz, 1988, p 327)

Following this analysis, and by way of conclusion, I will now explore how the Kantian and Nietzschean themes found within the DRM, should be held in tension, recognising that the conflict is irresolvable and that the values reflecting these themes are incommensurable. In the process, I examine further the implications of this for policy and practice and the values of equality and diversity explored throughout the book – that is, related to debates concerning postmodernism and its frequent retreat to value relativism, and criticisms by proponents within other social movements, that the universalism of the welfare state can be monolithic and oppressive, marginalising 'the voices' of those it is designed to help. In short, my argument is that recognising this incommensurable conflict between Kantian and Nietzschean values and themes would allow social movements, along Nietzschean lines, to sustain their critique of universalist reformers, but also, along Kantian lines, to prevent a postmodern collapse into value relativism and subsequent uncriticality.

Postmodernism and how irresolvable conflicts can be radical and dynamic

Postmodernism has multiple faces, but one characteristic uniting postmodern thought is its undermining of the enlightenment project by rejecting all 'totalising' or 'grand' theories – seen as misplaced attempts at discovering and then imposing order and unity through unitary and monolithic explanations. The assumption that there is a morally objective standpoint accessible via rational enquiry, found in, for example Kantian ethics, is therefore dismissed. Moral objectivism is then often substituted, explicitly or implicitly, with value relativism, where the moral significance of holding particular values is viewed as entirely relative to the holder, whether conceived of individually or in respect to particular cultures

(Habermas, 1990; Blackburn, 1996, p 326; West, 1996, pp 189-220; Calder, 2005). However, there is some dispute as to whether, or the degree to which, postmodernism is necessarily value relativist and what impact this has on policy and practice. For example, according to the social policy analyst Peter Taylor-Gooby, postmodernism inevitably collapses into value relativism, but because of its stress on subjective perspectives and preferences, it allows values associated with free-market consumerism to enter through the back door, so to speak (Taylor-Gooby, 1994). Other policy analysts, although they recognise these dangers, do not see postmodernism inevitably leading to this outcome, and acknowledge that elements of the postmodern critique can be used to underpin radical political stances (for example, see Fitzpatrick, 1996; Penna and O'Brien, 1996; Ellison, 1999, pp 57-85).

My argument is, to some extent, sympathetic with the latter interpretation of the postmodern critique, as reflected in the Nietzschean themes explored previously, but also views full-blooded value relativism as an incoherent and self-defeating expression of this critique. There is a notorious problem with postmodern value relativism, as its radical critique of moral objectivism, being an example of grand theorising, can be too indiscriminate. A radical critique, after all, locates itself outside of the paradigmatic framework being critiqued, and therefore claims a privileged position for seeing the world. Nevertheless, claiming any privileged position is precisely what grand theorising is being critiqued for. The dilemma faced by postmodern value relativists, therefore, is that to abandon grand theorising and moral objectivity, as its aim, risks abandoning the critique, as its method (Habermas, 1990; West, 1996, pp 189-220; Nussbaum, 1999, 2000). Nietzsche, being a forerunner of postmodern thought, faces the same dilemma, in that his particularism, explored previously, could lose its critical edge through a similar collapse into value relativism (see also Chapter One for an exploration of this problem for particularism more generally). Despite this difficulty, I think it is possible to defend an alternative position that accommodates some of the Nietzschean/postmodern critique of grand theory and ethical objectivism as being *over*-unifying and *over*-totalising, but at the same time does not collapse into the incoherence of a more full-blooded value relativism. Reflecting themes developed throughout the book, my main argument is that when the move is made from recognising particular differences to celebrating or affirming these differences, defending substantive conceptions of equality and rights is possible and can be promoted within a broadly Kantian framework. This defence, though, must fully acknowledge that the Nietzschean themes, also found within the DRM, are incommensurable with Kantian ethical commitments, but that this philosophical tension and conflict provides a dynamic and radical platform for developing egalitarian theory and practice.

It is important, however, first to highlight that recommending the 'celebration of difference' can be liberal in orientation, as well as Kantian. As explored in Chapters Three and Four, this recommendation recognises the moral significance of the distinction between persons, and the groups to which they belong, based on the premise that individual agents have particular life-plans and cultural backgrounds that matter to them and should be respected. Therefore, the arguments presented here are, partly at least, an attempt to reclaim some of the liberal, as well as Kantian, ground from the value relativist trends in postmodern thought, by articulating the liberalism found in the injunction that we should celebrate differences. Nevertheless, I also argue that the philosophical underpinnings of this politics of recognition found in the DRM and other social movements are right to acknowledge the limitations of this liberal and Kantian project. Using the postmodern critique, many within social movements have radically challenged welfare states, which promote social equality as a universal value, as this promotion over-generalises about the needs of groups defined as 'vulnerable' and 'disadvantaged', thereby reinforcing their social exclusion (for example, see Hughes and Lewis, 1998; Heredia, 2007; Ikaheimo, 2009). Consequently, universal liberal categories of rights and equality are often imposed on individuals and group members without sufficiently acknowledging the differences between them. For my part, and as defended in this chapter, a Nietzschean perspective to personal empowerment rejects universally imposed rules, and so counters these over-generalising tendencies, but is a perspective that must also be hedged by the universal moral injunction that differences should be celebrated. My main contention is that this latter injunction makes better sense of the former rejection, but only assuming the expectation that persons benefit from multi-dimensional relational experiences with radically different others as a result – that is, relationships characterised by reciprocation (see also Smith, 2001a, 2002a, 2002b, and Chapters Three, Four and Five here). I will now explore further how this principle of reciprocity, while promoting particularism, can also be coherently promoted as a universal value – that is, as a valued state of affairs that is promotable across and between various cultures and individual life experiences.

In summary, then, the argument so far recommending a celebration of difference implies at least three sorts of appeal. First, a very liberal and Kantian appeal to a universal moral category is permitted, one that promotes and compares goods where diversity is seen as *better than* sameness. Consequently, the celebration enjoins different individuals and groups not only to assert their own particularised differences, but also to promote the equal capacity or right of other individuals and groups to assert their differences too. Second, a more thoroughgoing Nietzschean appeal to particularism is also allowed, but one where promoting a range of incommensurable or incomparable differences is regarded as a morally preferable state of affairs to promoting goods that are always uniform and comparable, and/or strictly prioritised – that is, given the value of reciprocity, anticipating a mutually enriching encounter between persons and groups who are incomparably different. Third, the principle of reciprocity therefore operates as an overarching shared value across a plural society, providing a wider justification for promoting radically diverse forms of life, many being incommensurable. Consequently, it is a principle that establishes moral parameters concerning the definition and content of healthy social relations, across which a range of incommensurable values can be legitimately promoted. I will now provide a brief outline of the definition and content of reciprocal social relations, as these relate to the promotion of value incommensurability and radically diverse forms of life – and as a prelude to the themes explored in the final chapter.

I have argued elsewhere that, through individual or social forms, mutual acts of giving and receiving between persons, characterising reciprocal relations, are not solely defined by the production of valuable 'objects' that can then be used by others (Smith, 2001a, 2002a, 2002b; see also Chapters One, Three and Four here). Certainly, central to establishing reciprocal relations is acknowledging the value of 'things produced' for mutual exchange. However, this value cannot, I believe, be assessed independently from what I have called the ontological stance of givers and receivers. In other words, it is how people *are* with others – not just what they produce *for* others – that defines and shapes reciprocal relations. For example, if a person defines herself, or is defined by others, as having little or nothing to contribute in mutual exchanges, as is often the case with disabled people, then possibilities of both acknowledging and developing reciprocal relations are diminished, whereas if non-disabled people are open to receiving a wider variety of benefits from what disabled people have to offer, reciprocal exchange is more likely. This is so even if the giver, a disabled person, has the same to offer in both contexts. How, though, does this understanding of reciprocity relate to the arguments presented so far?

First, it can be seen how establishing reciprocal relations in large part relies on fostering an attitude of mutual self-worth derived from a positive assessment of what the first person can offer to the other, and what the other can contribute for the benefit of the first person. Consequently, there is a recognised equal status between persons based on these assumptions of mutuality and exchange. Second, this recognition of equal status allows for differences between individuals to be celebrated, anticipating the possibilities of increased reciprocity, even if existing social relations might unjustly reinforce the correlation between particular differences and social disadvantage. This is based on the assumption that the presence of difference provides for a wider variety of exchanges to take place, across economic, political and cultural domains, as well as through emotional exchanges in more intimate or personal relationships (again, see Chapter Two for further exploration of these and related issues). Third, the adjacent claim is that this multilayered understanding of reciprocity provides normative justification for the injunction that we should celebrate differences, and political and sociological space for disempowered groups to assert their identity on an equal basis to others, against more dominant and oppressive constructions of identity. More specifically, in relation to the DRM, it allows a full-blooded assertion of disabled people's rights to equality and inclusion, reflecting the universalism and moral objectivism of Kantian ethics, at the same time promoting a robust affirmation of individual particularised identity for disabled people, reflecting the subjectivism of Nietzsche.

With these latter points in mind in particular, I turn to the final chapter, where I argue that establishing these kinds of reciprocal relations accommodates a philosophically coherent and politically plausible response to the conflicts between the values of equality and diversity when promoting radical causes. This fully recognises that there is no rational or complete 'answer' to the various paradoxes of human experience and agency, the unpredictable and nuanced ways in which individuals become attached to valued objects, and the subsequent development and shaping of their identities. I conclude, following the Nietzschean and postmodern themes, and the continental tradition more generally, that we must accept that there are unfathomable aspects of human experience that cannot be explained via reason or moral theory. But I also contend, following the Kantian and universalist themes, and the Anglo-American analytical tradition more generally, that this acceptance permits a universal acknowledgement and celebration of incommensurable forms of life – anticipating that human beings are often enriched by their surprising encounters with others who are radically different.

Notes

[1] See also my other arguments in Chapter Five and how, for example, self-reported liberation from dominant norms is not peculiar to disabled people, but is found in other oppressed and marginalised groups too.

[2] See also my critique of liberal egalitarian teleology in Chapter Four promoting well-being as an end, and Nietzsche's critique of well-being promoted as an ultimate human goal in, for example, Nietzsche (1975a, pp 135-6) and Chapters Four and Five here.

[3] An example of this principle being reflected in policy and practice is found in direct payments, where money is given to disabled people to buy in their own care, as distinct from the provision of services organised by a 'care manager', usually a social worker; see also Giddens (1998) and Gray (2001) for other explorations of active agent-based conceptions of citizenship and the implications for policy and practice.

[4] It is pertinent to note that there is considerable debate within the DRM as to whether a disabled person should be referred to as a 'disabled person' or a 'person with a disability'. Mostly, the preference in the UK is for the term 'disabled person', on the grounds that it unashamedly recognises that a person has an identity associated with disablement – personhood, in other words, cannot be abstracted from the specific particularised experience of disability. By contrast, welfare professionals such as social workers, and some in the DRM (most notably from the US), often use the term 'person with a disability' – based on a more generalised and universal assumption that a person with a disability, like all persons with or without disabilities, is a person first who has an impairment second. As can be seen from the arguments presented here, the latter use broadly reflects universal Kantian ethics, which emphasises the universal abstract character of personhood, while the former reflects Nietzschean particularism, which emphasises the highly subjective and non-universal character of individual human experience. My main claim is that recognising these two uses as conflicting goes a long way to explaining these and similar conflicts

within the DRM, and also the conflicts between the DRM and the aspirations of welfare practitioners (see also Chapter One for further development of these and related themes).

[5] From this Nietzschean perspective, I argued in Chapter Two that particular valued attachments are made via a background of random and accidental events – that is, events without intrinsic meaning and purpose – and that these attachments in turn largely *create* meaning, mattering deeply to specific persons. I also argued that because these attachments matter to all persons, this leads paradoxically to universal reasons for valuing these attachments.

[6] It is the case that much of the postmodern anti-universalist critique of liberalism, and western philosophy and morality more generally, is anti-essentialist for similar reasons. It is also a critique found in the work, among many others, of Butler (1990), Saraga (1998) and Foucault (2001), and explored further in Chapter One.

[7] From the previous exploration, it can be seen that, by implication, Kant too is an anti-essentialist, in that he resists the reductionism of the medical model, which defines disabled people as essentially deficient. Kant and Kantians focus instead on the abstracted person as chooser, that is, separate from her phenomenal attributes of impairment (also see note 4). Kant's anti-essentialism, however, does not extend to the anti-universalism and particularism of Nietzsche, given Kant's argument for universal moral principles founded on recognising persons as choosers (again, see Chapter One for further exploration of these and related issues).

[8] See also Nietzsche's similar critique of charity (Nietzsche, 1975a, pp 98-9) and Chapter Four here.

[9] Again, see Saraga (1998), and other postmodern and post-structuralist critiques, for an exploration of how these types of oppressive dualities are experienced by minority groups generally.

[10] The highly moot question remains as to whether this strategy for interpreting Nietzsche makes his philosophy less profound (Devigne, 1999).

[11] See also Thompson (2008) for an interesting defence of what he calls existentialist ethics being applied to professional social work practice, which includes an examination of Nietzsche.

SEVEN

Paradox and the limits of reason

Introduction

A paradox is a proposition that may be empirical, philosophical or normative in character and appears to be based on uncontroversial assumptions and reasoning, but is also seemingly contradictory, so exposing possible problems when using conventional rules of logic and/or scientific observation (Blackburn, 1996, p 276; Palmquist, 2000, pp 64-102). Before exploring specific examples, I will outline two broad philosophical responses to paradox relevant to the wider themes of the book. First, paradox masks a mistake in reasoning and/or scientific investigation, and so is solvable by a clearer and more correct application of logic and empirical investigation. Second, a paradox, if unsolvable after logical and scientific applications are exhausted, suggests insights beyond reason's and science's explanatory scope, so indicating that truth or 'truths' relate in complex and problematic ways to reasoning, human observation and experience.

At the risk of over-simplification, the first response to paradox in the main tends to reflect the view of analytical philosophy. Within this tradition, conceptual analysis is central to philosophical progress, where the underlying logical structure of language and meaning is seen as representing or 'modelling' the empirical world we observe and experience (Russell, 1971; Honderich, 1995, pp 28-30; Blackburn, 1996, pp 14-15).[1] Consequently, claims regarding the suggestive character of paradox appear at best over-inflated. Instead, the Aristotelian law of non-contradiction and non-identity is invoked, initially at least, roughly stating that meaning is gained from making clear and unambiguous distinctions between things, and so avoiding contradiction or what would be understood as nonsense. Therefore, the response from the analytical tradition to a contradiction within a paradox is to solve it – exposing flaws in premises, highlighting equivocations and invalid steps in argument, making more appropriate empirical distinctions, and so on. The answer to paradox is therefore found within the process of logical reasoning and/or scientific investigation itself, contributing to the clarity of what exactly is being communicated, and subsequent descriptions of the world.

For example, Hillel Steiner, reflecting the analytical tradition in normative political philosophy, unravels what he calls the paradox of 'original or universal self-ownership' – if we own ourselves, we must also own the products of our labour, including the products of procreation; but it is the case that we are all procreated by our parents and so we cannot own ourselves, including our procreated labour (Steiner, 1994, pp 240-8). Steiner tries to solve this normative paradox using analytical argument, establishing self-ownership and equal rights to self-ownership, as a primary political value, acquired in adulthood, but excluded for children. The logical structure of the paradox is supposedly revealed and clearly described through analytical inspection, categorising and defining precisely who can hold rights to self-ownership and the extent to which parents can have ownership over their children – which, for Steiner, given the value of self-ownership and equal and universal rights to self-ownership, is necessary for the normative defence of his position (Steiner, 1994, pp 240-2).

In contrast, those from what might be sometimes misleadingly termed the non-analytical tradition (see next section), argue that the efficacy of paradox demonstrates the limits of conventional reason and analytical logic, especially perhaps when applied to empirical observations. For example, take Sorites' paradox – one grain of sand is not a heap, and therefore every additional grain of sand to any number of grains that are also not a heap can never result in a heap of sand, as what is added to is just as much not a heap as the one additional grain of sand. For many contemporary philosophers, this paradox is unsolvable, reflecting the inevitable vagueness of language, and the inadequacies of conventional logic in explaining the empirical world. While classic logical argument relies on predicates of either truth or falsehood, what is recommended here instead is the use of 'fuzzy logic' – establishing degrees or shades of truth, and reflecting the vagueness of reason and logic when understanding the world we inhabit (Blackburn, 1996, pp 151 and 357). Moreover, it is possible to take a further step away from the analytical tradition, and assert that the Aristotelian law of non-identity and non-contradiction does not, in any event, supply meanings that are profound, as understandings and insights about the world are gained by uniting or synthesising what has been mistakenly analysed as distinct or even opposite (see also Palmquist, 2000, pp 64-102). The proper response to paradox is to accept it as an intractable contradiction, so suggesting a profundity or insight that cannot be explained by reason and/or science. This is reflected in, for example, many artistic or poetic creations that often combine opposites, and/or distort what is 'real' and distinct about objects, as a way of suggesting meaning beyond what can be conventionally explained, expressed or portrayed.[2] Many religious beliefs also combine distinct objects to articulate doctrine, found in, for example, the orthodox Christian belief that the infinite has become its opposite, the finite, in the person of Jesus Christ – a doctrine that for Christians is mysterious and unexplainable via reason, but suggestive of profound empirical and normative truths about the character of human beings and their relationship with the world and their Creator (also see G.A. Cohen's exploration of how the finite and infinite relate in the Judea-Christian tradition more generally, in Cohen, 2000, pp 80-4).

Following these and related themes, philosophers have also often explored how the activity of philosophy itself mistakenly attempts to explain important values, by relating these values to the infinite and/or 'transcendent'.[3] For example, as explored throughout the book, existentialism – alongside other strands of contemporary continental philosophy – has explicitly rejected the analytical assumption that objective 'truth' and 'meaning' is found in underlying logical structures, reasoning or scientific discovery (also see Warnock, 1970; Honderich, 1995, pp 161-3; West, 1996, pp 117-53; and certain interpretations of Ludwig Wittgenstein's work in Shields, 1997; Clack, 1999; Tanesini, 2004, pp 53-8).[4] According to existentialists, distinctions only occur because of subjective human analysis. Existence on its own, so to speak, without our analysis, has no distinctions, categorical divisions or essential meaning, and so loses, to quote Jean-Paul Sartre '... its harmless appearance as an abstract category ... the diversity of things, their individuality, [being] only an appearance, and veneer' (Sartre, 1980, p 183). Therefore, 'truth' and 'meaning', instead of being found in the distinctions made by logic and science, are created by the choices human beings make in their particularised commitments to specific valued and named objects that are classified accordingly, but without essential meaning (see also Chapter Two for further exploration of these and related issues). One of existentialism's principle paradoxes, derived from this understanding, is that we have no choice but to choose in a world with no essential value or meaning. The point here is that this paradox of freedom is not presented by existentialists as an empirical and/or normative puzzle, solvable through reason and analytical argument, where the 'truth' of human existence and normative social relations is revealed through underlying logical structures and precise definitional categories. Rather, human action and experience has a deeply perplexing empirical and normative ontology. 'Being free' is integral to the human condition, but paradoxically this human condition is unavoidable and burdensome. Free acts are therefore normatively opaque, as well as indescribable and indefinable, given that being free has no essence or logical necessity underpinning it, as it is a brute, unanalysable fact of existence integral to the condition of 'being human'. In other words, although we exist *as* free creatures – without the need for establishing proceeding causes and motives to explain human action – living in this condition, we are limited by freedom itself, given that we are not free to stop being free. According to Sartre:

> If the fundamental condition of the act is freedom, we must attempt to describe this freedom more precisely. But at the start we encounter a great difficulty. Ordinarily, to describe something is a process of making explicit by aiming at the structures of a particular essence. [But] freedom has no essence. It is not subject to logical necessity.... How then are we to describe an existence which perpetually makes itself and which refuses to be confined in a definition?... [M]y freedom is perpetually in question in my being; it is not a quality added on or a *property* of my nature. It is very exactly the stuff of my being ... I am condemned to exist forever beyond my essence, beyond the causes and motives of my act. I am condemned to be free. This means that no limits to my freedom can be found except freedom itself or, if you prefer, that we are not free to cease being free. (Sartre, 1995, pp 438-9; emphasis in original)

What, then, of the arguments defended here, given these very different responses to empirical, philosophical and normative paradoxes? My main claim in this final chapter is that the conflict between the values of equality and diversity reflect, at least in part, four normative paradoxes in social relations that have been outlined and explored throughout the book. These paradoxes expose normative contradictions or tensions in the way individuals and group members value particular 'objects', based on what I believe are plausible empirical assumptions about the identity of these individuals and group members, and the specific manner in which persons relate to each other in any given community. I also argue that these contradictions and tensions are especially apparent in those societies that allow the equal right to choose and/or pursue diverse objects of value, making them especially apparent in liberal communities. What, then, are these four normative paradoxes? And, to what extent is it possible to solve and unravel them, if at all?

I begin by outlining the four paradoxes below:

1. The more it is objectively and universally asserted that heterogeneity and diversity is better than sameness and monolithic uniformity when persons, as agents, choose their lives – so comparing the value of these 'states of affairs' – the more a highly subjectivist and anti-universal view of human agency and particularised commitment is asserted, thus eliminating, or at least diminishing, the capacity to compare radically different lives led in this community (see especially Chapters One and Two).
2. The more attempts there are to imagine the life of 'the other' and empathically recognise the detrimental consequences of being disadvantaged, the more likely it is that some forms of inequality will be reinforced through various hierarchical misunderstandings between the 'better-off' and the 'worst-off'; but the fewer the attempts made to imagine the life of the other and empathically engage with the lives of 'the disadvantaged', the less likely it is that egalitarian values will be promoted rectifying these disadvantages (see especially Chapters Three and Four).
3. The more an individual or group possesses 'outsider status', the more likely it is that this will lead to social exclusion and the undermining of opportunity, as the range of potential lives that might be led by that individual or group is reduced; but the more excluded these individuals and groups are, the more possible it is in principle not to conform to dominant norms and practices, where positive subjective affirmations of particularised identities concerning the actual lives led by individuals who belong to these groups are asserted (see especially Chapters Five and Six).
4. The more commonality, connectedness and closer proximity there is between individuals and groups, the more aware these individuals and groups become of the differences that exist between them; but the more these differences are acknowledged, the more possibilities there are both for entrenched divisions as differences are highlighted, and for long-lasting commonality and

connectedness, as individuals and groups living in close proximity affirm the increased possibility of sharing and learning from others precisely because of these differences (to be explored further in this chapter).

Before I examine the fourth paradox in more detail, I will outline how, despite my demarcation earlier, the divide between analytical and so-called non-analytical philosophy is, in some ways at least, exaggerated – which in turn has implications for my second question concerning the extent to which, if at all, these paradoxes can be solved or unravelled.

The exaggerated divide between analytical and continental philosophy

The claim is often made that the divide between analytical and non-analytical/ continental philosophy outlined earlier is exaggerated and artificial. For example, the label non-analytical, while useful in stressing the difference between analytical philosophers and other philosophical traditions, is misleading if it implies that continental philosophers do not engage in detailed argument and analysis, which, of course, they frequently do (see arguments later). However, the counter-claim is that this divide, although in some ways exaggerated, still marks a clear separation between radically different views regarding the efficacy of philosophical, scientific and normative understanding (as explored previously). Reflecting the first view, David West sees Immanuel Kant as a pivotal thinker, so straddling both traditions (West, 1996, pp 16-27). Reflecting the second, many in the continental tradition see Kant as excessively rationalist and analytical, failing to appreciate the non-rational, instinctive or, latterly, the socially constructed character of human experience (West, 1996, pp 24-34). For example, in contemporary social philosophy, Derrida and Foucault have radically decentred what is regarded as the overly abstract and universal Kantian 'subject', instead focusing on the contingencies of human subjective experience, and the arbitrary exercise of power in social relations (Honderich, 1995, pp 160-3; West, 1996, pp 154-88; see also existentialists such as Nietzsche, for example, as explored in Chapters Two and Six, and my arguments later in this chapter).

While I have some sympathy with the latter claims, I explore the possibility of more fruitful interchanges between these two philosophical traditions, and how these may then affect the responses to those paradoxes outlined previously. Certainly, both traditions in their extreme forms respond to the problem of paradox very differently, but I will argue that the assumptions entailed, when using paradox to provide philosophical insights, are often similar, revealing significant and important overlaps between them. For example, Kant famously delineated what he identified as important paradoxes or 'antinomies', concerning the acquisition and limits of human knowledge and reason. He explored how humans can know, via *a priori* reason (reason that does not refer to experience), that things are unknowable 'in themselves', because we are limited in what we know by our experiences of them (Kant, 1993). Paradoxically, then, we can know about the limits of our knowledge of things without referring to our experiences, that is, via *a priori* reason, but only because we understand *via reason* that we know our knowledge of these things is mediated through our experiences. The point for Kant is that the goal of reason is to seek the 'unconditionally necessary' – in other words, to seek knowledge that does not depend on subjective experience, personal interest or perspective, such as universal moral laws, for example – while recognising that rational introspection also reveals that this kind of necessity is ultimately unachievable. The best that reason can achieve, therefore, is to find a 'concept' – a term by which universal understanding is maintained, reflecting those analytical distinctions outlined previously – that is paradoxically compatible with this assumption. Consequently, and reflecting the conclusions of the continental tradition, Kant states that:

> [The] satisfaction of reason is only further and further postponed by the continual enquiry after the condition. Reason, therefore, restlessly seeks the unconditionally necessary and sees itself compelled to assume this without having any means of making such necessity conceivable; reason is happy enough if only it can find a concept which is compatible with this assumption.... And so even though we do not indeed grasp the practical unconditioned necessity of the moral imperative, we do nevertheless grasp its inconceivability. This is all that can be fairly asked of a philosophy which strives in its principles to reach the very limits of human reason. (Kant, 1993, p 63)

Nevertheless, for Kant, despite these limits, there is a lot reason can achieve as a guide to moral action and more abstract philosophical understanding, and so in this way, and others, he parts company with many continental thinkers. As already highlighted, philosophers from existentialists such as Kierkegaard, Nietzsche and Sartre, to later poststructuralists and/or postmodernists such as Foucault and Derrida, all cast doubt, not only on reason's explanatory scope, as does Kant, but also on its universal credentials in guiding human action and explanation (see also Copleston, 1994, pp 352-442; West, 1996, pp 117-53; Calder, 2005). For example, Kierkegaard, being commonly regarded as the founder of existentialism, is scathing of the claim that exercising reason is universally consistent with living an authentically faithful religious life. He argues that exercising faith is qualitatively different from conforming to reason, natural inclinations or even morality, exhibited in Abraham's willingness to sacrifice his son Isaac because the God he has faith in commanded it – even though this action is contrary to reason, to the natural inclination to protect ones offspring, and even to divinely revealed morality that forbids murder (Kierkegaard, 1994, pp 3-108). Exercising faith is therefore 'taking a leap' beyond, and possibly contrary to, reason, natural inclinations and morality, but is for Kierkegaard the foundation for living an authentic religious life of unpredictability, risk and mystery (see also West, 1996, pp 117-53).[5]

On a different tack, but partly following Nietzsche (and explored in Chapters Two, Four and Six) contemporary poststructuralists and postmodernists claim that science and reason presents itself as 'objective' and 'universal' and supposedly neutral and non-political, but in so doing, disguises how science and reason is used to oppress and impose world views on the powerless and dispossessed. Foucault, for example, sees medical experts manipulating science and reason who, in the modern era, control discourses and practices around mental illness and other forms of bodily and cognitive 'dysfunction' (for example, see Foucault, 2001; Faubion, 2003). While pre-modern religious perspectives understand these conditions as caused by satanic possession and sin, modern descriptions identify causes in rational and scientific terms. The point for Foucault is that, in either case, the languages or discourses describing these conditions have no essential or objective meaning, as the scientific rationalists assert; rather, they are controlled by group members and vested interests, mainly professional men who have power over the way knowledge and understanding is produced and the various social practices that are subsequently recommended (see also Saraga, 1998; Faubion, 2003).

However, again, despite these antagonisms between analytical and continental perspectives concerning the precise role reason and science plays in producing knowledge and understanding, there are also, I believe, important overlaps between them. For example, both traditions often use reason to say something substantial about the human condition, and the physical and social worlds human beings inhabit. This 'saying', though, leads to a notorious circularity in the continental strategy, given that reason is used to *reveal* that reason imposes a particular world view. Consequently, although continental philosophers often do not pay the same kind of attention to classical logical syntax and structure as advocates of the analytical tradition, certainly other forms of reason are used to communicate or persuade. For example, Nietzsche, while attacking philosophical reflection as prejudicial assertion, also uses reasoned argument as a way of articulating his position. In *Beyond good and evil*, he states:

> Most of a philosopher's conscious thinking is secretly directed and compelled into definite channels by his instincts. Behind all logic too and its apparent autonomy stands evaluations, in plainer terms physiological demands for the preservation of a certain species of life … for the most part [philosophers] are no better than cunning pleaders for their prejudices, which they baptise 'truths'. (Nietzsche, 1975a, pp 17–18)[6]

Therefore, for Nietzsche at least, philosophical reflection and logic does not reveal the underlying essential structure of 'truth' and 'meaning' – as claimed by many in the analytical tradition – but is a means of imposing prejudicial evaluations on others. Yet, to defend his position, a rational argument is presented, intending to reveal that so-called 'essential truths' have no universal content, derived from assumptions concerning what most philosophers are really doing, namely asserting their prejudices, despite their pretensions to the contrary. This defence produces, in other words, a Nietzschean paradox when considering philosophical pursuit, namely that 'truth' is never fixed or permanent, and so any philosopher claiming otherwise is always telling and, even living, a lie – with the paradox being that the permanence and fixedness of 'never' and 'always' underlies Nietzsche's own philosophical 'truth claim' that truth is *not* permanent or fixed.[7] One typically analytical response to this Nietzschean paradox is to argue that Nietzsche is inconsistent and incomprehensible, and so simply does not make sense. The paradox, therefore, has no profundity, instead revealing the *non*sense of Nietzsche's position. Reflecting the continental tradition, I would counter that this response is too quick, missing, among other things, the way insights are often presented ironically by Nietzsche – so the Aristotelian law of non-contradiction, being the most obvious route to truth, is indeed reflected in Nietzsche's own argument, but one he ironically rejects according to his own logically defended position. Consequently, the 'apparent autonomy' to logic, which, according to Nietzsche, philosophers both assume and use to their advantage, reveals the profundity and perplexity of the claim that universal truth claims *merely* reflect evaluative prejudice. So, if all truth claims are exposed to this judgement, this would, initially at least, include the claim that there are no truth claims. In other words, and often despite himself, Nietzsche, like Kant, is exposing the limits of logic and reasoning, while not necessarily rejecting entirely the methods that logic and reasoning use when communicating meaning. Certainly, more full-blooded continental philosophers would state that this reading of Nietzsche's perspectivism, as it is sometimes called, is itself deceptive. It might be said, therefore, that logical consistency is manifested via social networks of power, where specific *forms* of consistency are privileged over others, given that particular language and discourses dominate in communities (for example, see Foucault, 2001, referred to earlier). However, my claim here is that while the latter may occur as a sociological phenomena, this does not necessarily imply that all autonomous laws of logic and reasoning should be abandoned – as the latter posture ironically starts looking like, to use Kantian language, a necessary condition approaching a universal truth. Other more subtle and nuanced strategies are also available, for example, to perspicuously observe how reason and logic is used in different social and political contexts, thus articulating more fully what can be legitimately said, or not said, about these uses.

I will now explore a Wittgensteinian-type distinction between 'saying' and 'showing' that I believe is helpful in understanding further the latter point. Simply put, saying is a verbal attempt at describing underlying logical and empirical characteristics *of* the world, and so is a descriptive statement pertaining to it, whereas showing is an unanalysed demonstration of a person's or group's place *in* the world, revealed by particular human actions or gestures (Kenny, 1983, pp 45-7; Grayling, 1996, pp 47-9; Wittgenstein, 2000a, 2000b; Tanesini, 2004, pp 53-88). Reflecting the analytical tradition, I have argued that a proper view of paradox, in some significant ways, relies on the Kantian-type assertion that reason and logic is essential for defining the parameters of understanding – that is, defining from the *inside* of reason outwards what is meaningful. Consequently, understanding starts from what sense we can say meaningfully and rationally, with reason remaining silent when we have reached the limits of language and logic, beyond which is entirely speculative or just plain nonsense. Nevertheless, reflecting more the continental tradition, I have also argued that it is precisely within this latter context that a paradox is produced – as on the borders of sense and nonsense there can be gestures towards deeper but more opaque insights concerning the human condition and human observations. For many Wittgensteinians, attempts at gesturing toward these opaque 'truths' – beyond the explanatory scope of logic and reasoning – is precisely the problem of philosophy and should be resisted (for example, see Tanesini, 2004, pp 53-88). However, other Wittgensteinian interpretations would argue that his philosophical analysis focuses on the limits of logic and language, but not on the limits of what *life* can offer in its opaqueness, mystery and wonder (for example, see Shields, 1997; Clack, 1999; and, more ambivalently perhaps, Russell, 1971).[8] I will now explore further how the implications of these latter interpretations of Wittgenstein can be used to build a bridge between the existentialists and value incommensurabilists defended throughout the book.

A bridge not too far between existentialists and value incommensurabilists

Mindful of the various themes outlined in the proceeding section and relating these to the existentialist themes explored so far, Jean-Paul Sartre, representing the continental tradition, claims that there are two types of description. There are those that describe essences – highlighting the common descriptions between two phenomena, providing distinguishing information about the external world; and those that describe 'the existent itself in its particularity' – having no essential commonality with other objects (Sartre, 1995, p 438). According to Sartre, and as already highlighted, describing freedom essentially is impossible, thereby revealing the limits of reason and logic in understanding the condition of freedom. However, recognising this impossibility also reveals the common characteristic of *my* being human, and that others like me are human too, but also part of my 'external world'. Consequently, even though freedom is indefinable and unnamable in essence, it is not necessarily indescribable in existence, given this description of what is common to the human condition (Sartre, 1995, p 438). In *Being and nothingness*, for example, Sartre makes fine conceptual distinctions in its 600-plus pages, in part to define 'more precisely' what freedom is (Sartre, 1995, p 438). During this endeavour, he identifies different types of philosophy, many of which he wants to distance himself from, to reveal his existentialist non-essentialist understanding as the most insightful description of the human condition.

I will now explore how other theorists, very much associated with analytical liberal political philosophy, have also explored the inability of reason and logic to explain everything, as well as its ability to explain *some* things concerning the character of freedom. Mainstream liberal thinkers such as Isaiah Berlin, Joseph Raz, William Galston and Elizabeth Anderson, and other value incommensurabilists cited in Chapter Two and defended here, explicitly reject the assumption that reason can provide a complete account of value as a harmonious or coherent whole or 'ideal'. As with Sartre, Nietzsche and Wittgenstein, their arguments consistently rally against any such claims for reason, and, in their defence of liberalism as they see it, promote the notion that individual choice operates both within and outside of reason's confines. The main claim is that many forms of rational calculation mistakenly pursue completeness and wholeness as an ideal, and risk producing 'answers' that falsely reconcile all human ends – so making redundant the purpose of freedom to choose from a wide range of conflicting values. For example, Berlin asserts that there is:

> ... no warrant for assuming or supposing (or even understanding what would be meant by saying) that all good things, or all bad things for that matter, are reconcilable with each other.... Indeed, it is because this is their situation that men place such immense value upon the freedom to choose; for if they had assurance that in some perfect state, realisable by men on earth, no ends pursued by them would ever be in conflict, the necessity and agony of choice would disappear, and with it the central importance of the freedom to choose. (Berlin, 1969, p 168)

Berlin's reference to the 'necessity and agony of choice' has a distinctly existentialist, as well as liberal, flavour to it – the implication being that choice is a burden carried by humans but, paradoxically, *must* be endured if choice, quite rightly for Berlin and the existentialists, is properly valued (see also Ferrel's interpretation of Berlin, in Ferrel, 2008). Developing these themes, and Berlin's claims that values are incommensurable, Raz also asserts that:

> Where the considerations for and against two alternatives are incommensurate, reason is indeterminate. It provides no better case for one alternative than for the other. Since it follows that there is no reason to shun one of the alternatives in favour of the other, we are in a sense free to choose which course to follow. That sense of freedom is special, and may be misleading.... Incomparability does not ensure equality of merit or demerit. It does not mean indifference. It marks the inability of reason to guide our action, not the insignificance of our choice. (Raz, 1988, pp 333-4)

Freedom of choice, in other words, for these liberals and existentialists, occupies a space reason cannot fill, given that without a rational calculator as a guide to action, humans have to make decisions 'on their own' – that is, with the associated burdens of responsibility, blame or praise placed on the shoulders of the chooser, rather than on what would otherwise merely be a logical process of rational calculation.[9] Consequently, not only must we accept the paradox of having no choice but to choose, but also that to choose is to make free decisions that are beyond reason – a kind of leap in the dark, or at least a leap into the unknown and not yet realised. To put it more succinctly, and using Sartre's abstract turn of phrase, 'human reality is free to the exact extent that it has to be its own nothingness' (Sartre, 1995, p 453). So, where does this bridge between existentialist and liberal political philosophy lead us regarding the conflict between the values of equality and diversity explored throughout this book, and the fourth paradox outlined earlier? What sort of community is suggested as a result? And how do we understand the relationships between liberal social values, and between those individuals and group members living in a liberal community?

Equality, diversity and incommensurable values

Following the arguments of Berlin and Raz, and by implication those of Sartre, Nietzsche and other existentialists, diverse attachments and the resulting plurality and incommensurability of goods are a consequence of a person being free to choose and create for herself her own life, beyond the bounds of rational explanation and justification. However, I will now argue that this produces various philosophical and political tensions and conflicts that are reflected in the fourth paradox outlined earlier; that is, the more commonality, connectedness and closer proximity there is between individuals and group members, the more aware these individuals and group members become of the differences that exist between them. The more these differences are acknowledged, however, the more possibilities there are both for entrenched division as differences are highlighted, and for long-lasting commonality and connectedness, as persons living in close proximity affirm the increased possibility of sharing and learning from others precisely because of these differences.

First, I assert a speculative, but I think plausible, assumption that searching for sameness and commonality is in large part derived from the human motivation to identify with others, and so belong in relationship *with* others. This assumption is, I believe, deeply rooted in equality principles, however these are conceived, where the similarities between persons are emphasised, which then provides grounds for shared normative commitments – promoting, for example, universal liberal values such as equal rights, equal opportunities, equal freedoms and so on (see also Chapter One for further exploration of these and related issues). Second, I contend that this motivation for belonging helps the internal subjective character of a person to connect with the outside objective world – that is, a world that is outside of 'me' (*my* being a separated human being) – and with 'others' who are like me, but who are also exterior *to* me, ie both connected *with* others and separated *from* others.[10] My further claim is that without this second assumption regarding the maintenance of particularised identity – and the paradoxical assertion that subjective identity is both separate *to* and connected *with* the outside world – the world we inhabit would either seem overwhelmingly different, with the extreme otherness of the outside world being wholly alienating to asserting subjective identities with any measure of confidence; or it would seem overwhelming similar, and so emasculate any particularised traces of these identities that become subsumed within the outside world. Therefore, my third contention is that the outside world is a threat to particularised identity if, in our proximity to others, we do not become especially aware of our differences, while also maintaining a common connection with those who, like you, are recognised too *as* different. Consequently, experiencing a long-lasting commonality and connectedness within liberal communities – most particularly when individuals and group members are living in close proximity – will inevitably, and quite rightly, expose the differences that exist between persons but as a healthy aspect of maintaining, paradoxically, *both* one's separateness and connection with others.

To be sure, during this process various political problems often arise, as these differences can become very entrenched as well as exposed, putting considerable strain on relationships, as any commonality and identification with 'the other' risks breaking down. In establishing principles of social justice, for example, Philippe Van Parijs observes how the presence of divergent conceptions of the good can undermine reasons for redistributing resources from the better-off to the worst-off, as there is less common understanding of what is 'normally' aspired to – with this lack of commonality being further reinforced as a result of more minimal redistribution (Van Parijs, 1995, pp 58-88; also see Dwyer, 2002). However, I would argue that this outcome, while possible, is neither philosophically nor politically inevitable, and, in any event, is not the only response to these political problems of radical diversity and other related difficulties. The argument throughout this book has been that a heightened awareness of the differences between persons, as they live in close proximity, means that liberal communities seeking commonality between different individuals and group members also produce arenas for a deepened connectedness *and* separateness between them. Reflecting Parekh's defence of multiculturalism, my central philosophical claim, then, is that: 'Similarities and differences do not passively co-exist but interpenetrate, and [so] neither is ontologically prior or morally more important' (Parekh, 2000, p 239). As a result, political and social relations can be enriched by specific encounters with similarities and difference. Whether these encounters are through dialogue and public discourse, or through cultural activities (such as art, music, food, dress, sport, social customs and so on) or more emotional and physical encounters with others in intimate close relationships, they all, in turn, have the potential to positively shape and develop the different 'forms of life' that occur in such communities. Following this understanding, I have argued that the values associated with equality and diversity are therefore best viewed as incommensurable, but also inseparable – with many normative principles reflecting each value seen as neither better than, worse than, equal to, nor on a par with each other (see also Raz, 1988, pp 321-368; and Chapters One and Two here).

To summarise, my main assertion is that it is possible to find a deeper connectedness with others precisely because deeper differences are more fully recognised. Therefore, I am against those who argue that identifying with others mainly involves recognising similarities between persons and group members (see Chapters Three and Four for further exploration of these and related issues). I also acknowledge the limits of liberal universalism when recognising these differences between persons and group members, while also accepting the universalism of celebrating these differences as related to promoting the diversity of values. According to Raz:

> [If] hope for the future depends on philosophical enlightenment it depends in no small measure on understanding the limits of universality, and the source and nature of diversity. It depends on reconciling belief in universality with a correct understanding of the real diversity of values. (Raz, 2001, p 3; see also Chapters One and Two here)

Hence, a non-particularised commitment to a universal good that encourages diversity is inseparable from highly particularised commitments to promoting a diversity of incomparable and incommensurable goods. From this understanding, the political community suggested here is therefore based on two philosophical viewpoints that seem to pull in opposite directions. One offers an objective view of value, based on an objectively valued outcome that judges diversity as being better than uniformity, and so comparing these states of affairs. The other asserts a highly subjectivist view of human identity being born from particular choices and social conditions, refusing to compare *as a matter of value* the different lives freely led in this community as being either better than, worse than, equal to, or on a par with another. Consequently, universalism and radical diversity are both promoted but without reducing one to the other, as the objectivity of value is manifested through the presence of diversity and the subjectivity of lives that are freely led is manifested through highly particularised social conditions. Again, to cite Raz: 'Instead of arguing that since values depend on society they cannot be objective, the reversal argument ... makes a more paradoxical claim: since values are objective, they cannot be independent of social conditions' (Raz, 2001, p 62; see also Appel, 1999; and Devigne, 1999 for further exploration of these and related issues).

It is important to also highlight that this paradoxical claim stands on its head Iris Marion Young's wider concern that 'if reasons seek to know the whole of reality, then, it must apprehend all the particular perspectives from their particular point of view' (Young, 1990, p 102). The problem for Young is that impartial universal reasoning cannot do this in principle, because it abstracts out of rational calculation, particularised interests (Young, 1990, p 102; see also Griffin, 1997). For my part, both universal and particularised viewpoints should be promoted, revealing the full character of Raz's paradox, where liberal political communities celebrate particularised difference by promoting the delimited universal value of diversity. I will now, in my last remarks, explore this final paradox further concerning the way persons recognise each other as both similar and different, and how this political process of 'recognition' relates to the normative principles of reciprocity and mutual exchange when living in these liberal communities.

Recognition and reciprocity in liberal egalitarian communities

In Chapters Three and Four, I explored the limits of empathic imagination and the emotions of sympathy or pity with the 'suffering other' to establish the important role that agency and freedom play in a person's life. I argued that another person's agent-based responses to her experiences may be very surprising and positive even if her experiences are similar to one's own, and/or these experiences are universally understood as 'bad' or 'disadvantageous'. This is not to claim that agency always produces unpredictability, or that it inevitably leads to what might be called positive constructive coping in difficult circumstances (Hoggett, 2001, p 43; see also Fraser, 1997, pp 234-5); rather, it provides the possibility at least of radically different and/or surprising life-enhancing subjective responses to what are described by *others* as bad experiences. For example, concerning disability, I argued in Chapters Five and Six that given these various agent-based responses, this means it is possible, in principle at least, for 'all aspects of one's identity [to] become a positive force in one's life only if embraced and accepted as such' (Raz, 2001, p 34; also see Bowring, 2000, pp 314-15; Levitas, 2001, pp 449-50).

From this understanding, I believe it is also possible to meet Hoggett's challenge of identifying a 'radical model of agency [that] … must illuminate how people break out of social systems … and endure the risk that any radical change in one's life brings – risk of loss of belonging, loss of friendships, and loss of identity' (Hoggett, 2001, p 51). So, in Chapters Three and Four, I argued that personal gains are had from not conforming to oppressive dominant norms and practices, which means that these losses can be compensated for, as individuals both connect with *and* separate out from the society to which they belong in ways that are liberating and life-enhancing – a dual process that I claim is often integral to a positive affirmation of personal identity, most especially when affirming those identities that are otherwise oppressed or marginalised. In addition, I argued that as free agents we not only have experiences but also respond to them in various and often surprising ways, which also means that the profundity of the second paradox outlined in this chapter is made apparent and revealed again in the fourth paradox explored here – that is, the more we connect with others, the more we are reminded that persons can never be one of the same, *even if* they share similar experiences. In other words, it might be again paradoxically stated that as a *result* of closeness, we are more acutely reminded of our 'permanent distance' and our need to distinguish from others.[11] My argument is that this maintenance of distance is integral not only to the preservation of identity, but also paradoxically to how we belong to a community that encourages persons to recognise each other as radically, and even often incomparably, different.

What I argue now, though, is that out of this latter paradox possibilities for learning from 'the other' are created, as the otherness, being born partly out of agency and establishing self-respect in creating particularised identities, leads to new perspectives and responses to life that can enrich and enlighten those who fully recognise and accept the value of another person's separateness and incomparable difference.[12] Here, the liberal community suggested by these possibilities is characterised by relating with persons who are separate and different but engaged in some kind of positive 'relational encounter' based on a respect for self and other. Moreover, persons in this type of community would be likely to support a principle of reciprocity, acknowledging that mutual exchanges occur between human beings who often lead incomparably different and sometimes conflicting lives (see also Chapters Two and Three for further exploration of these and related issues).[13]

Following the latter conclusion, I will now provide a brief philosophical account of John Rawls' liberalism, as Rawls also argues that the principle of reciprocity should be central to any notion of 'justice as fairness'. Rawls' main innovation was to base his theory of justice on a hypothetical agreement between free and equal persons who are self-interested, but where fair decision making is guaranteed, as these persons are placed in a position of ignorance, not knowing, among other things, their individual conceptions of the good (what they value), their talents and their position within society (for example, Rawls, 1973, pp 44-5, pp 60-1). He argues that from this 'original position' two main principles of justice would be agreed between these self-interested individuals – roughly, that there be maximum and equal basic liberties for all, and that inequalities are only justifiable if they benefit the worst-off. Basic liberties are those freedoms fundamental to liberal societies such as freedom of speech, movement, holding private property and so on, and, supplementing the second redistributive principle, the notion that positions and offices should be open to all, establishing the value of equal opportunity.

What is poignant here is that, according to Rawls, these justice principles express a commitment to reciprocity, given that the agreement recognises that mutual benefit between persons takes place in any just society through acts of cooperation and exchange. Particularly in his earlier work, the importance of contract is, in turn, based on a Kantian notion that there ought to be equal respect for persons, which for Rawls 'heightens the operation of the reciprocity principle' (Rawls, 1973, p 494). This is because the value of mutuality is derived from a human 'tendency to answer in kind', without which the claim from Rawls is that 'fruitful social cooperation [is made] fragile if not impossible' (Rawls, 1973, pp 494-5). His later work develops this analysis of reciprocity further, while recognising and promoting what he calls the fact of political pluralism, acknowledging that individuals commit to very different substantial conceptions of the good. For example, in *Justice as fairness: A re-statement*, Rawls argues that:

> Reciprocity is a moral idea situated between impartiality, which is altruistic, on the one side and mutual advantage on the other ... in

> view of the fact of political pluralism .... [a] political principle of
> justice ... should express a principle of reciprocity, since society is
> viewed as a fair system of cooperation from one generation to the
> next between fair and equal citizens, and since the political conception
> is to apply to the basic structure which regulates background justice.
> (Rawls, 2001, p 77)

At the risk of over-simplification, it is possible, therefore, to interpret Rawls'
understanding of reciprocity as a politically realistic and perhaps 'middle-way'
justice principle between the altruism promoted by, for example, many forms of
socialism, and the self-interest advocated by classical liberals. For Rawls, reciprocity
accommodates political pluralism and some level of economic inequality, while
also emphasising the importance of cooperating with others to mutually defend
and promote all interests, including one's own (also see Gauthier, 1990, pp 209-
10, for a similar liberal answer to what he sees as the paradox of promoting
self-interest, which often includes promoting other people's interests, sometimes
before one's own).

From this Rawlsian analysis, the political injunction to 'celebrate difference',
defended here, in one way can be said to be profoundly liberal, as it recognises the
moral significance of clear distinctions existing between persons and the groups
to which they belong (see also Smith, 2002a, 2002b; and Chapter Three here).
For example, Brian Barry argues that the largely postmodern trend of promoting
particularism and multiculturalism fails to recognise that this accommodation of
difference is already made within liberalism, and within post-Rawlsian analytical
political philosophy especially – this failure betraying a deep misunderstanding of
contemporary liberalism (for example, see Barry, 2001, pp 68-72; see also Chapter
One here). Consequently, Barry's critique of multiculturalism from his liberal
egalitarian perspective does not exclude 'celebrating differences', provided there is
no abandonment of universal liberal egalitarian principles. So, during an interview
soon after the publication of his book *Culture and equality: An egalitarian critique
of multiculturalism*, I asked him what his views were of social movements intent
on celebrating differences, given the value of equality. Barry's reply was telling:
'As long as they stick to celebrating, that is surely not incompatible with liberal
institutions, which allow for all kinds of group activities as long as engaging in
them is voluntary' (Barry, 2002, p 100).

Therefore, following Barry, the arguments presented here are, in part, an
attempt to reclaim some of the liberal ground from these trends in postmodern
and particularist/continental thought, by articulating the liberalism found within
the slogan that differences should be celebrated. Consequently, I counter some
of the overreaching claims of recognition philosophers such as Iris Young, who
also mistakenly asserts that the '[liberal] ideal of impartiality in moral theory
expresses a logic of identity that seeks to reduce differences to unity' (Young,
1990, p 97). Briefly put, and reflecting my previous arguments, this assertion
ignores the nuance of liberalism in its various forms, and how liberal proponents

often accommodate *and* promote difference, both philosophically and in their political practice. For example, as explored earlier in this chapter – and reflecting the philosophy of the analytical tradition more generally – liberals are inclined to make increasing distinctions and differences between objects and persons, as they seek conceptual clarity and more precise differentiation. Politically, too, liberals commit to individual actors making unique and free choices, often recognising that this commitment also promotes difference as a centrally important social value.[14]

Nevertheless, responding to Barry, I will argue in my final remarks that the philosophical underpinning of the 'politics of recognition' must also acknowledge the limitations of liberalism, and, among other things, emphasise the importance of establishing and fostering a certain kind of community – that is, a community not based on a formalised, abstract liberal impartiality, but rather on reciprocity principles born out of particularised encounters with others who are often attached to incommensurable valued objects (see also Chapter Two for further exploration of these and related issues). Consequently, I recommend a type of reciprocity that – instead of emphasising an abstract Rawlsian understanding of selfhood based on contractually obliged and impartial self-interested choosers – promotes a conception of equality and citizenship emphasising the interdependent and solidaristic nature of our active engagement with separate others who are radically different. Following this conclusion, a dual normative principle is implied that states that we should share each other's fates, given the unjust consequences of objectively defined disadvantage restricting a person's ability or opportunity to live a range of potential future lives, and learn from each other's fates, given the diversity of subjectively defined and self-created responses to particular experiences and/or social conditions. The latter emphasis on learning *from* diversity, I argue, implies a conception of solidarity that places the onus on the advantaged to learn from the disadvantaged, given that the latter's positive identity is often undermined as a result of their disadvantage, which in turn suggests two further distinct but interrelated normative principles (see also Chapters Three and Four for a more detailed defence of this position). First, we should recognise the equal status of those who belong to disadvantaged groups, in part derived from the moral significance of us all being different. Second, we should recognise the unfair treatment of such group members based on the moral significance of claiming just distributions, acknowledging that restricting opportunities for members of disadvantaged groups to live a range of potential future lives should be remedied, even if the lives *actually* led are often (albeit not always) surprisingly enriched and enriching. Through separately assessing the implications of both these principles, an understanding of solidarity can be promoted that is both immediate and forward-looking. The value of reciprocity is weighted in the present – as we can mutually benefit from our differences as these occur now – while just social relations are promoted for the future – as opportunities to live a range of potential lives become more equally distributed.

In this latter context especially, I have argued that we should also understand individual and social relations as mutual and interdependent (also see Kittay and Meyers, 1987; Mackenzie and Stoljar, 2000; Daly, 2002; Tanesini, 2004; and Chapters Five and Six here). However, it is important to acknowledge that this mutuality and interdependency does not necessarily imply that differences are celebrated, as, for example, a self-interested individual might thoroughly regret both her state of interdependency with others, and that differences exist between persons (also see Ignatieff, 1999; Grover, 2007). Instead, my argument is that mutuality and interdependency, being integral to reciprocal relations, should be in the first place explicitly valued. Positively acknowledging mutuality is therefore imbedded in the value of diversity, reflecting in turn the multi-dimensional character of our social relations, where opportunities for benefiting from a wide range of lives led are as a result augmented. Of course, the regretful self-interested individual might claim that she is content benefiting from only a narrow range of lives led, given the uniformity and sameness between persons that is promised. Nevertheless, my very liberal contention is that although this position may be philosophically or logically coherent, for the business of practical living it is likely to lead to a more impoverished life than could be achieved otherwise, and so is self-defeating even for the self-interested individual. In short, this, I believe, is because our responsibility to each other and ourselves emerges from our network of relations with others, as well as from our positive encounters with others who are often radically different (again, see Kittay and Meyers, 1987, p 10; see also Levitas, 2001, pp 460-1).[15] My main claim is that, if differences are celebrated in this way, we should *expect* an enriching and multi-dimensional relational experience with others. Consequently, my vision of a liberal community is not born from a monistic ideal that is shared by all and reflected in a universal theory of value, which then reconciles the conflict between equality and diversity principles. Rather, it is born from recognising the plurality, and often incomparability, of values found in highly particularised relational encounters with radically differently situated others, who can, if social and political conditions are conducive, mutually benefit from these encounters.[16] Certainly, these forms of reciprocal exchange depend on promoting universal social attitudes of equal respect towards others who lead radical and often incomparably different lives. However, this is not a recommendation based on universal 'answers' being found to the conflict between equality and diversity principles. Rather, it is one that asserts that the values associated with promoting both equality and diversity are deeply irreconcilable and conflicting, both philosophically and politically, but paradoxically are also mutually reinforcing.

Notes

[1] For example, Bertrand Russell used this kind of analysis in establishing 'set theory', where objects are grouped as members of a particular class, reflecting an analytical method of classification that, in principle, is applicable to everything, including logical understandings. However, this method leads to a paradox in terms of how the 'class of all classes' is classified – known as Russell's Paradox. If classes themselves are to be analysed in this way, as part of what we know and understand *about* classes, this will be identified

as a class of classes, which implies a class that is 'the class of *all* classes'. The problem is that, if this last class is to be classified as a class, which it must be if it is to be called a *class* of all classes, it is a member of itself; but if it is a member of itself, it is not the class of all classes, as it is a member *of* this class. More succinctly, if it is a member of itself, it is not; and if it is not a member of itself, it is (see also Blackburn, 1996, p 336).

[2] See also Palmquist (2000) for a further exploration of how combining opposites generates meaning via what he calls 'synthetic logic'.

[3] Different types of transcendentalism are various and much disputed. However, here I use the term very generally, referring to those philosophies that stress that understandings of the world and human existence – recognising that there are limits to our understanding – are not entirely reducible to experience, scientific observation and logical analysis (see also Honderich, 1995, pp 878-79).

[4] Later in this chapter, I apply Wittgenstein's distinction between 'saying' and 'showing' to understand some limits to reason and logic in explanation.

[5] Contrast this with Kant's claim in his preface to the second edition of the *Critique of pure reason*: 'I have therefore found it necessary to deny knowledge, in order to make room for faith' (cited in West, 1996, p 24). The point here is that Kant is not claiming that knowledge and reason are inconsistent with faith – contrary to Kierkegaard, but rather, given that knowledge and reason is limited, that faith can be exercised, 'filling the gaps' of human experience and understanding, where faith and reason are different but complementary, and therefore reconcilable.

[6] See also my arguments in Chapter Six concerning how both Kantian and Nietzschean themes are found in the political demands of the disability rights movement.

[7] This is similar to the liar paradox. It comes in many forms, but is probably best articulated in the sentence 'This sentence is always false', which is false if it is true, but true if it is false (Blackburn, 1996, pp 217-18).

[8] Given what I have argued previously, my sympathies are with these latter interpretations, reflecting, among other things, the transcendentalism of some existentialists explored here and throughout the book. Wittgenstein acknowledges, he was profoundly influenced by existentialists – most particularly Kierkegaard (see also Tanesini, 2004, pp 74-5).

[9] At this point, liberal egalitarian political philosophy and debates concerning moral responsibility also overlap, responding to the concern of Matt Matravers, among others, that they often do not relate (Matravers, 2002, p 569; see also Roemer, 1993; Scheffler, 1997; Woodard, 1998; Fisher, 1999; Long, 1999).

[10] Albert Camus' interpretation of Hegel emphasises a similar point: 'The desire re-establishes its identity, when it demonstrates that the exterior world is something apart' (Camus, 1982, p 108). Also see G.A. Cohen's interpretation of Hegelian dialectics in Cohen (2000, pp 46-68). However, it is important to highlight that Hegel's solutions to the kind of paradoxes explored here are highly philosophical and rational in character (Hegel, 1942), and so do not follow the existentialist and value incommensurabilist arguments, as, for Hegel, any question has a rational answer when it is properly put; or, to use Cohen's words, 'it develops its answer as it develops itself' (Cohen, 2000, p 68).

[11] Compare *and* contrast this with what Nietzsche sees as the virtue of solitude and separation in Nietzsche, 1975a, pp 194-96, and explored in Chapters Three, Four and Six; with Young's conclusion that less dominant groups' views of themselves inevitably are shaped by how other more dominant groups see them (Young, 1990, pp 59-60); and, again, with Camus' existentialist interpretation of Hegel: 'Consciousness of self, to be affirmed, must distinguish itself from what it is not. Man is a creature who, to affirm his existence and his difference, denies' (Camus, 1982, p 107).

[12] This assumption also, to some extent, reflects Anthony Gidden's notion of the 'autotelic self' – that is, a self that exhibits inner confidence derived from self-respect or, what he calls, ontological security – which then allows for the positive appreciation of social difference (cited in Deacon and Mann, 1999). It also reflects Rawls' argument that self-respect is the most important 'primary good' in part because it generates respect for others (Rawls, 1973, pp 440-2; and see my arguments here and in Chapter One).

[13] In this way, I also provide a normative rationale for Derek Edyvane's recommendation that: 'The agent looks beyond her immediate attachments and learns to recognise and value conflict with those who care about things different from the things she cares about. This engagement in conflict will allow the agent to make sense of her commitments in their social context' (Edyvane, 2005, p 30). Furthermore, my conclusions are consistent with his claim that: 'The forces of pluralism can be harnessed so as to generate the motivation for a cooperative activity which could potentially form an integral part of a flourishing political community and a flourishing life' (Edyvane, 2005, p 54; see also McLennan, 2008 for similar arguments).

[14] Given this, it might be said that Young's concerns are indeed profoundly liberal, as she too resists the over-unification of meaning, manifested in social categorisations and the promotion of universal interests (for example, see Young, 1990, pp 156-91).

[15] Here, a further distinction can be made between 'moral atomism' – which assumes an individual is, at least to some extent, responsible for her actions and the life she leads, a position I have largely defended throughout the book – and 'social atomism' – which assumes individuals act independently from each other, a position I reject, as explored here and in Chapters Five and Six (for this distinction, see also Perry, 1997).

[16] This conclusion reflects Hendley's interpretation of Levinas' and Habermas' position in Hendley (2004, pp 153-73); see also Parekh (2000, pp 341-3), Stocker (1997) and my arguments in Chapters Two and Three here.

References

Anderson, E.S. (1997) 'Practical reason and incommensurable goods', in R. Chang (ed) *Incommensurability, incomparability, and practical reason*, Cambridge, MA: Harvard University Press, pp 90–109.

Anderson, E.S. (1999) 'What is the point of equality?', *Ethics*, vol 109, no 2, pp 287–337.

Anwander, N. (2001) 'Incommensurability, incomparability and practical reason', *Ethical Theory and Moral Practice*, vol 4, no 2, pp 193–95.

Appel, F. (1999) *Nietzsche contra democracy*, Ithaca, NY: Cornell University Press.

Arneson, R.J. (1993) 'Equality', in R.E. Goodin and P. Pettit (eds) *A companion to contemporary political philosophy*, Oxford: Blackwell, pp 489–507.

Arneson, R.J. (1997) 'Egalitarianism and the undeserving poor', *The Journal of Political Philosophy*, vol 5, no 4, pp 327–50.

Arneson, R.J. (2000) 'Discussion: luck egalitarianism and prioritarianism', *Ethics*, vol 110, no 1, pp 339–49.

Baker, J., Lynch, K., Cantillon, S. and Walsh, J. (2004) *Equality: From theory to action*, Basingstoke: Palgrave Macmillan.

Banks, S. (2001) *Ethics and values in social work*, London: Palgrave Macmillan.

Barnes, C. (1991) *Disabled people in Britain and discrimination*, London: Hurst and Calgary.

Barry, B. (1990) *Political argument: With a new introduction*, Hemel Hempstead: Harvester Wheatsheaf.

Barry, B. (1995) *A treatise in social justice, vol II: Justice as impartiality*, Oxford: Clarendon Press.

Barry, B. (2001) *Culture and equality: An egalitarian critique of multiculturalism*, Cambridge: Polity Press.

Barry, B. (2002) 'Liberal egalitarianism, impartiality and multiculturalism: an interview with Brian Barry', *Imprints: A Journal of Analytical Socialism*, vol 6, no 2, pp 100–7.

Barton, L. (ed) (1996) *Disability and society*, London: Longman.

Berger, P.L. and Luckman, T. (1991) 'The social construction of reality', in P. Worsley (ed) *The new modern sociological readings*, London: Penguin.

Berkowitz, P. (1995) *Nietzsche: The ethics of a moralist*, Cambridge, MA: Harvard University Press.

Berlin, I. (1969) *Four essays on liberty*, Oxford: Oxford University Press.

Berlin, I. (1991) Hardy, H. (ed) *The crooked timber of humanity*, London: Fontana Press.

Berlin, I. (2002) *Liberty: Incorporating 'four essays on liberty'*, Oxford: Oxford University Press.

Bhabha, H.K. (1994) *The location of culture*, London: Routledge.

Bickenbach, J. (1999) 'Models of disablement, universalism and the international classification of impairments, disabilities and handicaps', *Social Science and Medicine*, vol 48, no 9, pp 1173-86.

Birch, A.H. (1993) *The concepts and theories of modern democracy*, London: Routledge.

Bird, C. (2004) 'Status, identity and respect', *Political Theory*, vol 32, no 2, pp 207-32.

Blackburn, S. (1996) *The Oxford dictionary of philosophy*, Oxford: Oxford University Press.

Blackham, H.J. (1989) *Six existentialist thinkers*, London: Routledge.

Bowring, F. (2000) 'Social exclusion: limitations of the debate', *Critical Social Policy*, vol 20, no 3, pp 307-30.

Broome, J. (1997) 'Is incommensurability vagueness?', in R. Chang (ed) *Incommensurability, incomparability, and practical reason*, Cambridge, MA: Harvard University Press, pp 67-89.

Brown, L. (2009) 'The role of the medical experts in shaping disability law', in K. Kristiansen, S. Vehmas and T. Shakespeare (eds) *Arguing about disability: Philosophical perspectives*, London: Routledge, pp 169-84.

Bryson, V. (2003) *Feminist political theory: An introduction*, Basingstoke: Macmillan.

Buchanan, A. (1995) 'Equal opportunity and genetic intervention', in E.F. Paul (ed) *The just society*, Cambridge: Cambridge University Press, pp 105-35.

Butler, J. (1990) *Gender trouble: Feminism and the subversion of identity*, New York, NY: Routledge.

Calder, G. (2005) 'Postmodernism, pragmatism, and the possibility of ethical relation with the past', *Theoria*, vol 52, no 108, pp 82-101.

Calder, G. (2007) 'Theory, practice and "teaching" professional ethics', in S.R. Smith (ed) *Applying theory to policy and practice: Issues for critical reflection*, Aldershot, Ashgate, pp 87-102.

Calder, G. and Smith, S.R. (2011) 'Differential treatment and employability: a UK case study of veil-wearing in schools', in G. Calder and E. Ceva (eds) *Diversity in Europe: Dilemmas of differential treatment in theory and practice*, London: Routledge.

Camus, A. (1982) *The rebel*, Harmondsworth: Penguin.

Ceva, E. (2009) 'Just procedures with controversial outcomes: on the grounds for substantive disputation within a procedural theory of justice', *Res Publica: A Journal of Moral, Legal and Social Philosophy*, vol 15, no 3, pp 219-35.

Chang, R. (ed) (1997) *Incommensurability, incomparability, and practical reason*, Cambridge, MA: Harvard University Press.

Chang, R. (2002) 'The possibility of parity', *Ethics*, vol 112, no 4, pp 659-88.

Chang, R. (2005) 'Parity, interval value, and choice', *Ethics*, vol 115, no 2, pp 331-50.

Clack, B.R. (1999) *An introduction to Wittgenstein's philosophy of religion*, Edinburgh: Edinburgh University Press.

Clarke, L. (1994) *Discrimination*, London: Institute of Personnel Management.

Cohen, E. and Ben-Ari E. (1993) 'Hard choices: a sociological perspective on value incommensurability', *Human Studies*, vol 16, no 3, pp 267-97.

Cohen, G.A. (1989) 'On the currency of egalitarian justice', *Ethics*, vol 99, no 4, pp 906-44.

Cohen, G.A. (1995) *Self-ownership, freedom and equality*, Cambridge: Cambridge University Press.

Cohen, G.A. (2000) *If you're an egalitarian how come you're so rich?*, Cambridge, MA: Harvard University Press.

Cohen, G.A. (2003) 'Facts and principles', *Philosophy and Public Affairs*, vol 31, no 3, pp 211-45.

Cole, J. (2004) *Still lives: Narratives of spinal cord injury*, Chester, NJ: Bradford Books.

Conolly, O. (1998) 'Pity, tragedy, and the pathos of distance', *European Journal of Philosophy*, vol 6, no 3, pp 277-96.

Copleston, F.S.J. (1994) *A history of philosophy: Vol. VII*, New York, NY: Image Books.

Cullen, B. (1979) *Hegel's social and political thought: An introduction*, London: Macmillan.

Cyrulnik, B. (2009) *Resilience: How your inner strength can set you free from the past*, London: Penguin.

Daly, M. (2002) 'Care as a good for social policy', *Journal of Social Policy*, vol 31, no 2, pp 251-70.

Dancy, J. (1993) *Moral reasons*, Oxford: Blackwell.

Darwall, S. (1977) 'Two kinds of respect', *Ethics*, vol 88, no 1, pp 36-49.

Deacon, A. and Mann, K. (1999) 'Agency, modernity and social policy', *Journal of Social Policy*, vol 28, no 3, pp 413-35.

Devigne, R. (1999) 'Review of Fredrick Appel "Nietzsche contra democracy"', *American Political Science Review*, vol 93, no 3, pp 693-4.

Duncan, S. and Edwards, R. (1999) *Lone mothers, paid work, and gendered moral rationalities*, London: Palgrave Macmillan.

Dworkin, G. (1988) *The theory and practice of autonomy*, Cambridge: Cambridge University Press.

Dworkin, R. (1981) 'Part 1: What is equality?', *Philosophy and Public Affairs*, vol 10, no 3, pp 185-246.

Dworkin, R. (2000) *Sovereign virtue: The theory and practice of equality*, Cambridge, MA: Harvard University Press.

Dworkin, R. (2002) 'Sovereign virtue revisited', *Ethics*, vol 113, no 3, pp 106-43.

Dworkin, R. (2003) 'Equality, luck and hierarchy', *Philosophy and Public Affairs*, vol 31, no 2, pp 190-8.

Dwyer, P. (2002) 'Making sense of citizenship: some user views on welfare rights and responsibilities', *Critical Social Policy*, vol 22, no 2, pp 273-99.

Edwards, S.D. (2009) 'Definitions of disability: ethical and other values', in K. Kristiansen, S. Vehmas and T. Shakespeare (eds) *Arguing about disability: Philosophical perspectives*, London: Routledge, pp 30-41.

Edyvane, D. (2005) 'A back-turning harmony: conflict as a source of political community', *Res Publica: A Journal of Legal and Social Philosophy*, vol 11, no 1, pp 27-54.

Edyvane, D. (2007) *Community and conflict: The sources of liberal solidarity*, Hampshire Basingstoke: Palgrave Macmillan.

Ellison, N. (1999) 'Beyond universalism and particularism: rethinking contemporary welfare theory', *Critical Social Policy*, vol 19, no 1, pp 57-85.

Faubion, J.D. (ed) (2003) *Power: The essential works of Michel Foucault*, London: Penguin.

Ferrell, J. (2008) 'The alleged relativism of Isaiah Berlin', *Critical Review of International Social and Political Philosophy*, vol 11, no 1, pp 41-56.

Finnis, J. (1997) 'Commensuration and public reason', in R. Chang (ed) *Incommensurability, incomparability, and practical reason*, Cambridge, MA: Harvard University Press, pp 215-33.

Fischer, J.M. (1999) 'Recent work on moral responsibility', *Ethics*, vol 110, no 1, pp 93-139.

Fishkin, J. (2002) 'Liberty versus equal opportunity', in L. Pojman (ed) *Political philosophy: Classic and contemporary readings*, London: McGraw Hill, pp 404-12.

Fitzpatrick, T. (1996) 'Postmodernism, welfare and radical politics', *Journal of Social Policy*, vol 25, no 3, pp 303-20.

Flynn, T.R. (2006) *Existentialism: A very short introduction*, Oxford: Oxford University Press.

Foucault, M. (2001) *The order of things*, London: Routledge.

Fraser, G. (2002) *Redeeming Nietzsche: On the piety of unbelief*, London: Routledge.

Fraser, N. (1997) *Justice interruptus: Critical reflections on the post-socialist tradition*, London: Routledge.

Fraser, N. and Honneth, A. (2003) *Redistribution or recognition? A political-philosophical exchange*, London: Verso.

Galston, W. A. (2002) *Liberal pluralism: The implications of value pluralism for political theory and practice*, Cambridge: Cambridge University Press.

Gauthier, D. (1990) *Moral dealing: Contract, ethics and reason*, Ithaca, NY: Cornell University Press.

Giddens, A. (1998) 'The future of the welfare state', in M. Novak (ed) *Is there a third way? Essays on the changing direction of socialist thought*, London: Institute of Economic Affairs, Health and Welfare Unit, pp 25-9.

Gilroy, P. (1993) *The black Atlantic: Modernity and double consciousness*, Cambridge, MA: Harvard University Press.

Gilroy, P. (2004) *After empire: Melancholia or convivial culture*, London: Routledge.

Gowans, C.W. (1987) *Moral dilemmas*, New York, NY: Oxford University Press.

Gray, A. (2001) 'Making work pay: devising best strategies for lone parents in Britain', *Journal of Social Policy*, vol 30, no 2, pp 189-207.

Gray, J. (1996) *Isaiah Berlin*, Princeton, NJ: Princeton University Press.

Grayling, A.C. (1996) *Wittgenstein*, Oxford: Oxford University Press.

Griffin, J. (1986) *Well-being: Its meaning, measurement, and moral importance*, Oxford: Oxford University Press.

Griffin, J. (1997) 'Incommensurability: what's the problem?', in R. Chang (ed) *Incommensurability, incomparability, and practical reason*, Cambridge, MA: Harvard University Press, pp 35-51.

Grover, C. (2007) 'The Freud report on the future of welfare to work: some critical reflections', *Critical Social Policy*, vol 27, no 4, pp 534-45.

Guttman, A. (ed) (1994) *Multiculturalism: Examining the politics of recognition*, Princeton, NJ: Princeton University Press.

Haan D.J. (2001) 'The definition of moral dilemmas: a logical problem', *Ethical Theory and Moral Practice*, vol 4, no 3, pp 267-84.

Habermas, J. (1990) *Philosophical discourses of modernity*, Cambridge: Polity Press.

Habermas, J. (1994) 'Struggles for recognition in the democratic constitutional state', in A. Guttman (ed) *Multiculturalism: Examining the politics of recognition*, Princeton, NJ: Princeton University Press, pp 107-48.

Hales, S.D. (1997) 'A consistent relativism', *Mind*, vol 106, no 421, pp 34-52.

Haworth, A. (2005) 'Liberalism, abstract individualism, and the problem of particular obligation', *Res Publica: A Journal of Legal and Social Philosophy*, vol 11, no 4, pp 371-401.

Hayek, F.A. (1993) *The constitution of liberty*, London: Routledge.

Hegel G.W.F. (1942) *The philosophy of right*, Oxford: Oxford University Press.

Hendley, S. (2004) 'Speech and sensibility: Levinas and Habermas on the constitution of the moral point of view', *Continental Philosophy in Review*, vol 37, no 2, pp 153-73.

Heredia, N. (2007) 'Eurocentrism, the philosophy of liberation and the social model of disability: the practice of a social movement within a Latin American context', in S.R. Smith (ed) *Applying theory to policy and practice: Issues for critical reflection*, Aldershot: Ashgate, pp 123-38.

Hevey, D. (1992) *The creatures time forgot*, London: Routledge.

Heywood, A. (2004) *Political theory: An introduction* (3rd edn), Basingstoke: Palgrave Macmillan.

Hill, T.E. (2002) *Human welfare and moral worth: Kantian perspectives*, Oxford: Clarendon Press.

Hoggett, P. (2001) 'Agency, rationality and social policy', *Journal of Social Policy*, vol 30, no 1, pp 37-56.

Honderich, T. (ed) (1995) *The Oxford companion to philosophy*, Oxford: Oxford University Press.

Honneth, A. (1992) 'Integrity and disrespect: principles of a conception of morality based on the theory of recognition', *Political Theory*, vol 20, no 2, pp 187-201.

Honneth, A. (2007) *Disrespect: The normative foundation of critical theory*, Cambridge: Polity Press.

Hughes, G. and Lewis, G. (eds) (1998) *Unsettling welfare: The reconstruction of social policy*, London: Routledge.

Hugman, R. and Smith, D. (1995) *Ethical issues in social work*, London: Routledge.

Hull, R. (2009) 'Disability and freedom', in K. Kristiansen, S. Vehmas and T. Shakespeare (eds) *Arguing about disability: Philosophical perspectives*, London: Routledge, pp 93-104.

Hursthouse, R. (1999) *On virtue ethics*, Oxford: Oxford University Press.

Huxley, A. (1971) *Brave new world*, London: Folio Press.

Ignatieff, M. (1999) 'Nationalism and toleration', in S. Mendus (ed) *The politics of toleration: Tolerance and intolerance in modern life*, Edinburgh: Edinburgh University Press, pp 77–106.

Ikaheimo, H. (2009) 'Personhood and the social inclusion of people with disabilities: a recognition-theoretical approach', in K. Kristiansen, S. Vehmas and T. Shakespeare (eds) *Arguing about disability: Philosophical perspectives*, London: Routledge, pp 77–92.

Jaggar, A.M. (2006) 'Reasoning about well-being: Nussbaum's methods of justifying the capabilities', *The Journal of Political Philosophy*, vol 14, no 3, pp 301–22.

Jones, P. (2006) 'Equality, recognition and difference', *Critical Review of International Social and Political Philosophy*, vol 9, no 1, pp 23–46.

Kant, I. (1993) *Grounding for the metaphysics of morals*, Indianapolis, IN: Hackett Publishing Company.

Kant, I. (1997) *Critique of practical reason*, Cambridge: Cambridge University Press.

Kant, I (1998) *Groundwork of the metaphysics of morals*, Cambridge: Cambridge University Press.

Kaufman, A. (1999) *Welfare in the Kantian state*, Oxford: Oxford University Press.

Kenny, A. (1983) *Wittgenstein*, London: Penguin.

Kierkegaard, S. (1994) *Fear and trembling: The book on Adler*, New York, NY: Alfred A. Knopf.

Kimball, R.H. (2001) 'Moral and logical perspectives on appealing to pity', *Argumentation*, vol 15, no 3, pp 331–46.

Kittay, E.F. and Meyers, D.T. (1987) *Women and moral theory*, New York, NY: Rowman & Littlefield.

Knowles, D. (2001) *Political philosophy*, London: Routledge.

Laegaard, S. (2005) 'On the prospects of a liberal theory of recognition', *Res Publica: A Journal of Legal and Social Philosophy*, vol 11, no 4, pp 325–48.

Levinas, E. (1985) *Ethics and infinity: Conversations with Philippe Nemo*, Pittsburgh, PA: Duquesne University Press.

Levinas, E. (1996) *Basic philosophical writings*, Bloomington, IN: Indiana University Press.

Levinas, E. (2006) *The humanism of the other*, Champaign, IL: University of Illinois Press.

Levitas, R. (2001) 'Against work: a utopian incursion into social policy', *Critical Social Policy*, vol 21, no 4, pp 449–65.

Liachowitz, C.H. (1988) *The social construction of disability*, Philadelphia, PA: University of Pennsylvania Press.

Lieter, B. (2002) *Nietzsche on morality*, London: Routledge.

Lishman, J. (ed) (2007) *Learning in social work and social care: Knowledge and theory*, London: Jessica Kingsley.

Lister, R. (1997) *Citizenship: Feminist perspectives*, London: Macmillan.

Lister, R. (2001) 'New labour: a study in ambiguity from a position of ambivalence', *Critical Social Policy*, vol 21, no 4, pp 425–47.

Lister, R. (2007) '(Mis)recognition, social inequality and social justice', in T. Lovell (ed) *(Mis)recognition, social inequality and social justice*, London: Routledge.

Long, R.T. (1999) 'The irrelevance of responsibility', *Social Philosophy and Policy*, vol 16, no 1, pp 118-45.

Louden, R.B. (2000) *Kant's impure ethics: From rational beings to human beings*, New York, NY: Oxford University Press.

Lovett, F. (2004) 'Can justice be based on consent', *The Journal of Political Philosophy*, vol 12, no 1, pp 79-101.

Lukes, S. (1997) 'Comparing the incomparable: trade-offs and sacrifices', in R. Chang (ed) *Incommensurability, incomparability, and practical reason*, Cambridge, MA: Harvard University Press, pp 184-95.

Mackenzie, C. and Scully, J. (2007) 'Moral imagination, disability and embodiment', *Journal of Applied Philosophy*, vol 24, no 4, pp 335-51.

Mackenzie, C. and Stoljar, N. (eds) (2000) *Relational autonomy: Feminist perspectives on autonomy*, New York, NY: Oxford University Press.

Madood, T. (2007) *Multiculturalism: Themes for the 21st century*, Cambridge: Polity Press.

Malone, E.M. (1993) 'Kuhn reconstructed: incommensurability without relativism', *Studies in History and Philosophy of Science*, vol 24, no 1, pp 69-93.

March, A.F. (2006) 'Liberal citizenship and the search for an overlapping consensus: the case of Muslim minorities', *Philosophy and Public Affairs*, vol 34, no 4, pp 373-421.

Matravers, M. (2002) 'Responsibility, luck and the "equality of what?" debate', *Political Studies*, vol 50, no 3, pp 558-72.

Matravers, M. (2007) *Responsibility and justice*, Oxford: Wiley.

May, S. (1999) *Nietzsche's ethics and his war on 'morality'*, Oxford: Clarendon Press.

McLennan, G. (2008) 'Progressive pluralism?', *Critical Review of International Social and Political Philosophy*, vol 11, no 1, pp 89-105.

McKinnon, C. (2006) *Toleration: A critical introduction*, London: Routledge.

Mendus, S. (ed) (1999) *The politics of toleration: Tolerance and intolerance in modern life*, Edinburgh: Edinburgh University Press.

Mendus, S. (2003) *Impartiality in moral and political philosophy*, Oxford: Oxford University Press.

Mill, J.S. (1991) *On liberty and other essays*, Oxford: Oxford University Press.

Millgram, E. (1997) 'Incommensurability and practical reason', in R. Chang (ed) *Incommensurability, incomparability, and practical reason*, Cambridge, MA: Harvard University Press, pp 151-69.

Morris, J. (1991) *Pride against prejudice*, London: Women's Press.

Munoz-Darde, V. (1998) 'Rawls, justice in the family and justice of the family', *Philosophical Quarterly*, vol 48, no 192, pp 335-52.

Nagel, T. (1989) *A view from nowhere*, New York, NY: Oxford University Press.

Nagel, T. (1995) *Equality and impartiality*, New York, NY: Oxford University Press.

Neenan, M. (2009) *Developing resilience: A cognitive behavioural approach*, London: Routledge.

Nietzsche, F. (1956) *The birth of tragedy and the genealogy of morals*, New York, NY: Doubleday Anchor Books.

Nietzsche, F. (1968) *Twilight of the idols and the anti-Christ*, London: Penguin.

Nietzsche, F. (1975a) *Beyond good and evil*, London: Penguin.

Nietzsche, F. (1975b) *Thus spoke Zarathustra*, London: Penguin.

Nozick, R. (1974) *Anarchy, state and utopia*, Oxford: Blackwell.

Nussbaum, M. (1992) 'Human functioning and social justice: in defense of Aristotelian essentialism', *Political Theory*, vol 20, no 3, pp 202-46.

Nussbaum, M. (1996) 'Compassion: the basic social emotion', *Social Philosophy and Policy*, vol 13, no 1, pp 27-58.

Nussbaum, M. (1999) *Sex and social justice*, New York, NY: Oxford University Press.

Nussbaum, M. (2000) *Women and human development: The capabilities approach*, Cambridge: Cambridge University Press.

Nussbaum, M. (2006) *Frontiers of justice: Disability, nationality and species membership* (The Tanner Lectures on Human Values), Cambridge, MA: Belknap Press.

Oakley, A. (1972) *Sex, gender and society*, London: Temple Smith.

Oakley, J. and Cocking, D. (2001) *Virtue ethics and professional roles*, Cambridge: Cambridge University Press.

Oliver, M. (1990) *The politics of disablement: Critical texts in social work and the welfare state*, London: Macmillan.

Oliver, M. (1996) *Understanding disability: From theory to practice*, London: Macmillan.

Oliver, M. and Barnes, C. (1998) *Disabled people and social policy: From exclusion to inclusion*, London: Longman.

Palmquist, S. (2000) *The tree of philosophy*, Hong Kong: Philopsychy Press.

Parekh, B. (2000) *Re-thinking multiculturalism: Cultural diversity and political theory*, Basingstoke: Palgrave Macmillan.

Parekh, B. (2008) *A new politics of identity: Political principles for an interdependent world*, Basingstoke: Palgrave Macmillan.

Parfit, D. (1987) *Reasons and persons*, Oxford: Clarendon Press.

Paul, E.F. (ed) (1995) *The just society*, Cambridge: Cambridge University Press.

Penna, S. and O'Brien, M. (1996) 'Post-modernism and social policy: a small step forwards?', *Journal of Social Policy*, vol 25, no 1, pp 39-61.

Perry, S.R. (1997) 'Libertarianism, entitlement, and responsibility', *Philosophy and Public Affairs*, vol 26, no 4, pp 351-96.

Peters, R.S. (1973) *Reason and compassion: The Lindsey memorial lectures*, London: Routledge.

Phillips, A. (2004) 'Defending equality of outcome', *The Journal of Political Philosophy*, vol 12, no 1, pp 1-19.

Piper, A. (1991) 'Impartiality, compassion and modal imagination', *Ethics*, vol 101, no 4, pp 726-75.

Pippin, R.B. (1991) *Modernism as a philosophical problem*, Oxford: Blackwell.

Rabinowicz, W. (2009) 'Incommensurability and vagueness', *Aristotelian Society Supplementary Volume*, vol 105, no 1, pp 71-94.

Rajezi, A. (2002) 'The moral theory behind moral dilemmas', *American Philosophical Quarterly*, vol 39, no 4, pp 373-83.

Rawls, J. (1973) *A theory of justice*, Oxford: Oxford University Press.

Rawls, J. (1993) *Political liberalism*, New York, NY: Colombia University Press.

Rawls, J. (2001) *Justice as fairness: A re-statement*, Cambridge, MA: Harvard University Press.

Raz, J. (1988) *The morality of freedom*, Oxford: Clarendon Press.

Raz, J. (1997) 'Incommensurability and agency', in R. Chang (ed) *Incommensurability, incomparability, and practical reason*, Cambridge, MA: Harvard University Press, pp 110-28.

Raz, J. (2001) *Value, respect and attachment*, Cambridge: Cambridge University Press.

Reath, A. (2006) *Agency and autonomy in Kant's moral theory*, Oxford: Oxford University Press.

Reeve, D. (2009) 'Biopolitics and bare life: does the impaired body provide contemporary examples of *homo sacer?*', in K. Kristiansen, S. Vehmas and T. Shakespeare (eds) *Arguing about disability: Philosophical perspectives*, London: Routledge, pp 203-18.

Regan, D. (1997) 'Value, comparability and choice', in R. Chang (ed) *Incommensurability, incomparability, and practical reason*, Cambridge, MA: Harvard University Press, pp 129-50.

Reynolds, J. (2006) *Understanding existentialism*, London: Acumen.

Ripstein, A. (1994) 'Equality, luck and responsibility', *Philosophy and Public Affairs*, vol 23, no 1, pp 3-23.

Roemer, J. (1993) 'A pragmatic theory of responsibility', *Philosophy and Public Affairs*, vol 22, no 2, pp 146-66.

Russell, B. (1971) *The problems of philosophy*, Oxford: Oxford University Press.

Salih, S. (ed) (2003) *The Judith Butler reader*, Oxford: Blackwell.

Sandel, M. (1982) *Liberalism and the limits of justice*, Cambridge: Cambridge University Press.

Saraga, E. (ed) (1998) *Embodying the social: Constructions of difference*, London: Routledge.

Sartre, J.P. (1980) *Nausea*, London: Penguin.

Sartre, J.P. (1995) *Being and nothingness*, London: Routledge.

Sangiovanni, A. (2007) 'Global justice, reciprocity, and the state', *Philosophy and Public Affairs*, vol 35, no 1, pp 3-39.

Sawyer, C. (2010) 'Distribution, disability, and normality' *Imprints: Egalitarian Theory and Practice*, vol 10, no 3, pp 229-56.

Scanlon, T.M. (1998) *What we owe to each other*, Cambridge, MA: Harvard University Press.

Scheffler, S. (1992) 'Responsibility, reactive attitudes, and liberalism in philosophy and politics', *Philosophy and Public Affairs*, vol 21, no 4, pp 229-323.

Scheffler, S. (1997) 'Relationships and responsibilities', *Philosophy and Public Affairs*, vol 26, no 3, pp 189-209.

Scheffler, S. (2003) 'What is egalitarianism?', *Philosophy and Public Affairs*, vol 31, no 1, pp 5-39.

Schwartz, J.D. (1993) 'Pity and judgement in Greek drama: a response to professor Alford', *Political Research Quarterly*, vol 46, no 2, pp 281-7.

Scruton, R. (2001) *The meaning of conservatism*, Basingstoke: Palgrave Macmillan.

Sen, A. (1985) 'Well-being, agency and freedom: the Dewey lectures', *The Journal of Philosophy*, vol 82, no 4, pp 169-221.

Sen, A. (1992) *Inequality re-examined*, Oxford: Oxford University Press.

Sen, A. and Williams, B (eds) (1982) *Utilitarianism and beyond*, Cambridge: Cambridge University Press.

Shakespeare, T. (2006) *Disability rights and wrongs*, London: Routledge.

Shields, P.R. (1997) *Logic and sin in the writings of Ludwig Wittgenstein*, Chicago, IL: University of Chicago Press.

Shorten, A. (2005) 'Toleration and cultural controversies', *Res Publica: A Journal of Legal and Social Philosophy*, vol. 11, no 3, pp 275-99.

Smith, S.R. (1997) 'Disarming the ideological conflict between the centre-left and the new right: the implementation of UK social security policy', *Journal of Political Ideologies*, vol 2, no 1, pp 79-97.

Smith, S.R. (1998) *The centre-left and new right divide? Political philosophy and aspects of social policy in the era of the welfare state*, Aldershot: Ashgate.

Smith, S.R. (1999) 'Arguing against cuts in lone parent benefits: reclaiming the desert ground', *Critical Social Policy*, vol 19, no 3, pp 313-34.

Smith, S.R. (2001a) 'The social construction of talent: a defence of justice as reciprocity', *The Journal of Political Philosophy*, vol 9, no 1, pp 19-37.

Smith, S.R. (2001b) 'Distorted ideals: the "problem of dependency" and the mythology of independent living', *Social Theory and Practice*, vol 27, no 4, pp 579-98.

Smith, S.R. (2002a) *Defending justice as reciprocity: An essay on social policy and political philosophy*, Lampeter: Edwin Mellen Press.

Smith, S.R. (2002b) 'Fraternal learning and interdependency: celebrating difference within reciprocal commitments', *Policy and Politics*, vol 30, no 1, pp 47-59.

Smith, S.R. (2005a) 'Equality, identity and the disability rights movement: from policy to practice and from Kant to Nietzsche in more than one uneasy move', *Critical Social Policy*, vol 25, no 4, pp 554-76.

Smith, S.R. (2005b) 'Keeping our distance in compassion-based social relations', *Journal of Moral Philosophy*, vol 2, no 1, pp 69-87.

Smith, S.R. (2007a) 'Applying theory to policy and practice: methodological problems and issues', in S.R. Smith (ed) *Applying theory to policy and practice: Issues for critical reflection*, Aldershot: Ashgate, pp 1-18.

Smith, S.R. (ed) (2007b) *Applying theory to policy and practice: Issues for critical reflection*, Aldershot: Ashgate.

Smith, S.R. (2007c) 'Review of Mark Stein's (2006) "Distributive justice and disability: Utlitarianism against egalitarianism"', *Philosophy in Review*, vol 27, no 1, pp 74-6.

Smith, S. R. (2008) 'Agency and surprise, learning at the limits of empathic-imagination and liberal egalitarianism', *Critical Review in International Social and Political Philosophy*, vol 11, no 1, pp 25-40. Available at: www.informaworld.com.

Smith, S. R. (2009) 'Social justice and disability, competing interpretations of the medical and social models', in K. Kristiansen, S. Vehmas and T. Shakespeare (eds) *Arguing about disability: Philosophical perspectives*, pp 15-29.

Smith, S.R. and O'Neill, M. (1997) 'Equality of what and the disability rights movement', *Imprints: A Journal of Analytical Socialism*, vol 2, no 2, pp 123-44.

Snow, N.E. (1991) 'Compassion', *American Philosophical Quarterly*, vol 28, no 3, pp 195-205.

Solomon, R.C. (2001) *From rationalism to existentialism: The existentialists and their nineteenth century backgrounds*, New York, NY: Rowman and Littlefield.

Squires, J. (1999) *Gender in political theory*, Cambridge: Polity Press.

Stainton, T. (1994) *Autonomy and social policy: Rights and mental handicap*, Aldershot: Avebury Press.

Stein, M. (2006) *Distributive justice and disability: Utilitarianism against egalitarianism*, New Haven, CT: Yale University Press.

Steiner, H. (1994) *An essay on rights*, Oxford: Blackwell.

Stocker, M. (1997) 'Abstract and concrete value: plurality, conflict, and maximization', in R. Chang (ed) *Incommensurability, incomparability, and practical reason*, Cambridge, MA: Harvard University Press, pp 196-214.

Stoesz, D. (2002) 'The American welfare state in twilight', *Journal of Social Policy*, vol 31, no 3, pp 487-503.

Sugden, R. (2009) 'On modeling vagueness, and on not modeling incommensurability', *Aristotelian Society Supplementary Volume*, vol 105, no 1, pp 95-113.

Sunstein, C.R. (1997) 'Incommensurability and kinds of valuation: some applications in law', in R. Chang (ed) *Incommensurability, incomparability, and practical reason*, Cambridge, MA: Harvard University Press, pp 234-54.

Swain, J., French, S. and Cameron, D. (eds) (2003) *Controversial issues in a disabling society*, Buckingham: Open University Press.

Tanesini, A. (2004) *Wittgenstein: A feminist interpretation*, Cambridge: Polity Press.

Taylor, C. (1992) *Multiculturalism and the politics of difference*, Princeton, NJ: Princeton University Press.

Taylor, C. (1994) 'The politics of recognition', in A. Guttman (ed) (1994) *Multiculturalism: Examining the politics of recognition*, Princeton, NJ: Princeton University Press, pp 25-73.

Taylor, C. (1997) 'Leading a life', in R. Chang (ed) *Incommensurability, incomparability, and practical reason*, Cambridge, MA: Harvard University Press, pp 170-83.

Taylor, R.S. (2003) 'Rawls's defence of the priority of liberty: a Kantian reconstruction', *Philosophy and Public Affairs*, vol 3, no 4, pp 246-71.

Taylor-Gooby, P. (1994) 'Postmodernism and social policy: the great leap backwards?', *Journal of Social Policy*, vol 23, no 3, pp 385-464.

Thompson, N. (2008), 'Existentialist ethics: from Nietzsche to Sartre and beyond', *Ethics and Social Welfare,* vol 2, no 1, pp 10-23.

Toppinen, P. (2005) 'Critical reflections on social justice and recognition', *Res Publica: A Journal of Legal and Social Philosophy,* vol 11, no 4, pp 425-33.

Tully, J. (2004) 'Recognition and dialogue: the emergence of a new field', *Critical Review of International Social and Political Philosophy,* vol 7, no 3, pp 84-106.

Urmson, J.O. (1974) 'A defence of intuitionism', *Proceedings of The Aristotelian Society,* vol 75, no 1, pp 111-19.

Van der Linden, H. (1988) *Kantian ethics and socialism,* Cambridge, MA: Hackett Publishing Company.

Van Parijs, P. (1995) *Real freedom for all: What (if anything) can justify capitalism?,* Oxford: Clarendon Press.

Vehmas, S. and Makela, P. (2009) 'The ontology of disability: a discussion of the natural and social features', in K. Kristiansen, S. Vehmas and T. Shakespeare (eds) *Arguing about disability: Philosophical perspectives,* London: Routledge, pp 42-56.

Warnock, M. (1970) *Existentialism,* Oxford: Oxford University Press.

West, D. (1996) *An introduction to continental philosophy,* Cambridge: Polity Press.

Whelehan, I. (1995) *Modern feminist thought,* New York, NY: New York University Press.

Whitebrook, M. (2002) 'Compassion as a political virtue', *Political Studies,* vol 50, no 3, pp 529-44.

WHO (World Health Organization) (2001) *Second international classification of functioning, disability and health,* New York, NY: United Nations.

Williams, B. (ed) (1981a) *Moral luck,* Cambridge: Cambridge University Press.

Williams, B. (1981b) 'Moral luck', in B. Williams (ed) (1981) *Moral luck,* Cambridge: Cambridge University Press, pp 1-23.

Wittgenstein, L. (2000a) *Tractatus: Logico-philosophicus,* London: Routledge.

Wittgenstein, L. (2000b) *Philosophical Investigations* (3rd edn), Oxford: Blackwell.

Woodard, C. (1998) 'Egalitarianism, responsibility, and desert', *Imprints: A Journal of Analytical Socialism,* vol 3, no 1, pp 25-48.

Wright, M.V. (2002) 'Narrative imagination and taking the perspective of others', *Studies in Philosophy and Education,* vol 21, no 5, pp 407-16.

Young, I.M. (1990) *Justice and the politics of difference,* Princeton, NJ: Princeton University Press.

Index

The letter f indicates a figure, n an endnote and t a table